Escape from Leviathan

Escape from Leviathan

Liberty, Welfare and Anarchy Reconciled

J. C. Lester

First published in Great Britain 2000 by
MACMILLAN PRESS LTD
Houndmills, Basingstoke, Hampshire RG21 6XS and London
Companies and representatives throughout the world

A catalogue record for this book is available from the British Library.

ISBN 0–333–77756–5

First published in the United States of America 2000 by
ST. MARTIN'S PRESS, LLC,
Scholarly and Reference Division,
175 Fifth Avenue, New York, N.Y. 10010

ISBN 0–312–23416–3

Library of Congress Cataloging-in-Publication Data
Lester, J. C.
Escape from leviathan : liberty, welfare, and anarchy reconciled / J.C. Lester.
p.   cm.
Includes bibliographical references (p.) and index.
ISBN 0–312–23416–3
1. Liberty. 2. Libertarianism. 3. Welfare economics. I. Title.

JC585 .L37   2000
320'.01'1 — dc21

00–025475

This book is printed on paper suitable for recycling and made from fully managed and sustained forest sources.

10   9   8   7   6   5   4   3   2   1
09   08   07   06   05   04   03   02   01   00

Printed and bound in Great Britain by
Antony Rowe Ltd, Chippenham, Wiltshire

To my parents

Nothing in the state,
everything against the state,
everything outside the state.[1]

---

1 This reverses Benito Mussolini's definition of fascism (as quoted in *The Blackwell Encyclopaedia of Political Thought*'s entry on 'fascism' [Miller 1987, 150]). Anarcho-libertarianism, or private-property anarchism, is the opposite of fascism.

Contents

Preface
and acknowledgments

I am indebted to the following people for valuable criticism: David Barker, Mark Brady, John Charvet, Jonathan Le Cocq, Antony Flew, David Gordon, Jan Narveson, and David Ramsay Steele. I have also benefited considerably from the comments of several anonymous reviewers of parts, or all, of what follows.

I have a particular debt to David McDonagh. His arguments first persuaded me to extreme, or consistent, classical liberalism or anarcho-libertarianism. He has also indefatigably continued to argue with me over many parts of this book.

Responsibility for errors remains, of course, mine.

I thank the relevant publishers for permission to quote from the following:

Berlin, Isaiah. 1968. *Four Essays on Liberty*. Oxford: Oxford University Press.

Frey, R. G. (ed.) 1985. *Utility and Rights*. Oxford: Basil Blackwell.

Gauthier, David. 1986. *Morals by Agreement*. New York: Oxford University Press.

Gray, John. 1989. *Liberalisms: Essays in Political Theory*. London: Routledge.

Hahn, Frank, and Martin Hollis. 1979. *Philosophy and Economic Theory*. Oxford: Oxford University Press.

Hare, Richard Mervyn. [1963] 1972. *Freedom and Reason*. Oxford: Oxford University Press.

Hare, Richard Mervyn. [1952] 1986. *The Language of Morals*.
Oxford: Oxford University Press.

Nozick, Robert. 1974. *Anarchy, State, and Utopia*. Oxford: Basil
Blackwell.

Rawls, John. [1972] 1983. *A Theory of Justice*. Oxford: Oxford
University Press.

Sen, Amartya K., and Bernard A. O. Williams (eds.) 1982.
Utilitarianism and Beyond. Cambridge: Cambridge University
Press.

Watson, Gary. (ed.) 1982. *Free Will*. Oxford: Oxford University
Press.

I also thank the editors of the following publications for permission
to incorporate versions of my writings that they have previously
published:

Aristoi

For and Against the State: New Philosophical Readings

Journal of Applied Philosophy

Journal of Social and Evolutionary Systems

Journal of Social Philosophy

Journal of Value Inquiry

1. Introduction

1.1. The Classical-Liberal[1] Compatibility Thesis

There is only one thing that is seriously morally wrong with the world, and that is politics. By 'politics' I mean all that, and only what, involves the state. By 'the state' I mean an organization that coercively imposes ultimate control on some persons and property. If you tell me what most worries you about the world, then I can often tell you how politics is the sole cause of it, or how politics considerably exacerbates it, or why you should change your illiberal opinions.

It was coming to accept this outlook that turned my focus from general philosophy to political philosophy. In particular, I came to view most political disagreement as caused by thinking that human liberty, human welfare, and the free market are often at odds with each other. All I read, including the explicit criticisms of libertarianism, seemed to me to corroborate the view that there is no practical clash among these. I call this the 'classical-liberal compatibility thesis', or 'compatibility thesis' for short, though I here defend a more explicit and more extreme version than any original classical liberal.

The classical liberals,[2] modern libertarians,[3] and pro-market economists generally,[4] often appear to argue – at least implicitly – for the practical compatibility of liberty and welfare in the market.[5] However, such arguments are rarely clear, consistent, comprehensive, and non-moral[6] (people usually feel obliged to take moral sides – unnecessarily, I shall argue – with either liberty or welfare). My book attempts to rectify this by clarifying the philosophical aspects of the compatibility thesis: its main intention is to be a philosophical complement to the relevant social scientific literature. It would be impossible also to explain or even to cite all that literature. When dealing with specific criticisms and alternative positions, I shall outline and cite ideas and works insofar as it would seem incomplete not to do so, so that the reader can have some idea of the overall libertarian outlook. There will not, however, be a comprehensive attempt to defend libertarianism in empirical terms. And though many of the cited works will have relevant arguments and evidence, very few of them will be consistently or comprehensively libertarian.

The compatibility thesis seems generally less popular among today's libertarians than it was in the nineteenth century. Today, libertarian economists tend to focus on the 'economic efficiency' or welfare side of markets while libertarian philosophers are more likely to emphasize libertarian 'rights'. Perhaps this is partly due to greater subject specialization in modern times.[7] The compatibility thesis is obviously much more convincing if it can be explicitly and clearly maintained.[8] This book is thus a deliberate attempt to defend the compatibility thesis in a more explicit, extreme, and interdisciplinary way – though the emphasis is clearly on the philosophy.

The compatibility thesis suffers especially from vagueness and error concerning conceptual and practical connections among four things in particular: rationality, liberty, welfare, and anarchy. These will, therefore, be the subjects of the four main chapters. There is a cluster of major problems here: there is no clear account of (classical liberal or libertarian) liberty or what it entails; want-satisfaction, as a theory of welfare, often suffers unsound criticisms or is misinterpreted in practice; some pro-market economists' conclusions can appear to rely on a dubious assumption of instrumental rationality; the theories of liberty, welfare, and anarchy defended in this book also require a rationality assumption; there are erroneous prejudices concerning the nature and practice of politics and anarchy. There are also various subsidiary problems, such as whether there is weakness of will, and the nature of free will and of moral sentiments.

I shall now attempt to state the extreme compatibility thesis more clearly (no doubt various objections will readily spring to the reader's mind, but these will have to wait until the relevant chapters): in practice (rather than in imaginary cases) and in the long term, there are no systematic clashes among interpersonal liberty, general welfare, and market-anarchy, where these terms are to be understood roughly as follows: 'interpersonal liberty' is 'not being imposed on by others'; 'general welfare' is 'people having their unimposed-wants satisfied'; 'market-anarchy' is 'unrestricted libertarian trade'; and the underpinning conception of 'rationality' is 'agents always attempt to achieve what they most want under the perceived circumstances'.

I shall not, I hope, fall into the trap of barren essentialism or mere verbal analysis, as criticized in many of Karl Popper's books,[9] instead of discussing the truth or falsehood of theories. My view is not that there are 'essences' or 'true meanings' of these things but that there is often at least one of the following errors concerning them: a sound commonsense understanding or plain English usage is being flouted for no valid reason (such as 'coercion' being extended beyond 'the use of force'); there is no clear account of the real phenomenon which some word denotes, and a better account is needed to avoid confusion (such as 'weakness of will'); there is no clear meaning to some word and so a better definition, only partly stipulative, can assist in clarifying what people must intend (such as the libertarian use of 'liberty'); there are important logical and practical connections among these ideas and the things they denote in the world, which are no more 'merely verbal' than are, say, the theories of geometry (such as anarchy being intrinsically liberal). Thus I intend my approach not to be the mere linguistic analysis of normal usage but what W. W. Bartley, following Popper, calls 'diacritical analysis' (1984, 125).

An important aspect of the compatibility thesis is the nonmoral approach that I take throughout. It might help to give an early and explicit explanation of this somewhat unusual idea of eschewing moral advocacy.

1.2. Why Moral Advocacy is Avoided

In modern Western societies, thanks mainly to classical liberal thinkers, there are two dominant criteria of what is socially desirable: liberty and welfare (under some interpretations of these). Most people, including moral and political philosophers, have moral and political views that tend to limit welfare promotion for libertarian reasons or to override liberty[10] because of welfare considerations – and do both on different issues. Other general social values – depending on their interpretation – usually fit roughly on one side or the other, or are regarded as promoting both in some way: democracy, equality, human rights, civil liberties, 'social justice', autonomy, and so forth. At the extremes of the two views we have natural-rights libertarians (such as Robert Nozick, at least in his 1974, and Murray Rothbard) and utilitarians (such as R. M. Hare and Peter Singer). So if it is possible effectively to defend the congruence of liberty and welfare in practice, then there is no practical need for an ultimate moral defense of either. A moral defense is necessary only insofar as critics have moral ends that trump both human liberty and human welfare. Such critics are rare and can have little effect in practice. Therefore, in this book on political philosophy, it is possible to avoid any defense of liberty or welfare as ultimate moral goals while still having a substantive thesis. I certainly do not mean to belittle moral arguments as such. It is simply that to bring in moral arguments would distract from my arguments for *objective* compatibility.

An analogical defense of this non-moral thesis occurs to me. Suppose two undiscovered primitive tribes living in the same region. One tribe thinks that eating any part of animals without hearts is immoral. The other tribe thinks that eating any part of animals without kidneys is immoral. They have heated debates about both the moral issues and the empirical facts about which animals have which organs. They feel moral contempt for each other and continually attack each other in attempts to enforce their moral views. Peaceful association suffers considerably. An anthropologist with some knowledge of biology discovers them. He explains that all animals have either both a heart and kidneys or neither.[11] This view has been widely tested by biologists, and they also have plausible theoretical reasons for explaining that this will always be so (except in the case of genetically engineerable animals, we may suppose[12]). Therefore, he argues, the bitter disagreements and struggles can cease, to the great benefit of all. It would surely be irrelevant for the tribes to insist that the anthropologist say which side he is really on, and give his tacit moral arguments. He need not be on either side. It would probably only cloud the issue of the important thesis he is stating for him also to bring in moral arguments.

The politically typical reader might now be thinking that I have hardly made a case that the compatibility thesis is plausible, and that I ought to carry on at some length to establish this if I am to persuade him to take it at all seriously. This is where epistemological reasons oblige me to disagree. If the compatibility thesis is true, then it is surely important; but I do not think that there would be any point in attempting to establish its plausibility. For another unusual aspect of this book is its use of the critical-rationalist method. An early explanation of this too might go some way to defusing those critics for whom it appears obvious that someone with a thesis must attempt to demonstrate, establish, prove, justify, or ground it.

1.3. A Critical-Rationalist Apologia

Critical-rationalist epistemology is used throughout the book. This theory of knowledge was developed by Karl Popper (see, for example, his 1978 and 1979 books) and slightly extended in scope by W. W. Bartley (1984).[13] Although always a general epistemology in principle, Popper soon concentrated on science – which he saw as involving more interesting problems and in a sharper form – and only later went back to elaborating the broader implications. The following very brief exposition will follow the same route.

The fundamental idea is that all knowledge is ultimately conjectural. Because of the intrinsically unlimited nature of universal theories, we can never make them more probable (in an epistemological sense) by finding new examples that fit with what they predict. We can never give our theories firm foundations of any sort. To attempt to do so is the inductivist or, more generally, foundationalist fallacy. However, any single counter-example is sufficient to show that a universal theory is false. So the best instrumentally rational approach is to conjecture theories that are as bold as possible and then attempt to test them rigorously. In this way we can at least have theories that are as large in content as our best tests will allow. Such bold universal theories might be false, and probably are: in an infinite universe it is statistically unlikely that we have stumbled on the truth. However, given our apparent success in dealing with the world, there seems no reason to suppose that we have totally failed to understand it. By rejecting falsified theories we might be reaching ones with ever greater truth content.[14] Without this approach we have no course of action that is not ultimately arbtrary.

In the broader sense of this epistemology, criticism is what takes on the role of empirical tests. One does not need to specify what would count as a falsifying criticism,[15] and in philosophical matters the very specification (in precise terms, at least) might already constitute the falsification. Nor does criticizability require that the thesis could be false: for if there are necessary truths then they cannot be false, but we can concede that we might err in thinking that we have discovered one, as sometimes happens with mathematical proofs (Bartley 1984, 238–41). It is sufficient that one seriously attempts to answer criticism. For instance, the critical rationalist approach in a defender of classical logic such as the logician David Miller, is to read and answer critics of classical logic while trying not to beg the question (though he is always likely to appear to his opponents to be vulnerable to that charge). He says he cannot specify precisely what would be a refutation without producing one, which he thinks is impossible. It is the real openness to criticism that is the core of Popper's epistemological method (Miller 1994).

If critical rationalism is not, as Popper thought, the solution to the problems of induction and foundationalism, then it is at least a pragmatic way of dealing with theories. It is not necessary for critical rationalism to be the absolutely correct epistemology for this process to be valuable. This is not a limited approach. Most people recognize the value of criticism. It is just that it might irritate those who like a bit of 'justification' first to find that what they would have put in that role arises only in response to criticism. Where, they might ask, do the refutations of others' arguments leave us? Merely unrefuted. But where, they might demand, is the account going? Nowhere, we are already there: we have a thesis to defend, not to arrive at or build up.

Therefore, this book does not start with first principles and attempt to build up to well-justified conclusions.[16] This is not an attempt to prove, demonstrate, or show that liberty and welfare are congruent in a market. It is merely a philosophical and economic defense of this bold conjecture from an unavoidably limited number of views and criticisms that are inconsistent with it. The approach with all the relevant conceptions is to state the respective theses clearly and briefly and then to attempt to defend and reconcile them by considering major and typical criticisms. Why do I attempt to explain errors in the authors tackled? Why do I take up particular issues? Only because these seem significant criticisms that require a reply. The idea is to show that the chosen conceptions and the compatibility thesis can withstand such criticisms and comparisons, and so are improvements that remain, as yet, unrefuted.

That this book follows the critical-rationalist method is the reason that critics dominate the arguments in what follows. If I were merely to build a castle of consistent theory then that would probably leave these critics, and those with similar opinions, quite unmoved. It seems that one must in practice take on prevalent and powerful criticisms. One can do this tacitly, by writing with known views in mind or by postulating criticisms. In some cases I have resorted to postulation, though only in self-criticism or at the suggestion of another. Generally, I have tried to tackle real critics in the relevant literature. This has made it necessary to deal with myriad awkward points. In this way, I hope to be seriously testing the compatibility thesis.[17] (The philosophers and economists being examined tend to run together their discussions of the issues, so it would be too confusing and repetitive to discuss each conception of the thesis in strict isolation and only then to attempt to reconcile them.)

In the books and articles discussed, I do not usually first give a thorough account of the writers' views and then go on to attempt comprehensive replies: these views often include unrelated matters and points of agreement, or involve crucial mistaken assumptions which make their general arguments irrelevant. I take a more dialog-like approach by tackling what seem to be important and separable points with respect to the compatibility thesis. The overall impression might be of a 'set them up and knock them down' method, as one critic put it. For critical rationalists, however, that is just what one ought to be doing, though as fairly as one can (I might define 'justificationism' as a 'build it up and ignore them method'). So if what follows looks somewhat like the meeting of endless debating points, then that is because, in a sense, that is what critical rationalism is about. These points need not relate to each other in any integrated way: each merely needs to be inconsistent with the thesis.

This book is primarily in the area of political philosophy. I include problems in moral theory, epistemology, metaphysics, and economics in proportion to how far they are important to the general political philosophical theory. So, for instance, there is a relevant discussion of so-called weakness of will, but it is obviously severely limited in its length and comprehensiveness. The

breadth of the subject matter involved has also inevitably re-
sulted in many approximate solutions to important problems. It
would certainly be necessary to revise these approximations in
the light of a more detailed approach and further criticism. The
result in any particular area may be 'too quick' for the specialist,
but it seemed more important to attempt an overall defense of
the general theory than to write definitively on any aspect.

Despite attempting to avoid moral issues, I shall now state
my general moral position, though I shall not be advocating it in
this book. I do this for various reasons. This should make even
more sense of why I am defending the compatibility thesis, and
it should stop people mistakenly reading morality into the arguments that follow (or help them to catch me out if I have
brought it in despite my intentions[18]). Also, I want people to understand how it is possible to be a libertarian who is not a natural rightist, nor a utilitarian, nor a contractarian.

I am not a preference utilitarian: I would defend unimposed-
want satisfaction only as a plausible and practical welfare criterion that does not clash with liberty and anarchy. But neither do
I subscribe to natural rights-based libertarianism in the strong,
objectivist and moral-cognitivist, sense that some suppose can
bridge the gap between values and facts (though it would be irrelevant for me to discuss such theories in this book). I do, however, think that people have a moral right to liberty and all that
follows therefrom in the subjectivist sense that I feel it immoral,
in normal practice rather than in any conceivable situation, to
deny them this. I also see moral differences not as arbitrary
clashes of sentiment but as capable of employing the same critical-rationalist method: arguing *as though* there were a truth of
the matter.[19] Both moral and factual arguments ultimately appeal to (inter) subjective evaluation of how things seems to be: it
seems right (good or true) or wrong (bad or false) to the individ-
ual(s).

My general moral position is of critical-rationalist libertarianism: I can see no good reason for limiting interpersonal liberty. I see liberty as the basic social rule within which other values must fit.[20] I do not base this moral position on anything; it is
as unsupported as universal empirical theories. If asked to say
in virtue of what liberty is valuable, one can only give a finite
list, which might miss some sources of its value. Even if someone
accepts this list, he can ask us in virtue of what those things are

valuable, and so on ad infinitum. A finite moral justification of liberty is impossible by that philosophical route. Or if someone asks us to demonstrate the empirical connections between liberty and the things that supposedly make it valuable, then we shall find it as impossible as demonstrating that a scientific theory is universally true. The only sensible course of action is to explain that the critic is asking for the impossible – you could ask the same of his moral position – and instead request a single sound reason why it is not desirable to respect liberty.

When defending this moral theory, outside this book, I use whatever arguments seem sound in the circumstances. Major types of arguments include defending liberty as intuitively morally right in itself in some cases, and showing that there is no clash with morally desirable welfare in others. I might also argue that it best promotes, or is at least consistent with, or ought to override, certain conceptions of autonomy, justice, equality, self-realization, equal opportunities, need-satisfaction, interest-satisfaction, perfect rationality, individual dignity, or whatever other moral values are under discussion.

So while I admit that I have moral motives and wider interests, I assert that this book is about only the critical-rationalist philosophical and, far less directly, social scientific defense of the objective compatibility thesis. However, it can also more generally be seen as one aspect, though a broad one, of a (critical-rationalist) defense of libertarianism.

Why should anyone take any interest in this book? I guess that for libertarians the incentive is either to find some philosophical arguments and conceptual tools with which to debate non-libertarians or against which to test their own ideas. The fact that anarchy is assumed to be feasible might seem highly problematic even to many libertarians. This should not put them off too much though. Anarchy is merely an extreme form of liberty and private property. If some form of minimal state were to prove necessary to protect these, that would not undermine all the conclusions in this book (though it would, of course, falsify the extreme compatibility thesis I am defending). It would simply mean that it would be necessary to find some way of establishing and funding a minimalist state that would be consistent with minimizing imposed costs (which would thereby continue to promote general welfare as much as is practical in the long term). Given that the laissez-faire empirical conclusions and arguments are merely outlined, why should non-libertarians take any interest? They might want to refute any philosophical arguments that attempt to defend such laissez-faire conclusions, or they might simply want to understand them. However, there might even be enough general argument for a non-libertarian to start taking the position seriously.

I shall start each main chapter with a brief statement of its general thesis; that is, the particular conception and how I shall attempt to defend and reconcile it. This should give an overview of what is to follow. For those unfamiliar with the literature being dealt with, this opening statement might be a bit hard to take in completely, but the issues should become clearer as one reads on, and readers can then refer back to the opening statement. I do not set out my own views in great detail before tackling criticisms; this is precisely because it is only the nature of the criticisms that determines what details are relevant. It should be clear that each position being examined is significantly inconsistent with the chapter conception and its part in the compatibility thesis.

We first look at the rationality assumption that underpins economics and this book's conceptions of liberty, welfare, and anarchy. Some readers might prefer to go straight to the more exciting liberty chapter (but many likely criticisms will have been anticipated in the rationality chapter).

2. Rationality

2.0. Chapter Thesis

The standard, modern, economic assumption of instrumental rationality holds people to be self-interested utility-maximizers. Economists usually intend this to mean egoistic preferences and perfect calculation over time. Insofar as people think this to be unrealistic, it throws doubt on the (generally pro-market) conclusions of the economists. Here we give the assumption of self-interested utility-maximization an aprioristic interpretation that may help to reconcile standard economics with Austrian School aprioristic economics. This a priori sense does not imply egoism and is not trivial. Economics requires this sense as a core assumption in order to link its results more convincingly to liberty, welfare, and anarchy. This book's conceptions of liberty, welfare, and anarchy also presuppose some such account. This chapter has proven the most troublesome and tentative aspect of the defense of the compatibility thesis, but an attempt was necessary. I hope that there is at least some general soundness in the approach.

First we shall look at the aprioristic view of rationality. Then we shall break the rationality assumption into parts and consider each part in turn. There will be a few words at the end on another key economic concept of particular relevance: demand.

2.1. Why Defend Aprioristic Instrumental Rationality?

This chapter is partly an attempt to reconcile two extreme views in economics: the (neglected) subjective, aprioristic approach and the (standard) objective, empirical approach. The Austrian subjective view of value, building on Carl Menger's theory of value, was developed into a theory of economics as being entirely an a priori[21] theory of action.[22] This probably finds its most extreme statement in Ludwig von Mises's *Human Action* (1949). By contrast, the standard economic view has developed into making empirical predictions about economic phenomena whereby the truth of the assumptions, especially about economic agents, is relatively unimportant: predictive fecundity is all. This finds an extreme statement in Milton Friedman's introductory essay in his *Essays in Positive Economics* (1953). However, some economists fall somewhere between the two extremes, such as Richard McKenzie and Gordon Tullock.[23]

As a consequence, Austrian economics has fallen out of favor with most economists for not being empirical, while standard economics has fallen out of favor with many non-economists for being insufficiently linked with the real subjective aspects of human values, especially welfare, liberty, and morality. I generally view the Austrians as correct on an aprioristic core. And it is also quite valid to argue ceteris paribus while drawing out the logical consequences of, say, rent control or minimum wage laws. It must be a mistake *completely* to dismiss such arguments in favor of empirical tests. But I shall not here be attempting the immense project of adjudicating between (or, perhaps, marrying the best parts of each of) the two approaches to economics in areas other than the rationality assumption.[24]

We need to look at the problem in more detail. Economics – particularly that of the Austrian, Chicago, and Virginia Schools – is the social science that has ostensibly done the most to link the free market with liberty and welfare. Instrumental rationality, a basic assumption of economics, can appear to be unrealistic or viciously vacuous (depending on how one interprets it), and so this has a tendency to undermine its conclusions. The concept of economic demand is more central still and sometimes appears to bias economics in the direction of market conclusions (as it only counts 'demand' where people can afford the price). This has not been so fiercely criticized recently, though its defense is illuminating. A version of the rationality assumption is also necessary for the conceptions of liberty and welfare used in this book. So if we can defend the rationality assumption and economic demand, then this should go some way to defending the conclusions of the (generally pro-market) economists, the conceptions of liberty and welfare, and thus the compatibility thesis.

The standard interpretation of instrumental rationality (as found in, say, Hirshleifer 1984, discussed later) has people as self-interestedly maximizing, over time, their utility – though we can only observe them revealing their preferences by their purchases (and other actions). This chapter is not about defending this standard outlook directly. In particular I readily concede here that people are not always 'self-interested' in the sense of being egoistic, for I deny that economics needs to assume this. I also admit that people can make mistakes concerning their long-term interests (but the empirical literature can in part show that people are better off making and learning from their own mistakes than having others control them, and some philosophical arguments can contribute to showing that this is so as well). Instead, I defend an aprioristic interpretation of the standard instrumental-rationality formulation.

I take the following to summarize the major objections to the ideas that agents are self-interested utility-maximizers and to economic demand (I shall later quote and discuss critics in each case, so shall not anticipate that by expanding the following points here):

1) The self and its interests: This requires a complex philosophical and empirical account of the self (which is malleable rather than fixed and which has multiple identities) and its interests (about which the self can be mistaken, or socially determined, or weak-willed).

2) Self-interest: People are not merely self-interested for they often consider the interests of others, notably in moral decisions. Complete self-sacrifice is possible.

3) Utility: However one interprets 'utility' (pleasure, happiness, and so on), it does not make sense as the single motive or goal. There are many things we want, and we cannot reduce them to a homogeneous desire or aim.

4) Utility-maximization: People do not maximize anything in particular, let alone 'utility'. Their diverse activities are incommensurable in terms of value.

5) Economic demand: People cannot always afford what they have a 'demand' for (in a more ordinary sense of the word). In particular, this conception neglects those important demands that we know as 'needs'. Moreover, much of what people do have an economic demand for they do not really need. This conception is thus inherently pro-market and anti-welfare.

This chapter deals with these criticisms in turn (though many examples of 3, 4, and 5 I leave to the welfare chapter, which also includes such issues).[25] It should help to give immediately a similar outline of each of these terms as I shall defend them (again, their full meaning and strength should become clearer as the discussion of criticisms proceeds):

1) The self and its interests: Any single thing is a self in a general and innocuous sense: 'the thing it*self*'. The term does not have to imply anything about the nature of persons or of personal identity. It is irrelevant that there are important philosophical and empirical problems about the 'self' in that sense.

Anything that has desires has interests in the sense intended: things it is interested in achieving.[26] It is not necessary that these desires be held self-consciously (or reflectively) and continuously; it is sufficient that some kind of desire motivates behavior

2) Self-perceived interest: The self-interest assumption is not to be contrasted with altruism, with which it is compatible, but with being an unconscious automaton or without a spontaneous will of one's own.[27] Agents, qua agents, follow their consciously felt, self-perceived interests or desires.

3) Utility: What one desires or wants to do, one has utility (psychological satisfaction) at the thought of doing. Striving for want-satisfaction, or to avoid want-dissatisfaction in the case of disutility, must be what motivates agents.

4) Utility-maximization: What one has the strongest desire to do, one has the strongest utility at the thought of doing. Agents aim at the goal the thought of which gives them the greatest utility, or least disutility, at the time of aiming at it (again, no great self-consciousness is being presupposed; for example, the 'thoughtless' scratching of an itch is more want-satisfying than any alternative action that occurs to us at the time).

5) Economic Demand: Mere evidence of the willingness and ability to pay a price for something is not inherently anti-welfare or pro-market. Moreover, no alternative need-based conception of demand could be practical.

Thus I am roughly, with the reservations below, defending the a priori, or subjective, approach to rationality (not to economics as a whole) as expounded in Mises 1949 and Israel Kirzner 1960. According to this view, introspection and reason show that agents are instrumentally rational in the sense of being purposeful maximizers. I prefer to interpret instrumental rationality explicitly as 'self-interested utility-maximization' in a clearer attempt to tie the aprioristic view to the standard view.

It might seem to many economists that I am defending a straw man. The literal truth of the rationality assumption is often thought to be unimportant for the general business of doing economics. Gary Becker (1962) has even argued that with no rationality assumption there would, with a high probability, still be downward-sloping demand curves due to limited income (and so economic analysis and empirical predictions). So one might question whether the economic work I want to defend need, or even can, be interpreted using an a priori conception of instrumental rationality. However, from a purely economic viewpoint, it seems that we need a defense of instrumental rationality as a descriptive account of what agents are trying to do efficiently (they are a priori instrumentally rational in the sense of trying to make the best of things; but they need not be instrumentally rational in the sense of succeeding in this aim); for if agents are not trying to be efficiently instrumentally rational, then it is hard to make any real sense of their behavior. Consequently, the prescriptive accounts (as given by economists in any advisory role) of efficient instrumental rationality (of what should be done to achieve certain ends) must carry very little weight. So shall all the results based on the additional rule-of-thumb assumptions (such as, individuals maximizing want-satisfaction over time and firms being profit-maximizers[28]) that also implicitly approximate to, or build on, the subjective instrumental rationality of agents. Standard economics cannot entirely abandon the core, a priori, subjective aspect of their science without producing mere predictions about prices and patterns of behavior that are impossible to relate to real human purposes.[29] Admittedly, this chapter does not go into the economic detail of the extent of the links between Austrian aprioristic rationality and, what I call, standard rule-of-thumb economic rationality, but perhaps the formulation of rationality defended here is a more explicit approach to such links than that offered by Kirzner, who is probably the leading advocate of this thesis among present day economists. It does, at least, tackle many of the broader philosophical issues.

Before dealing with criticisms of this formulation of aprioristic rationality, I should mention a few more important differences from Mises 1949 and Kirzner 1960 and 1990. Both Mises and Kirzner conflate two ideas: 1) we are always motivated to satisfy our greatest desire, or want, or appetite, or perceived interest; and 2) we always aim at the greatest psychological satisfaction, or pleasure, or happiness. 1 we can plausibly interpret as a priori true; 2 is plainly false. To aim at satisfying one's strongest desire is not the same as aiming at psychological satisfaction when that desire is satisfied. We can even desire things that *cannot* cause us psychological satisfaction once attained – such as posthumous fame. Mises, in particular, regularly conflates these two ideas in a way that makes his position hedonistic or eudamonistic and false instead of to do with want-satisfaction in the aprioristic sense I shall defend here (for example, Mises [1949] 1966, 92, 242). If we do not make this vital distinction, then we are open to the criticism that, as we have goals other than psychological satisfaction, the assumption is at best a rough approximation and all conclusions based on it are thereby suspect – exactly the sort of criticism that we want to avoid.

This book might also have a broader account of rationality than Kirzner has in mind, as I do not agree with his possible qualification of the role of rationality when he writes, more recently, in such terms as the following: '*to the extent that* "rationality" plays a role in human decisions ... ' (1990, 36) and 'to reject the scientific demonstration of the power of such systematic learning patterns, on the grounds of occasional or frequent human "irrationality," ... ' (1990, 36). If agents, qua agents, are bound to be instrumentally rational, then there seems no room for such 'irrationality'. Neither can I agree with Kirzner's view that 'the core of economic theory is the theory of markets' (1990, 33) (unless perhaps, as is quite possible, Kirzner intends 'core' to mean 'the most important part'). As Mises held, the core of economics (at least qua social science[30]) seems to be the rationality assumption itself: one needs it to make subjective sense of markets, and one can use it for analysing Robinson-Crusoe situations and non-market choices generally.

Apart from these reservations, and a few others implicit in what follows, I recommend Mises's and Kirzner's defenses and uses of a priori economic rationality, and I only hope that what follows is philosophically complementary.

We shall now examine the separate parts of the rationality assumption that have been distinguished.

2.2. The Self and Its Interests

a. Formal Definitions

Economists do not need a sophisticated account of the self in either the sense of what it is to be a person as such or to be a particular person. Some philosophers think there is a problem with the nature of the self in these senses. The idea has its modern origins, though it goes back much further, in the Cartesian dualism of the mind and the body. René Descartes used this distinction because he thought that there was something certain about one's experiences, at least that one is having them and cannot be deluded about the nature of them, in a way that the physical world is not certain. Despite having gone on supposedly to prove the non-delusional nature of our clear and distinct experiences, with help from the idea of a perfect being who is no deceiver, he was still left with the dualism of an immaterial mind and a material body.[31] The self is the mind that just happens to occupy this particular body but which, apparently, could in principle move to a different habitat. This idea remains popular in attenuated form, and causes the identification of the person or personality (one's conscious states or behavioral dispositions) with the 'self' (what one 'really' is).

'Self' does not need to be used to mean the person or personality. English does not absolutely demand this usage, and in one sense it is at odds with modern science: science seems to show that we are fundamentally biological organisms rather than beings that contingently inhabit these organisms.[32] One can speak of the self of an inanimate object as the same sort of self as that of a human being: 'self' can simply be used to mean 'thing' or 'entity': 'the chair it*self* was missing'; 'the man him*self* was missing'. Admittedly, it is odd to refer to chairs as having 'selves', but the economic use of the 'self', in 'self-interest', can coherently be seen as an innocuous reference to an entity without any implication as to the nature of that entity.

When 'interest' is added to 'self' we are simply informed that we are dealing with the idea of an entity that has conscious interests; there is no implication about the nature or structure of the self or the interests (or values or desires[33]). There are simply objective interests of the conscious entity in the sense that these are actually felt, rather than the interests that would or ought to be felt given more information or greater insight into how the world is. We humans are biological organisms that usually have a consciousness that includes interests. If one states that Mr Jones himself has an interest in economics, then one need mean no more than that physical entity itself, who happens to be the *Homo sapiens* we label Mr Jones, often desires to understand economics. If Mr Jones himself lost his interest in economics, then we need not speak of a change in his identity. Mr Jones is the same physical self who simply happens to have lost a particular interest.

I think that something like this materialist account is, at least part of, the solution to the philosophical problem of personal identity. Whether or not one accepts this, the physical conception of the self will do for economics to identify the particular agent. One might object that the body's cells are replaced throughout one's life, so that there is not even a permanent physical self. But people are not as physically different as the body's replacement of cells might lead one to think. The genetic structure remains and one's brain might not be renewed at all (this has recently been disputed), though a tiny fraction of brain cells die every day. In any case, the continuing physical process over time is also an adequate 'self' for our purposes.

Another philosophical idea that economics has no room for is that of divisions of interests within the self such that a more-valued interest can be overwhelmed by a less-valued one. This ancient belief in weakness of will remains popular and will be discussed later. There is also the related idea that there are competing consciousnesses within an individual.

What follows might seem to imply that there is a sophisticated alternative account of the phenomena to be discussed implicit in the rationality assumption being defended; that the rationality assumption is really very complicated because it entails all these responses. That is not so. It is simply necessary to develop a more sophisticated defense of the basic assumption when critics take sophisticated positions that are incompatible with it.

The above sketch is incompatible with that of very many philosophers. In a much longer book, it might be possible to deal with quite a few of them. Instead we deal with two who are typical, general, and rigorous in their criticism: Harry G. Frankfurt

(1982) and Gary Watson (1982). Both of these argue for positions that are incompatible with the assumption that human beings can always be treated as selves who are simply attempting to follow their own interests out of their own free will. All the main issues seem to arise in these two accounts. Frankfurt argues that being a person requires us to be able to *desire* that certain desires become our will, and that freedom of will means *successfully* choosing our will. Watson argues that there can be a clash between one's desires and values, and that only if the values win can we be free agents. If their criticisms are sound, then paternalism might seem to follow if one is to protect human beings who are not fully persons, or who are not always capable of free will or free choice (assuming that the state and its officials are immune to similar criticisms). So these critics merit a serious response from the point of view of the compatibility thesis. To the extent that it seems called for, various points will also be made concerning liberty, welfare, and anarchy.

b. Freewill and Persons

Frankfurt holds that an essential difference between persons and other beings is to be found in the structure of the will. He defines 'first-order desires' as 'simply desires to do or not to do one thing or another' (1982, 83). He argues that a being is not a person unless it is capable of having 'second-order volitions' (86). This means the ability to reflect on one's desires critically such that one can come to desire to make some desire into the thing that one wills. What one 'wills' is the 'effective desire' that one acts on or would act on in the appropriate circumstances, unless that desire changed. Beings without second-order volitions are called 'wantons': 'the essential characteristic of a wanton is that he does not care about his will' (86). This includes all non-human animals, very young children, and perhaps some adults. Apparently, all adult humans may be to some extent wanton for they can often lack second-order volitions concerning certain matters. A wanton 'may possess and employ rational faculties of a high order' (87).

Frankfurt then gives us the example of two narcotics addicts.[34] He supposes that one is an 'unwilling' addict: he has first-order desires both to give up and to take narcotics (both paths have their attractions), plus a second-order 'volition' to give up – but his addiction is too strong for this desire and so the desire to take the drugs becomes his first-order volition. The other addict is supposed to have the same conflicting first-order desires but one simply proves stronger than the other without a second-order volition of any kind. Frankfurt says of this latter addict that 'he has no identity apart from his first-order desires' (88).

This example is unfortunate. It looks tendentious insofar as Frankfurt has chosen an emotive subject where he demotes a narcotics user possibly to a non-person, or wanton, status. It seems that we might switch the situation around by supposing that one drug user could have the second-order volition to enjoy his drugs while the other one merely enjoyed them because his first-order volition was stronger (Frankfurt later considers this possibility, as we shall see).

Frankfurt says that the (second-order) 'unwilling' addict makes one of the first order desires 'more truly his own' such that he

> may meaningfully make the analytically puzzling statements that [1] the force moving him to take the drug is a *force other than his own* [emphasis added], and that [2] it is not of his own free will but rather [3] against his will that this force moves him to take it. (88)

Taken *literally*, Frankfurt is quite right that these statements are 'meaningful', for we can understand them and they are apparently false. With 1, it is clearly this addict's first-order volition that makes him take the drugs. Ex hypothesi, there is no force 'other than his own'. With 2, Frankfurt introduces the notion of 'free will' without any indication that he has a Pickwickian sense in mind, at least compared to the ordinary sense rather than philosophical senses. In the ordinary use of 'free will' it is clear that this is a case of someone's exercising free will, for he is not being forced by another.[35] With 3, it follows from Frankfurt's quite ordinary definition of 'will' as 'effective desire' that the narcotics user takes the drugs as a result of his will. Apparently Frankfurt means 'meaningfully' in some *metaphorical* sense. One can clearly accept Frankfurt's two-level structure of desire, as I do, without being committed to his view of free will. (Obviously, all this is implicitly to do with the so-called 'weakness of will' phenomenon; explicitly dealt with in the next section as an alternative to Frankfurt's account.)

Frankfurt goes on to link his view of personhood with 'freedom of the will' and to distinguish this from freedom of action:

> Now freedom of action is (roughly, at least) the freedom to do what one wants to do. Analogously, then, the statement that a person enjoys freedom of the will means (also roughly) that he is free to want what he wants to want ... to have the will he wants. (90)

And the congruence between his first- and second-order volitions must not be 'only a happy chance' (90) but real choices.

One can accept that one has freedom of action when one's actions are unconstrained. But it would be more usual to say that one has freedom of the will to the extent that there is no *external agent* who is dictating or constraining one's will (effective desires). As long as someone's will is as it is as a result of his being the being that he is, then we can say that his will is free. If someone had electrodes in his brain, which could be stimulated by someone else to create effective desires, then he would thus far be the puppet of the other agent rather than an autonomous or free one himself. Such a set up is possible but only usually occurs with animals in the scientist's laboratory.[36] This account has the virtue of allowing a compatibilist solution (in a different sense of 'compatibility' to that of this book's thesis) to the traditional free-will-versus-determinism debate.[37] One acts as a result of free will as long as one's will is unconstrained by others. But one's will is naturally constrained by the nature of the being that one is. Without this constraint one's actions would be entirely random rather than free. The school of thought that demands a kind of free will that escapes both determinism and mere randomness has never given an intelligible account of a third option, as far as I can see (but I cannot discuss cases here).[38] It follows from this compatibilist position that all animals have free will to the extent that they make choices (economic decisions) rather than follow some overwhelming instinct (though not all 'instinct' need rule out choice). Free will seems to require only choice, and human beings always have to choose their movements except for certain autonomic ones, such as the heart beat and reflex responses.[39]

There are often external physical barriers to what we want to do that limit us, and hence we are less free (in one sense of 'free'). There are also physical and psychological barriers within ourselves that limit us, and hence we are analogously less free than we might be. But to lack the ability to change our effective desires, or personality, is not to lack free will. The glutton who cannot make himself desire fasting has a completely free will – for no one is controlling his will but himself, what he is – but he does not have complete freedom of desire, any more than he has complete freedom of factual beliefs or moral feelings, because he is limited by his nature; by what he is. At any particular moment we find our desires, beliefs, and values by introspection. If one finds that one has a desire to change one's effective desire and that one cannot, then one has come up against a constraint on what one is (even if it is only an immediate constraint that might eventually somehow be overcome). One's will is free in the sense of 'free from external determination'; it could never be free in the sense of 'free of any constraint whatsoever'. To be a particular thing is to be a constrained thing. One must have constraints on what one is or one would not be anything at all. An unbounded object made of no particular stuff in no particular shape could not exist. Any real object, including an agent, is logically bound to have limits both physical and psychological (stones are severely limited psychologically; humans considerably less so).

There does seem to be something to the idea that self-reflection makes for personhood. But all a person's desires are constrained to some extent. Those who have the will they desire to have are lucky, for often they are more or less bound to have it (in the case of sexual preferences, for instance). They are not obviously thereby to be thought of as limited in some undesirable way. Frankfurt seems logically committed to viewing all effective desires that we could not change if we wanted to as thereby being undesirable examples of an 'unfree will'. I cannot see anything necessarily undesirable about such desires or anything that makes the will unfree in any important sense. Is it an unfortunate lack of free will for a man to be contentedly heterosexual just because he would be unable, if he were to try, to will himself otherwise? Frankfurt fails to deal with such ordinary examples.[40]

Frankfurt's account goes on to rule out higher order 'volitions' than the second level by 'commitment' at that level (91). But (as Gary Watson observes, in the next article to be answered) it is not clear why such commitment could not take place at the first level instead. And Frankfurt even admits that second-order volitions can be capricious, so the value of having his 'free will' is unclear.

We next meet a third addict who is a willing one who would take steps to reacquire the addiction if it should fade. Frankfurt makes this supposition to show that this addict would be morally responsible for affirming the addiction with a second-order volition. This addict is held to lack free will, nevertheless, for he would not be in a position to stop even if he wanted to. Well, this addict is not externally constrained and thus is like the other two. This would be so even if he were as addicted to his drug as everyone is born 'addicted' to air, food, and warmth. It must be mistaken to say that we lack free will because we need these mundane things in order to live, though this seems to be what Frankfurt would have to say to be consistent.[41]

I conjecture that Frankfurt has confused free will (voluntariness) with the ability to choose one's motivating desires. He was trying to find a way to prevent a person from ultimately being a 'slave' to some unchosen desire. But it is impossible to avoid ultimately unchosen desires: some desires must arise spontaneously in us or we would be without initial motivation to make any choice at all. Even if we could simply feel any effective desire that we chose to, we would still be left with an unchosen desire at a higher level: the desire that made us choose. Complete 'free will' in this sense would require an infinite regress.

Where does this leave us? Frankfurt's insights are 1) the ability to reflect upon one's desires is part of what we seem to mean by a 'person'; and 2) we sometimes find that we desire other effective desires than those we do have. Do these insights undermine the economic conception of the self and its interests in any way? No. 1) When the economist uses his conception of a self with interests he can usually be interpreted as meaning a person in so far as he is analysing human behavior. But, as explained, if this looks problematic, then he can equally well be interpreted as meaning any entity with interests or desires. No theory of personhood is implied. 2) The other economic assumption here is that of selves following their interests. This has not been effectively undermined by anything in Frankfurt's account. But this raises the topic of weakness of will that has been hovering around Frankfurt's position, and it now seems appropriate to discuss it explicitly as an alternative account.

c. Weakness of Will or Meta-Desire?

I do not deny 'weakness of will' in the sense of 'whim', or 'strength of will' in the sense of 'determination'. However, most would admit a prima facie inconsistency in the idea of 'weakness of will' in the sense of 'wittingly doing other than what, under the circumstances, one most desires, most wants, or thinks it best to do' (that is why it is a philosophical problem). The thesis of this whole chapter can be interpreted as meaning that to act at all is to do what one most desires, most wants, or thinks it best to do. So the whole chapter has to stand as more generally showing the myth of this sense of 'weakness of will'. Here I merely give an analysis of the apparent inconsistency and offer a general account of the phenomenon intended to dissolve it (much more could be said, in particular about the nature and the formation of meta-desires).

Relatively recently, in philosophical terms, R. M. Hare ([1952] and [1963]) has more or less argued for the impossibility of weakness of will, at least in moral cases, and thereby started a spate of new thinking on the subject. Long before this Socrates held weakness of will to be impossible. For this reason problems concerning this topic are sometimes known as the 'Socratic Paradoxes'. As William Charlton (1988) shows, 'weakness of will' can be broken down into various problems. Here there will be an attempt to tackle only the general problem. This is distinguished from the problem of whether it is possible to do what one feels to be immoral (which is discussed in 2.5.b). The solution suggested here is explained in terms of Frankfurt's idea of levels of desire.

Though it might be the case that we would like to have desires other than the ones that we actually do, we realize that we have to make the best of our existing desires (at least until, if possible, we can eventually change them[42]). A smoker might like not to desire smoking so much, but given that he does desire it so much he regards himself as better off by smoking than by not smoking. He might want to cultivate a stronger desire to stop because, for instance, he wants to live a little longer. But if he cannot cultivate a stronger desire to stop, and chooses not to contract into a penalty system, then he is unlikely to thank any-one who attempts to deprive him of what he must, on balance, still want.

Introspection might show that not doing what one most de-sires, wants, or thinks best, under the circumstances, is psycho-logically impossible, but the point is really conceptual given the assumption of a unitary conscious self; that is, without 'hidden' desires.[43] We might sometimes feel inclined to *say* that we are doing something we do not really desire to do, but this assertion must be mistaken or we would not be doing it. This assertion is really a sop to our critics or an inaccurate way of expressing the feeling that we would be better off without the general circum-stances or the desire itself.

It might be asked why I desire not to have a certain desire other than because, in some way or to some degree, I do not de-sire the desired object. It might be felt, for instance, that it is possible that a confirmed smoker might be glad if a world-wide permanent tobacco blight meant that he could never smoke again. He might feel that his 'true' desire would now be better met. Well, it is fine to say that I desire not to have a certain de-sire because *in some way* or *to some degree* I do not desire the desired object. Decisions are always made on the *perceived bal-ance* of costs and benefits. We perceive that some goal has unde-sirable aspects but think that these are outweighed by the desir-able ones (though we are sometimes confused enough to deny that we ever really loved the advantages when we are left with only the disadvantages). What happens in particular where we desire not to will[44] X is that we have two quite consistent feel-ings (these need not be put into words):

> 1) We feel that it is better on balance to give in to desire X given that we do have the desire to such a degree (it would be too costly not to give in to the desire).

> 2) We feel that giving in to desire X will have consequences that we desire less than our ability to desire X (in fact we need not at all desire the 'ability' to desire X).

A test for the sincerity of 2 would be whether we would take some relatively cheap way of destroying the desire if that were to become possible.

For instance,

1) A woman strongly desires chocolate and feels that life without it is too miserable to forgo it.

2) She knows that chocolate makes her fat and feels that being fat is worse than losing her desire for chocolate. (She does not feel that under the actual circumstances being fat is worse than giving up chocolate or she would give it up.)

A test would be whether she would take a pill to lose her desire for chocolate if an inexpensive one were to become readily available.

So could the smoker consistently welcome the tobacco blight that stopped his smoking? Of course he could *sometimes* feel that way, such as immediately after smoking to satiation or at some time after the blight had occurred and his craving had subsided. But *while* his stronger desire for tobacco exists he will necessarily not, on balance, be glad to be deprived of his tobacco. The smoker's so-called 'true' desire is really his desire about his effective desire or will. However, both the smoker and the chocolate-lover might prefer to cut down the costs of their desires (a cure for cancer and an effective slimming pill, and so on) rather than give up their desires. It is usually the costs of our desires that we hate first. We only dislike our desires when changing them seems less costly than reducing the costs associated with them.

What we cannot do consistently is sincerely feel that something is on balance undesirable and yet still desire it in reality, rather than merely feel some residual desire for it. When we think we are doing this we are conflating our effective (or strongest) desire (our will) with our desire about our effective desire. Once these different levels of desire are disentangled, the apparent contradiction, that is the philosophical problem, disappears. And the opposite ability, to have the will we desire to have because of *stronger meta-desires* that become the will, explains the phenomenon of 'strength of will' or 'self-control'. (The first-order desire merely decreasing by some means would not be called 'strength of will' though the effect would be the same.)

The fact that people can be unhappy with their desires may be a serious practical problem for them. It is a mistake to turn this practical problem into a paradox. Once one sees that the problem is practical one can go about trying to solve it: by trying to find better reasons for changing – or accepting – one's desire, or attempting slow change, or contracting into a penalty system, or lessening the costs. Of course, it is *logically* possible that coercing adults into 'good' personal habits will give them, and possibly other people, reason to thank us in the long term. But that is an entirely separate empirical thesis that is not related to the assertion that people suffer from genuine 'weakness of will' such that they think X is most desirable while doing Y instead. On the issue of this separate logical possibility, with the compatibility thesis in mind, I refer any illiberal readers to the disastrous history of state interference with personal habits.[45] Should a charitable observer at least give less weight to desires that the individual himself does not like having? Not if he is concerned with the person's welfare in the sense of *real* want-satisfaction, as defended in the welfare chapter. However, such concern is quite compatible with offering assistance with the practical problems of undesired desires.

It is usually other people who appear to gain from 'protection from themselves' (if it is desired in one's own case then one can, as suggested, contract into constraints without interfering with others). I suggest this appearance is commonly based on two mistakes: the conceptual confusion that people can be unwilling victims of their own desires; and the failure to investigate the reality of well-considered choices in those activities that are too easily dismissed as 'wanton', or some such pejorative. These things combine to create such an intolerance of, typically minority, activities that people can, like Frankfurt, even question whether these human beings are fully persons.

Having looked at *levels* of volition, we now look at *sources* of volition.

d. Desires versus Values?

Gary Watson (1982) wants to make a distinction between desiring and valuing such that actions are unfree where the agent is

> unable to get what he most wants, *or values*, and this inability is due to his own 'motivational system'. In this case the obstruction to the action that he most wants to do is his own will. (97)

This account differs from Frankfurt's in that one's motivation is supposed to be affected by competing sources of volition rather than different levels of volition.

Watson outlines Hume's view that reason is purely the instrument of the passions that calculates how to feed them, and contrasts this with Plato's view that reason can itself determine what has value: where reason itself is a source of motivation, generating desires for 'the good'. Watson sees this latter position as being that of making a conceptual distinction between desiring a state of affairs and thinking it to be of value. Valuing 'is essentially related to thinking or judging good' (99). Wants that are values are rational and provide reasons for action. They are to be contrasted with 'desires, whose objects may not be thought good and which are thus, ... blind and irrational ... mute on the question of what is good' (99). So what is desirable (naturally pleasurable) contrasts with what is valuable (rationally best). These are independent sources of motivation, because what you desire to do you do not necessarily have a reason to do.

Is this distinction valid? For economics, desire, interest, and value can be seen to be more or less identical in just the way that R. B. Perry has it, as quoted by Watson (100 n5):

'This, then, we take to be the original source and constant feature of all value. That which is an object of interest is *eo ipso* invested with value.' And 'interest' is characterized in the following way:' ... liking and disliking, desire and aversion, will and refusal, or seeking and avoiding. It is to this all-pervasive characteristic of the motor-affective life, this *state*, *act*, *attitude* or *disposition of favor* or disfavor, to which we propose to give the name of 'interest'.' (*General Theory of Value*, Harvard University Press, 1950, ch. 5)

However, there is a real distinction that can be made in this area, and perhaps it is this that Watson is mislabelling as a distinction between desire and value. This distinction is between those things we desire without verbal reflection and those things we desire on which we have verbally reflected. Such is the power of language that it can look as though we have two radically different sources of motivation. This is not so. A reason does not have to be put into words and examined to be a reason. If a being has any kind of idea why it wants to do a thing rather than not do it then it has a reason for doing it. Ideas, or thoughts, or propositions, do not have to be verbal in form. The hungry dog believes that the substance before it is edible and so it has a reason to eat it. People often have the same belief and reason without putting it into words.

I do not intend to imply that 'desire' and 'value' are always linguistically interchangeable. Additional words are sometimes required to make the equivalence clear. For instance, it sounds odd to say that valuing something of natural beauty, such as the Lake District, is the same as desiring it and desiring it now. When we say we value it we must mean such things as that we desire that it be preserved, or that we desire that we, or others, can see it sometimes, or some such desire. The desire is implicit in the claim to value. We are not necessarily effectively motivated by any particular desire or value, as the cost of acting on it might be too high.

Of course, one can reason about a thing to different degrees in the sense that one can simply consider more ideas and criticisms about some matter. But here one is doing *more* reasoning rather than simply reasoning as opposed to not reasoning. The fact that rigorous reasoning often requires the use of language as a tool is what might make it look as though only verbal thought is rational. But the cat that is examining a hole in the floor is using its reason on inputs from its various senses to test the idea that there may be something worth catching inside it. When it concludes that there is insufficient evidence, it departs. Animals certainly use logical forms of thought to achieve their ends. No choice can be made without the use of these. Neither humans nor animals usually find it necessary, or even possible, to make that logic verbally explicit. But without tacit *modus ponens* or *modus tollens* (the use of if-then structures of thought in some form) an agent, qua agent, could not move purposively at all.

Watson is right that valuing 'is essentially related to thinking or judging good'. He is also right to think that desires may not be thought good. But 'good' and 'valuable' and 'desirable' are here more or less synonymous – or at least Watson is not using any real distinction between them. Watson is, rather, using the terms at different levels (in the manner of Frankfurt, but unwittingly) such that he is misled into thinking that they show different sources of motivation. The grain of truth is the same as Frankfurt's: we do not necessarily value some values, or desire some desires, or think it good that we think something good. Using different terms in each phrase cannot mark a real distinction in terms of source of motivation. The source of motivation is the individual's desire or value.

So a desire or value is always, contra Watson, a prima facie reason for action. But there is an ambiguity about 'reason'. A 'reason' can be a felt motivation, or it can be an argument. All desires or values are reasons for action only in the appetitive sense. They are things that we find that we simply want, or would want in appropriate circumstances. Some of these will be natural and some will be fabricated, to some extent, by argument. But desires and values are always found and not chosen (even when we find that we have brought them into existence by argument or by cultivation). The thing that we *can* choose to do is to examine these reasons with arguments. But when we are 'reasoning about our reasons' here we are using 'reason' in two radically different senses. This expression can be disambiguated into 'intellectually examining our desires (or what we value)'.

Watson's account is linked to the idea that people are not always free agents, 'because what one desires may not be what one values, and what one most values may not be what one is finally moved to get' (100). We are given examples where one can, supposedly, desire something and assign no value whatever to it:

> a woman who has the sudden urge to drown her bawling child in the bath; or ... a squash player who, while suffering ignominious defeat, desires to smash his opponent in the face with the racquet. (100–1)

Watson insists, 'It is not that they assign to these actions an initial value which is then outweighed by other considerations' (101). As has been argued, to have an urge or desire is precisely to value, in some way, the thing one feels the urge or desire for. These are, though sometimes with different phrasing necessary, two ways of saying the same thing. But for Watson only a persistent value that has been reasoned about is a 'value'.[46]

This 'estrangement' from a desire can also involve a persistent and pervasive one: 'a man who thinks his sexual inclinations are the work of the devil' (101) will positively disvalue them. Again, does this really split desires from values, rather than meta-desires? Could we not as well say that 'he does not desire his sexual desires'? Watson tries to drive the wedge in with the view that

> the man who is estranged from his sexual inclinations does not acknowledge even a prima-facie reason for sexual activity; that he is sexually inclined toward certain activities is not even a consideration. (101)

Here 'reason' is again apparently being used in the sense of a value that we have arrived at verbally. That, at least, is the only real sense I can make of Watson's distinction. This may be a consistent way of talking about things, but it is confusing. For in plain language, it is absurd to say that someone is inclined to do something yet does not have even a prima facie reason to do it. If he can see no reason *whatever* to do it, then he can hardly desire it. Desire is at least a prima facie reason to do a thing. In Watson's examples the benefits of acting on such desires are really seen as hugely outweighed by the costs.

Watson then gives some examples of desires that are supposed to be not appetitive or passionate but which can still be independent of evaluation. The disinclination to move away from one's family is supposed to be able to be due to 'acculturation' rather than 'a current judgement ... reflecting perhaps an assessment of one's "duties" and interests'. Or one might be 'habituated' to think that divorce is wrong 'even though one sees no justification for maintaining one's marriage'. These examples of acculturation exist 'independently of the agent's judgement ... acculturated desires are irrational (better non-rational) in the same sense as appetitive and passionate desires' (105).

This looks like Hayek's idea, in his social thought, that people follow traditions by force of habit.[47] But people must clearly perceive certain advantages in traditions, evaluate them as superior, if only in terms of the costs and benefits associated with those who keep them and the costs and benefits associated with those who break them. It is true that most people do not go in for radical criticism of all customs or habits they practise. They often give very little consideration to some of these, its being sufficient that they are content with them and see, on occasional reflection, no advantage to mending, at a cost and some risk, what does not seem broken. But introspection suggests that it is almost never true that people have not evaluated certain options, at least Hobson's choice of taking it or leaving it, and opted for what seems the better. (Again, ultimately the whole chapter has to stand as a fuller defense of the thesis that we must act on the basis of what we find most want-satisfying, otherwise a lot more detail might be desirable, or valuable, here.) It seems an unstoppable function of the brain to suggest and evaluate, as regards worth or truth, different possibilities. This is the very process of being conscious. In fact the genetic advantage of consciousness is just that it allows us, indeed obliges us, to fabricate and evaluate different possibilities in our imaginations so that our theories can 'suffer and perish' instead of ourselves.[48]

I must agree that to the extent that we have a tradition or habit of dogmatism, we are more intellectually limited than where criticism is fostered. But it is unduly pessimistic to view traditions and habits as by their very natures non-rational constraints on people. Hayek errs in the opposite direction here in his theory of spontaneous order, where criticism is seen as a threat to the liberty that only traditions and customs make possible.[49] A third possibility is seeing traditions and habits as more like obvious opportunities and standard solutions to problems, which we might well find useful but may ultimately reject if something better occurs to us. Watson is partly taking a stand for the worth of fairly radical criticism of the things we desire or value. This is just what we might expect in a philosopher, but it is as though he prefers not to advocate the extremely critical life openly. Instead, he stipulatively, but covertly, defines the things we value without scrutinizing them as not being valued at all.

A *free* agent is held to be one who weighs up alternatives on the basis of his values and then makes judgements. An agent's 'intentional' actions are 'free' actions when his 'valuation system' is in accord with his 'motivational system' (106). Given that no real distinction has been made between values and desires, as has been argued, there can be no real clash between the 'valuation system' and 'motivational system'. *All* agents are able to weigh up the alternatives on the basis of their values, or desires, and so all can be *free* agents. Watson seems to have the gist of the truth about the nature of free will or agency in the idea that a free agent must 'assign values to alternative states of affairs, that is, rank them in terms of worth' (105). In fact each agent must rank his desires in terms of subjective worth, or strength of desire. The ranking need not be very detailed or long term. The agent usually realizes that certain levels of calculation are simply too fastidious under the circumstances and so to be avoided. Some alternatives have to be ranked as among the infinite possibilities that are not worth further consideration, or we should never get around to acting. So for all agents there is always some, at least implicit, assignment of value to alternative states of affairs.

As I have acknowledged, Watson has a valid criticism concerning the fact that Frankfurt's two-level system cannot account for free will. But his own account abandons the insight that there *are* levels of desire in favor of a distinction that, if it does anything at all, unwittingly makes 'values' a verbal subset of 'desires' (though not of 'effective desires', or 'will'). His account of free agency is thus even more awry.

It might illuminate matters to look at the issue that Watson raises at the start of his piece: Isaiah Berlin's question that if you believe that someone is causally determined to choose as he does then

> what reasons can you, in principle, adduce for attributing responsibility or applying moral rules to him ... which you would not think it reasonable to apply in the case of compulsive choosers – kleptomaniacs, dipsomaniacs, and the like? (Berlin 1984, xx-xxi)

Watson answers Berlin with the idea that 'compulsive choosers' have desires and emotions 'more or less radically independent of [their] evaluational systems' (110). So, as with Frankfurt, it looks as though we are not dealing with properly functioning persons. In fact, all human beings are supposed to be free agents only in some respects, for their appetites and passions are sometimes in conflict with and overrule their practical judgements. In which case, perhaps those who see what people's 'real' values are have grounds for coercing them in terms of their own values alone; the coercer would not be imposing his values on those he would be controlling. And who is better placed to decide what a

person's 'real' values are than those who examine values for a
living? This idea of the value of the philosopher king is an aspect
of Platonism that appears implicit in Watson. Whatever Watson's real views on paternalism, his account invites such ideas.

A better answer to Berlin would be to *defend* the responsibility of 'compulsive choosers' along the following lines. People can
certainly find that they do not desire their effective desires. And
such effective desires can sometimes be caused by physiological
abnormalities that might one day be correctable by medical
means. In the meantime, it might be wise to avoid 'medicalizing'
what is really a type of behavior of which we disapprove (as psy-
chiatry once did with masturbation, homosexual activity, bear-
ing illegitimate children, and even Negro slaves escaping).[50] Persistent thieves and drug users are not ipso facto mentally ab-
normal. Such people might wish to alter these aspects of their
lives, or they might not. Until they find the thought of these activities less attractive, they will choose to continue them. Even if
there is a physiological basis, that does not mean that the agent
is not doing what he most wishes under the circumstances; that
he is not in conscious, chosen, control of his own actions. There is
no reason to give them involuntary 'treatment', but if they insist
on imposing on others then there is, equally, no reason for not
'attributing responsibility or applying moral rules' to 'compulsive
choosers'.

It might still be thought that there are some obvious cases
where people are not acting out of free will. It is not possible to
tackle a definitive list, but what about acts done in circumstances of diminished responsibility due to perception- or emotion-altering drugs, or the consequences of love potions or post-
hypnotic suggestions (assuming that such things exist)?

Acts done in circumstances of diminished responsibility are
still done out of free will in the sense being defended here. Free
will does not decline simply because strange circumstances
make us act abnormally. Perception- or emotion-altering drugs
do not make people act without following what they think to be
their interests. They might even kill a friend owing to a misper-
ception about who he is or what he is doing. They would be acting out of free will but making a mistake. One does not need to
be drugged to make such mistakes. If someone imposes drugs,
love potions, or post-hypnotic suggestions *that we do not agree*

to, then they thereby do things to us against our will; our free will is interfered with *at that point*. But we *thereafter* act on the basis of these things out of free will (though we are less culpable because of the original interference). There is an ambiguity about 'diminished responsibility' in these cases. The person who cannot function normally and spontaneously may have diminished responsibility in a *factual* sense (he is less capable). But perhaps he has diminished responsibility in a *moral* sense (he is less culpable) only if he did not knowingly initiate or risk this diminished condition. In both cases, however, he is acting in pursuit of his perceived interests, which is to act out of free will.

None of this has been intended to be a criticism of the reality of values in the moral sense. It is clear that there are moral values which are not on a par with just any old desire. However, any such moral value, if genuinely held, has ultimately to be a particular kind of thing that is desired; a subset of the more general category. If we are to avoid a lot of inconsistent confusion, it is necessary to understand this. This view should become much clearer in the next section.

One of the most controversial aspects of the rationality assumption of economics is its interpretation of what it means to be 'self-interested'. It is often held to be either substantive and false, or tautological and vacuous. Now I defend the view that it is a priori but illuminating.

2.3. Self-Interest and Altruism

First I shall examine the ways that self-interest and altruism are thought incompatible and explain the aprioristic view. Then we look at the problem posed for this aprioristic view by the way that the nature of morals is often (mis)understood. This account is then briefly tested against a few typical options incompatible with it. It is important to bear in mind here that the compatibility of Austrian economics's aprioristic sense of self-interest and altruism is intended to be a purely conceptual point about agents' choices. The critics discussed often miss the point by interpreting the issue as about empirical human nature.

a. The Logic of Altruism

Many early writers on economics and most modern economists
have assumed that men are egoistic; thus they have ruled out altruism.[51] If they use the term 'self-interest', they mean only
egoism. They are here taken to be, at least implicitly, against the
aprioristic idea that economics can use an assumption of self-
interest that means merely interests of the self, or self-perceived
interests, and which coherently embraces both egoism and altruism without thereby being vacuous.

For instance, in *Leviathan,* Thomas Hobbes assumes that 'of
all Voluntary Acts, the Object is to every man his own Good'
([1651] 1943, 78). All apparent acts of altruism are to be explained as disguised self-seeking. Hobbes found the idea of a
person's benefiting another for the other's sake to be at best an
implausible, and possibly a priori inconsistent, view of human
motivation. In John Aubrey's *Brief Lives,* we are told that when
asked why Hobbes had given alms to a beggar, Hobbes replied
that it was to relieve his own distress at seeing the beggar's distress.

F. Y. Edgeworth states that 'the first principle of Economics
is that every agent is actuated only by self-interest' (1881, 16).
Though he later admits that in reality 'man is for the most part
an impure egoist, a mixed utilitarian' (104). So the assumption is
merely a generally useful one for Edgeworth. Gary Becker rigorously and consistently applies basic economic assumptions to areas normally considered outside the field of economics (e.g.,
Becker 1976).[52] He admits the existence of altruism (and that it
is part of 'rationality'), but even he assumes that this must be a
separate motive, with others, from self-interest as used by economics, which is 'assumed to dominate all other motives, with a
permanent place also assigned to benevolence to children'
(Becker 1971). So Becker follows Edgeworth's one-hundred-
years-older opinion in finding the self-interest assumption extremely fruitful though not completely true.[53]

We even find a moral philosopher, David Gauthier, telling us
that

> this conception, of persons as taking no interest in one an-
> other's interests, is fundamental not only to economics, but

also to moral theory. For we agree with Kant that moral constraints must apply in the absence of other-directed interests
.... (1986, 100)

So, as Kirzner (1990) and Tibor Machan (1989, 25–30) have
also observed, using other examples, it looks logically necessary
to many economists and their critics that the assumption of self-
interest cannot be made compatible with altruism. But this is
not so.

Let us distinguish two false views on altruism:

1) People are necessarily psychological egoists and hence
never altruists. The argument can be put thus: one cannot help
others unless one thereby achieves personal satisfaction, in some
sense, so apparently altruistic people give up nothing for they
are following their self-interest as much as anyone else.

2) The assumption of self-interest must be false or vacuous
because it is obvious that people are often selflessly altruistic.[54]

Why are these two views false? 'Altruism' means 'other-
regardingness' or 'other-interestedness' in the sense of seeing
another as an end in himself. 'Self-interest' is popularly used to
mean *purely* self-regarding or self-interested, and so is incompatible with altruism. There is nothing categorically incorrect
about using 'self-interest' in a sense that means what is also
called 'egoism'. That is obviously a more common way to use the
term. But being self-interested can be interpreted in the aprioristic economic sense as merely following *whatever* interests one
has oneself. It is possibly clearer for economic apriorists to interpret 'self-interest' as 'self-perceived interest' to help to avoid
confusion. The point is that it is not necessary to understand
economic 'self-interest' in the narrow sense. In the aprioristic
sense, 'self-perceived interest' can embrace altruism; for altruism then means having an interest in others as ends in themselves.

This position can be set out as follows:

Self-perceived interest: in the broad aprioristic sense, all interests (or desires, wants, values; these are not distinguished
here) are interests *of* the self. We cannot have *purely selfless* interests for we must feel an interest that is *ours* to the extent that
we are proper agents with motives.

But such interests of the self can still intelligibly be divided thus:

Egoism: an interest in one's own ends and in other people or things, if at all, as mere means to one's own ends.

Altruism: an interest in other people, or even things, as ends in themselves.

Consider Hobbes's action of giving alms to a beggar. He stated that he gave only to relieve his own distress. That Hobbes took any interest in the beggar means that the self-perceived interests of Hobbes's included the circumstances of the beggar's. Thus his action was self-interested in the broad aprioristic sense. We can go on to ask whether Hobbes was being egoistic or altruistic. If Hobbes were merely upset at the ugly sight of the beggar, and would rather that he had never seen him, then we can say that his behavior was egoistic: he did not view the beggar as a valuable thing in himself but as a nuisance. This is a natural interpretation to put on Hobbes's explanation of his behavior. But if Hobbes was really taking pity on the beggar as an end in himself, and would wish him to be better off whether or not Hobbes knew about it, then his behavior was altruistic. In both cases we have self-interest in that Hobbes himself has the beggar as one of his interests. In reality, it might well have been that Hobbes both found the beggar a nuisance and had some sympathy with him. So perhaps his gift would be motivated by both irritation and pity. Neither feeling would be more real than the other in the sense that the irritation showed him not to be really altruistic at all or the pity showed him not to be really egoistic at all. Both his egoistic interests and his altruistic interests are objectively his self-perceived interests.

In my experience, some professional economists see the above argument as a mere proof of psychological egoism. A thought-experiment might show the reality of altruism more clearly. The devil stops time during a family car crash and offers the husband a choice of 1) the rest of the family dying but his happily forgetting them, or 2) the rest of the family surviving but his miserably thinking them dead. That 2 would be a possible, even likely, choice shows that real altruism is possible. To choose 2 must be to desire the good of others as ends in themselves rather than for any satisfaction, in whatever sense, they might bring us. But this does not show that we are not 'self-interested' in the aprioristic economic sense.

Contrary to the popular view, economics is not obliged to assume egoism or P. H. Wicksteed's 'non-tuism' (though that assumption is certainly allowable if it usefully simplifies matters). There need be no particular problem with allowing that people can have interests that embrace promoting (or destroying, come to that) the interests of others. Of course, it will sometimes be useful for economic analysis to distinguish what kinds of self-perceived interests are in operation; but there is no need to think that the altruistic kinds (ideology, charity, and so on) are ipso facto beyond economic analysis.

It is difficult for some people to accept that altruism can *innocuously* be seen as part of self-perceived interest. Part of the problem relates to a conception of morality that is rather prevalent, but from which I dissent. First we shall look at that, and then at some typical critics of aprioristic self-interest.

b. The Intentional Structure of Moral Sentiments

Here I discuss the intentional structure of moral sentiments (the categorical nature of morals is dealt with in 2.5.b). In doing this, I hope to focus on the form or nature of morals as such; in what sense they exist, rather than the content of particular moral views. Thus this book remains non-moral, or non-ethical, as regards advocatory content. Why are these discussions here? They explain how morals are compatible with economics. Thus morals do not trump economic analysis, or vice versa. While not crucial to the overall compatibility thesis, these accounts are, I hope, clearly relevant. If they are not purely descriptive, due to the nebulous nature of moral sentiment, then they are at least maximally rationalist: they allow more and bolder views to count as moral views, while implying that it is worth talking to people with different moral views instead of coercing them (for if they genuinely hold a moral value, then they will and must live up to it – and, of course, we might be the ones who are persuaded).

Morality is correctly seen as having to be impartial in some sense. Yet it seems that morality has to be held as a personal value and is thus also partial in some other sense, or there would be no motivational explanation. Immanuel Kant reacted to the threat to morality posed by the Hobbesian-type of self-interest argument by trying to make morality almost a purely logical affair (1785). He held that an act is moral only to the extent that all can will it without contradiction. There must be no personal desire involved, though he does allow respect for the moral law. Thus Kant correctly perceived that morality is impartial in some way, but he opted for a pure impartiality that leaves no clear room for motivation.[55] (Though the Kantian test of whether something is done morally can charitably be interpreted as whether we would have done it even if we felt no *egoistic* desire for it, plus whether it is universalizable.)

Bishop Butler's response to Hobbes seems approximately correct [1726]. He agreed with the insight that all interests must be interests *of* the self but denied that this entails that we are self-interested in any egoistic sense, that we must be interested *in* the self alone. He held that Hobbes had overlooked the real distinction we have in our goals.[56] But Hume's view of moralizing seems to capture the correct account better. He writes that we feel 'some sentiment of blame or approbation, whence we pronounce the action criminal or virtuous' (1739–40, Book III, Part I). This thus views moralizing as (1) the personal emotional evaluation of a type or principle of behavior (2) irrespective of the interests of a particular agent. It therefore catches both (1) the partial and (2) the impartial aspects of moralizing. To be clearer, the account needs to be elaborated.

(1) We have partiality in one way. For the very fact that the individual sees a certain groups of agents and type of behavior as being of value, or disvalue, shows that he is partial to these. This partiality is usually overlooked, or felt to make a moral view somehow less moral, because people often feel that moral views must somehow be completely impartial.[57] But without this partiality we have no motivation (how the individual becomes partial to certain groups or types of behavior is a separate issue).

(2) We have the impartiality in the altruistic sense that the evaluation is not specific to the agent and his immediate and personal goals. The agent has to be able to affirm the evaluation even when he does not know who in particular is involved. But the groups among whom he is impartial in his judgement need not be as large as *all* human beings.[58] He is impartial within the domain of some group that matters to him.[59] The group might also be *larger* than that of all human beings and include animals and plant life or even inanimate matter. It is even morally coherent to discriminate against human beings as being immoral or worth less than other species or some abstract goal.

One might think that an attempt to respect, say, justice as such would mean that I could not discriminate between my group and other groups. But justice is a formal concept, like desert and impartiality. One needs principles and groups, and that entails discrimination, before one can use the formal concept. Perhaps this is obscured by two popular views: that either the group in moral matters ought always to include all human beings or that the principle must be utilitarian. But these views clearly discriminate in favor of a particular group or principle, and thus discriminate against other groups or principles.

Thus every moral sentiment is group- and principle-*partial* but also individual-*impartial*. I am 'self-interested' in that I am bound to want only things *I* value, but some of the things I value are altruistically and morally valued. This is not supposed fully to capture the nature of moralizing, but it should be relevantly more accurate than that of the critics of aprioristic self-perceived interest that we are about to examine.

Throughout this book I am obliged, for reasons of space, to pick out what I take to be the few key points in people's arguments and then give what I think to be a few pertinent replies. I emphasize that here, as I shall often be giving (even) less space to many people's arguments than I gave to Frankfurt's and Watson's. Wherever I might have misconstrued the relevant arguments, I fear that I would have made the same error if I had dealt with them at greater length – and become (more) tedious into the bargain. So it seemed better to be 'too quick' than 'too slow'. The reader is, of course, at liberty to check the original works if he doubts my interpretation.

c. Commitment, Motive-Stimuli, and Vacuousness

Amartya Sen (Sen 1979b), C. D. Broad [1950], and Tibor Machan (1990) want a pure impartiality that excludes any clear self-referential motive (though Sen and Machan are criticizing economics from the viewpoint of morals, while Broad is criticizing psychological egoism). David Ramsay Steele (1992) does not discuss morals but agrees with Machan in finding the aprioristic approach to be vacuous. I shall now consider their criticisms.

In his 'Rational Fools', Amartya Sen asserts that economics's self-interest assumption rules out 'commitment' or is vacuously true (Sen 1979b). As he thinks that people obviously do feel real commitment, he rejects the motivational exclusiveness, or vacuousness, of the self-interest assumption. Sen holds that economics must be supplemented with a richer view of human nature that allows room for morals in economic analysis. He appears to conflate the Hobbesian assumption of egoistic self-interest – for he mentions Butler's criticism of this – with economics's revealed preference theory, whereby 'if you are observed to choose x rejecting y, you are declared to have "revealed" a preference for x over y' (91–2). Sen complains that

> no matter whether you are a single-minded egoist or a raving altruist or a class conscious militant, you will appear to be maximising your own utility in this enchanted world of definitions. (92)

And he objects to the idea that choices are only 'rational' if they 'can be explained as the choosing of "most preferred" alternatives' (92).

Sen apparently believes that we sometimes do what we do not, under the circumstances, most prefer to do. He offers an alternative approach that takes account of commitment, which includes morality 'in a very broad sense' (97). He suggests that 'commitment' can be defined as occurring where a person chooses 'an act that he believes will yield a lower level of personal welfare to him than an alternative that is also available to him' (95). That sounds acceptable *at first*, for it has been argued that we do sometimes forgo *egoistic* welfare to help others for their sakes. But Sen continues:

> commitment does involve, in a very real sense, counterpreferential choice, destroying the crucial assumption that the chosen alternative must be better than (or at least as good as) the others for the person choosing it. (96)

How can we make a 'counterpreferential choice'? How can we choose to do what we do not in some sense prefer to do? Must not the chosen alternative be better for us in *some* sense? Otherwise, where is the personal motivation? Sen goes further and approvingly quotes a character who says of his action, 'I had no motive and no interest' (97). Sen seems to have replaced an 'enchanted world of definitions' (where all actions can be seen as analytically self-interested) with a world without any motives at all. He feels he has to do this as he cannot allow sympathy to be part of 'commitment' because 'behaviour based on sympathy is in an important sense egoistic, for one is oneself pleased at others' pleasure and pained at others' pain' (95).

He wants to make sense of a pure impartiality that entirely escapes sympathy. But Sen's 'commitment' (that is, morality) must involve being impartial in some way within the group to which one is partial. If my earlier account of morality is correct, then one cannot have a moral commitment that escapes sympathy (in a broad sense of 'sympathy'). Even the more general sense of, subjective, 'commitment' just seems to mean feeling emotional engagement of some kind. Without personal sentiment we would not be committed and so could not act out of commitment.[60] Sen will not allow an aprioristic-type interpretation of self interest because he accepts the mistaken conception of morality discussed earlier: he hankers after a 'pure' impartiality in morality that is impossible because it leaves no room for the necessary sentimental, or emotional, motive. So Sen's views on definitions in economics only partly repeat what Butler wrote in response to Hobbes. For Sen overlooks Butler's insight that Hobbes's position on personal motivation is essentially correct but still leaves room for real altruistic goals.

C. D. Broad ([1950] 1971) is correct to criticize psychological egoism, as held by Hobbes, as a false theory of human motivation. He is mistaken in failing to see that altruism must still be self-interested in the sense under discussion. Like Sen, he appears to opt for altruism without the necessary self-referential motive, for he also seems mistakenly to think that Butler refuted Hobbes on this issue. Broad admits that the desire of a mother for the good of her child 'is self-referential, because the fact that it is her child and not another's acts as a powerful motive-stimulant' (252). This is fine as far as it goes. Broad is right in seeing that such altruism refers back to the self. He is wrong in failing to see that all altruism refers back to the self in a similar sense.

Consider Broad's main example:

> a person who deliberately chooses to devote his life to working among lepers, in the full knowledge that he will almost

certainly contract leprosy and die in a particularly loathsome
way. (256)

It can immediately be conceded that the real motive might be
that the man simply wants to help the lepers. And it can be
agreed that this is an other-regarding motive: he values the lepers for their own sakes. But, to use Broad's terminology against
himself, we can say that the lepers are indeed acting as a 'powerful motive-stimulant'. Broad tries to rule this out by stipulat-
ing that the lepers are not the man's 'relatives nor his friends
nor his benefactors nor members of any community or institution to which he belongs' (257). But it seems that the man must
view them as members of his (moral) community in some sense
(perhaps the 'community of mankind') or he would not so act.
Some people may be so constituted that they care as much about
strangers as most people do only about their immediate family.
Unless this individual has some such feeling he would not act as
described. So we must extend Broad's notion of the so-called
'egoistic motive-stimulus' (256) to cover his otherwise motiveless
altruistic actions. The man is motivated by finding that the
thought of helping the lepers *for their own sakes* more satisfies
his wants than not helping them – or he would not do it. The
self-referential motivation that Broad explicitly tries to rule out
is a *necessary* part of being altruistic.

Tibor Machan is an interesting critic of the aprioristic interpretation of self-interest in economics. He is sympathetic with
the free-market results of mainstream economics, and he is
sympathetic with the idea that people should be positively egoistic (he is a libertarian influenced by Ayn Rand). He is familiar
with the recent suggestion from some Public Choice economists
that it is sensible to include ideological factors to explain politicians' behavior. He knows that the 'economic imperialists' are
happy with self-perceived interest embracing morality, but he is
not. The sticking point for Machan is the idea that a mere definition can be so pervasive. As Machan puts it:

> Any factor or model that explains anything whatever –
> for example, self-defeating as well as self-serving conduct –
> simply explains nothing much! If the model fully explains the
> bank-robber as well as the banker, what can we learn from
> the explanation? In no science would this kind of approach be

admitted; the melting of ice explained by the same factor as the freezing of water,[61] private interest! ...

In order to avoid this vacuousness, the 'ideological variable' has to be seen as adding a dimension, namely what kind of conduct human beings take to be proper, what they see as binding on them quite apart from what they prefer. (1990, 25–6)

I have already dealt with the idea that there could be 'conduct human beings take to be proper ... quite apart from what they prefer'. Here the charge of 'vacuousness' is considered. Is the concept of self-perceived interest tautologous? It depends on how it is interpreted. If it is taken to mean that *people* are motivated by their self-perceived interests then it is not tautologous. We can make sense of a person's 'behaving' (in the sense of physically moving) in a non-self-interested way, and thus we can conceive of falsifications. For instance, if people's bodies were controlled by other minds then they would not be pursuing their own self-perceived interests; nor would they if their bodies spontaneously behaved in ways they could not consciously control, as happens to some extent with epileptic fits, twitching nerves, and reflex actions. Sustained constructive examples ought to sound far-fetched. The idea that *people* are motivated by self-perceived interest is supposed to be an almost universal truth, but it is not a tautology.

If, on the other hand, the idea is the aprioristic economic one that all *actions* are self-interested, then it is, roughly speaking, tautologous; or if not strictly tautologous (for it is not clear that the meanings of the terms make it true) then a priori (for it can be known independently of experience). For any action to be an action it must mean that an individual is moving his body as a result of his self-perceived interests. If the body were moving automatically or as a result of another's will then the individual himself would not be *acting*. So the idea that *people* are motivated by self-perceived interest can be seen as a highly accurate approximation that is based on the apriorism about *agents*.

However, this apriorism is not viciously vacuous or any kind of a threat to the scientific nature of economics. On the contrary, it is an enlightening apriorism that allows fruitful economic analysis to proceed. The fact that an individual is assumed to be thus self-interested does not in itself tell us anything about the

particular values and beliefs of the individual. The hard work of
explaining what is going on in some economic situation is often
in making shrewd guesses and testing them (whether empirically or critically). Having a theoretical framework is not the
same as already having an explanation. If an engineer is called
in to discover why a bridge fell down, then he might already
have the theoretical tools for the job but he will hardly have the
specific explanation. Only in an innocuous sense are the theoretical tools of the economist and engineer 'vacuous', because the
application of these tools to the particular circumstances has not
yet been done.

David Ramsay Steele voices similar objections to Machan's:

> A determined praxeologist can account for every vagary (as
> Mises did: 1966, 103) by positing a different end-means
> scheme in each case, and in that way rescue the apodictic cer-
> tainty of praxeology, but this would be at the cost of render-
> ing it inapplicable because all too promiscuously applicable.
> (Steele 1992, 98)

On the contrary, action that does not fit the supposed end-means
scheme is primarily begging for the, possibly difficult, task of
suggesting a plausible, testable, enlightening new theory of the
motive in operation. The alternative too often is idly, promiscu-
ously, and unenlighteningly to assert some non-specific 'irrationality'. Fortunately, aprioristic rationality can only fail to apply if the individual fails to be an agent. It has to be admitted
that mental confusion (such as a failure to grasp the economic
concept of sunk costs) and imperfect calculation of what is prudent (such as is caused by a poor grasp of statistics) are possible
and sometimes occur. However, these are also completely compatible with the aprioristic view of what people are *attempting* to
do and they should, similarly, not be assumed too readily, non-
testably, or non-specifically.

As Kirzner writes:

> The description of all human *action* as rational constitutes a
> proposition that is, in fact, incapable of being falsified by any
> experience, yet does, nevertheless, convey highly valuable in-
> formation. ([1960] 1976, 172, emphasis added)

But again, this view is not specific to any notion of economic *man*. There is no substantive theory of human nature here. This notion of self-interested motivation is naturally applicable to all beings capable of action.

Some might find all this a plausible enough position but doubt that it can be connected to economics in any useful way. I can only refer them here to the economic literature that explicitly embraces this approach. The writings of Mises, Rothbard, and Kirzner would be a start. However, as we shall see, the conceptions of liberty, welfare, and anarchy defended in this book also require some such conception of instrumental rationality independently of whether economics can convincingly be connected to it.

It has been difficult to put off discussing utility and utility-maximization. Now that we come to them I shall deal with them fairly briefly for the time being, as many of the relevant points concerning them arise more naturally in the discussion of want-satisfaction in the chapter on welfare.

2.4. Utility

What one desires or wants to do, one has utility (felt satisfaction, in a very general sense) at the thought of having, achieving, or doing. This requires *conscious* (though not necessarily self-conscious) desires to motivate us as agents. We can also be said to achieve 'utility' if we are successful in attaining our goal; though this is merely 'want-satisfaction' in the sense of achieving what we want whether or not that goal involves any personal psychological satisfaction in itself. Many economists became worried that utility is not empirically detectable. But they thought that if someone has more satisfaction, in either sense, from one thing rather than another then we can at least say that he prefers it, and preferences are empirically revealed by a person's choices. This is supposed by many to be an advance such that any psychological aspect of 'utility' can be more or less abandoned.

Take a typical and well known example. Jack Hirshleifer is aware of the criticisms concerning the elusive subjectivity of utility and so dismisses Bentham's idea (as he calls it). Instead, Hirshleifer asserts that 'what modern economists call "utility" reflects nothing more than rank ordering of preference' (1984, 61). If he means that economics can *completely* abandon cardinal utility as a background assumption, then this seems to be a mistake. It seems clear that if one prefers A to B to C then these things are decreasingly want-satisfying, or wanted. What is more, one can often say, with great certainty and intuitive sense, that one prefers A much more than B but prefers B only a little more than C. To assert that there is a rough cardinality of protean and fleeting utility, is not to imply that it is amenable to precise arithmetic. The difficulty of measuring a thing is not a sufficient reason for denying the validity of talking about it.[62] Without the cardinal notion of utility we are left without the notion of conscious beings. A mere machine might be programed with preference-like, and even weighted, tasks; but we do not feel that these are like an *agent's* goals precisely because they lack the psychological aspect that utility must represent. Thus the idea of conceptually restricting economics to involve only behaviorally exhibited preferences not only makes it impossible to discuss real want-satisfaction in economics (and thereby welfare and liberty insofar as they involve want-satisfaction), but it also seems to fail clearly to distinguish conscious beings from unconscious automata. I have no objection to economists restricting themselves to observable phenomena for many purposes. But if they say that they require no conceptual link to the psychological, then they are throwing out the baby with the bathwater.

As Hirshleifer continues his account of economics it is clear that the notion of utility as really involving some kind of psychological satisfaction is implicitly needed for economic analysis to have any practical significance for us. For instance, when he draws utility functions he writes,

> The assertion that people experience diminishing marginal utility, as consumption income rises, is an empirical one .... It corresponds to our commonsense notion that more income makes us happier, but we usually get more of a thrill from our first million than our tenth. (64)

Note that there is also, rough, cardinality even in Hirshleifer's example. I accept that it might not be possible or useful for economics qua science to attempt to quantify it precisely. I do not need to defend that. Cardinal utility and economics will be discussed in more detail in the welfare chapter.

There are also philosophical objections to utility. Some of these objections are responses to the interpretations that utilitarians have put on the term. Classically, utilitarians have interpreted 'utility' as happiness or pleasure. But these interpretations are too narrow. One characteristic of happiness is that it is a general state that is not achieved by simply any gain of a desired thing. And 'pleasure' usually connotes a much more specific state of mind relating to the fulfilment of bodily desires rather than intellectual or moral goals. 'Utility' is better understood as want-satisfaction in the broadest sense. All sorts of things can be want-satisfying and in different ways, but in some sense we must be motivated by what satisfies our wants.

Can one speak consistently of someone's being motivated towards disutility? Would he give himself physical and emotional discomfort with no other object than so doing? It would seem unavoidable to conclude that, by definition, such a person just found utility, want-satisfaction, in giving himself pain. It is inconsistent to hold that one can be motivated by disutility (currently wanting not to have one's current wants satisfied).

That one can find utility in 'horrible' ways might seem to undermine its intrinsic plausibility as a welfare criterion. It can still be argued that worse consequences seem to result when people try to interfere with 'perverse' or 'perverted' objects of utility. This is what preference-utilitarian (that is, want-satisfaction) welfarists *must* argue: for the *motive*-utility of aprioristic economics (that we must *aim* at what it most satisfies us to aim at) becomes the *goal*-utility of preference-utilitarian welfare (that we are better off if we really *achieve* what it most satisfies us to aim at). This argument must also be reserved for the welfare chapter. Now the idea of what it '*most* satisfies us to aim at' requires some brief explanation.

2.5. Utility-Maximization

a. The Commensurability of One's Want-Satisfactions

It is a logically separable part of the rationality assumption being discussed that people attempt to *maximize* their utility. It can be admitted that very different things satisfy our wants at

different times. And these things give us different types of satisfying feelings, or *none at all* if we do not realize that the want is
objectively satisfied. But when we are deciding whether to opt
for one thing rather than another, then we naturally weigh up
which is *more* want-satisfying to us at the time. We find that different want-satisfactions are usually quite commensurable. We
are only incapable of making definite choices when the decision
is too finely balanced, or complicated, or the outcome is too unpredictable.

This is a claim about the phenomena of these decisions. It is
not supposed to be true only by definition. We can imagine beings who look like us who do not make decisions as we do but
have fixed responses to various stimuli. Or we could make decisions in different ways. We might, for instance, find that whenever we consider two possible choices (one after the other) the
one we think of second automatically becomes our will. Thus this
theory is not tautological. It is not empirical in the shared external sense, but it is introspectively knowable and thus a priori.

Introspection shows that this weighing-up process is contin-
ual. We do not flip from one activity to another without having
decided that it would *here and now* be more want-satisfying to
change to the second (we feel a greater want for the second). In
fact it is more want-satisfying than *anything else* available that
we can think of at the time. There does not seem to be a single
sort of sensation with a homogeneous quality that can be compared; yet as we compare possible choices we cannot help but
take the option that in some way feels to be the most want-
satisfying, or least want-dissatisfying, at the time.[63] (This is not
to say that we are attempting to maximize such want-
satisfaction over an extended time period, though economics
might find that a useful rule-of-thumb assumption for interpreting behavior.)

Of course, all of this glosses over the qualitatively different
natures of many choices as we experience them. It does not,
however, caricature these or do them any violence to insist that,
in the end, we seem to experience the *greatest* desire or want
(given the possibilities under consideration) for the one finally
chosen. Even to choose for an explicitly qualitative reason is to
do so because we find that is what, in a sense, we *most* desire to
do (pace Charles Taylor in his 1982). The fact that we can often

put a list of utterly disparate possibilities into a clear order of desirability shows the comprehensive nature of this faculty. That agents are motivated by utility-maximization in this sense might also prompt the accusation of being vacuous; for whatever happens, we will seek to explain it in a utility-maximizing framework. But again, this 'vacuity' is, apparently, not obvious to everyone and is needed for (making sense of) the fruitful science of economics.

We can now consider an interesting question in this area (which might otherwise have been discussed immediately after 2.3.b, The Intentional Structure of Moral Sentiments): how can utility maximization be squared with the categorical or absolute nature of morals? Does one override the other?

b. The Utility-Maximization of Categorical Morals

The view of morals to be defended here is quite controversial today but is certainly not without historical precedent. That there is objective moral knowledge, and that fully to know the moral thing is to do it, was argued by Plato. Here we are not defending objective moral knowledge but only the idea that *fully* to hold a moral obligation sentimentally, not to feel it uncertainly or as a slight pricking of the conscience, is *always* to act on it in appropriate circumstances. We might call this thesis 'Humean-Platonic morality'. This view is present to a considerable extent in the writings of R. M. Hare, who argues for it in much more detail than I do here though he does express reservations.[64] The relevant issue in this chapter is how utility maximization relates to this view of the categorical nature of morals. But to say that even moral motives have to fit this general theory of motives is not to attempt to belittle them or to reduce them to something else (as utilitarianism really does[65]).

A crucial distinction here is between moral sentiments (moral values or desires consciously felt and acted on) and moral theories (abstractions that we can advance and discuss). What we are considering here are moral sentiments. It is possible to defend moral theories intellectually while not really feeling them. Without seeing this, one can fail to realize that one's 'official' or 'theoretical' moral position is a sort of public recommendation that one might not personally feel, value, or desire. In what follows, we focus on actions subjectively evaluated as 'immoral' (or categorically unacceptable) because 'moral' is often used to mean merely permissible (rather than categorically obligatory).

The general argument can be put as follows. Morals are trumps in the sense that we cannot knowingly do what we feel, at that moment, is immoral; this would mean acting in a way that we viewed as being categorically undesirable. In this way moral values or desires are mistaken for being incommensurable when compared with other values or desires. The moral and non-moral desires *are* compared by desirability, but the moral are bound to win for they are categorically (absolutely, unconditionally) desirable or undesirable when they are held (though they may cease to be held). When we feel that something is immoral under the circumstances, we feel that it is more desirable to avoid it than to give in to any incompatible non-moral desire (even the desire to save one's own life). That morals are trumps may make it look as though we are dealing with something qualitatively different from desires: trumps are not apparently weighed against other non-trump cards for they automatically beat it. But one can view the lowest trump as effectively one point higher than any ordinary card; and one can view a minimal moral desire as just a point or two ahead of non-moral desires. Of course, moral desires also have to have certain features other than 'trumping' to be *moral* desires, but they are ultimately desires or sentiments nevertheless. We feel stronger utility and disutility about, respectively, moral and immoral actions than we do about non-moral actions.

It might help to distinguish two ways in which moral sentiments can be argued to be categorical (or absolute): 1. the conceptual, and 2. the psychological.

1. Conceptually, what is felt to be immoral is *what we feel no one should ever do in the circumstances*; it is a *categorical sentiment* about a type of behavior in some group. One cannot at the same time (at least, not without confusion) do what one feels no one should do. Moral values must be obeyed because if disobeyed they are, ipso facto, not held *categorically*. Most moral philosophers seem to agree that morals are at least categorical whatever else they are. One source of confusion here is where our general moral feelings (such as feeling that lying is usually immoral) differ from our specific moral feelings (such as feeling that some particular lie is moral). This seems to occur because

such general morals are usually held ceteris paribus, at least tacitly so. Strange circumstances, including very trivial infractions combined with very great rewards, give rise to genuinely different moral feelings that are only superficially examples of inconsistency.

2. Psychologically, can you recall doing anything that *clearly* felt immoral at the time that you did it? Do not conflate this with a slight feeling of moral dubiousness, or knowing that it is conventionally immoral, or that you feared punishment, or that you felt shame at the possibility of being caught, or that you would not have wanted to argue that you had been moral, or that you felt you had done wrong immediately *afterwards* (moral values are in flux, as are our beliefs and tastes). You might even have been honest in thinking the very words 'This is wrong' *in the theoretical sense* as you did a thing: you felt you could not fault the *intellectual* moral position with a sound criticism. But as morals are fundamentally about our sentiments, can you have fully felt the sentiment of categorical impermissibility at the time of permitting yourself the action?

Apart from being more extreme, this account thus also differs from Hare's in another important way. Hare ([1952] 1986, 167) makes a threefold distinction that I have also made here, among (I paraphrase) (1) conventional or social morals, (2) one's personal, psychological or felt, morals, and (3) one's explicit value judgements or theories put into words. However, Hare then focuses on 3 as determinative of action – *if sincere*. But if they are *sincere* then they are in realm 2, *whether or not* they are explicitly expressed in realm 3. Because Hare's book is about the *language* of morals, he fails to see clearly that 2 is the realm that is determinative of action (Hare takes language too seriously; perhaps he should have written about *The Nature and Concept of Morals* instead).

In the final part of this chapter we look at the assumption of economic demand. This assumption is even more fundamental to the science of economics than the assumption of economic rationality. It is often thought to be inherently and arbitrarily biased in favor of the market. Given the pro-market conclusions of much of economics, especially any explicitly or implicitly used in this book, successfully to defend economic demand would significantly assist the compatibility thesis.

2.6. Economic Demand

In standard economic theory, the demand for a good is defined in terms of effective demand: the consumer is willing and able to pay the price. The idea of economic demand is not currently criticized as often and as comprehensively as the idea of economic rationality, though it is more fundamental to most economic analysis. Perhaps this recent lack of criticism is because this idea is not taken at all seriously by those who have already rejected economic rationality. Here there is a brief explanation and defense of the idea. What follows is really only a version of the defense of the market that is sometimes known as the 'economic calculation argument', which can be found in Mises's *Socialism* (originally published in 1922).

The gist of the economic calculation argument is as follows. All economic resources are, by definition, 'scarce' (there is not a superabundance of them) and each can satisfy more than one end. All societies must avoid waste of such resources. To avoid waste you need to know the relative value of resources (their ability in terms of each other to satisfy consumer ends). In practice this requires a common denominator or numeraire. In complex societies this role is performed by money. The primary function of money is to be a medium of exchange and so facilitate that very extensive division of labor which permits an enormous increase in production. Profit-and-loss is the only known indicator of general social productivity. The price system provides the only known social method of determining economic (waste-avoiding) efficiency as opposed to technical (single-goal) efficiency. How, without a market in resources, is one to choose between another hospital and another school? Between building with bricks or concrete? Between using more labor or more capital? Between choosing this sort of capital or that? We cannot abolish economic scarcity and then simply produce what is technically efficient. Choices have to be made. This is a fact of life and it does not look as though it could change, for more resources permit the satisfaction of new demands. On these questions a society of altruists would be unable to answer on the basis of needs alone. Competing (effective) demands for resources determine relative prices in the market, and these are necessary for the calculation.

None of this itself undermines the notion of needs. From a benevolent point of view needs are important. But the present standard economic definition of 'demand' does not preclude criticism of the results in welfare terms, nor state or charitable 'corrections'. Any seriously competing definition of 'demand' in terms of needs would have to show itself to be more useful. While the standard definition gives us something precise and easily monitored in real situations (prices, and profits-and-loss), any replacement 'needs' definition would be vague and slippery for several reasons:

1. Individual people have different hierarchies, with different weightings, for even the most basic goods; such as security, health, and longevity. A comprehensive non-price ranking system is unknown that can determine where all people have their ever-changing individual preferences.

2. If the price of one basic good changes sufficiently relative to others, then people will often need, and be able, to reallocate their spending to receive their new, best, overall mix of such goods. But without prices how could we even tell that relative resource costs had changed, let alone how much reallocation might be necessary?

3. Infinite resources could theoretically be allocated to any of these basic categories. Ever more could be done to make one live that little bit longer (by researching for new drugs perhaps) or be that little bit more secure (maybe by employing extra police). But we have to stop devoting resources to one of these things at some point or we shall suffer a greater cost with the other. The price mechanism is the only known system for determining what pattern of such basic production is generally preferred.

4. The price system co-ordinates all the polycentric, and anarchic, changes in demand due to the changes in individual circumstances. These changes cannot be registered by any known single central mechanism or polycentric non-price mechanism.

The defense of economic demand and the price mechanism at first looks like only the thin end of the wedge of defending the free market. But to read the literature[66] and appreciate more fully the allocative efficiency of market pricing (*including* the efficient long-term meeting of needs) is to find that one is then put into a position of finding it very hard to think of good reasons for deviating, except by charity, from the market-pricing outcome on any occasion (to go into this literature in any detail here would be to write pure economics instead of political philosophy). A strong presumption in favor of the market then carries one a considerable distance towards anarchy without further argument. I guess that this is part of the reason for the remarkable British phenomenon of Marxian (anti-money) socialists who master the economic calculation argument only to find themselves intellectually catapulted, past various state-interventionist ideologies, to market-anarchy.[67]

Despite the fact that there is more discussion of utility in the welfare chapter, we shall now go straight to the subject of liberty. This is because we have said enough about utility for the purpose of elaborating the theory of liberty, and many of the philosophical ideas in the liberty chapter are required in the one on welfare, which focuses more on the reconciliation of liberty, welfare, and anarchy. The libertarian philosophical problems are also the most interesting.

3. Liberty

3.0. Chapter Thesis

The classical liberal, libertarian, and principal commonsense conception of interpersonal liberty is of people not having constraints imposed upon them by other people. Such liberty is here formulated as people not having a subjective cost initiated and imposed on them (that is, without their consent) by other people. Or, for short, *liberty is the absence of imposed cost*. In the event of a mutual clash of imposed costs, *observing liberty entails minimizing imposed costs*. These two formulae are defended as capturing the conception clearly, consistently, comprehensively, and non-morally. They are used to derive property implications and to solve philosophical problems associated with this conception of liberty. Maximizing such liberty requires contingently deontological[68] libertarianism, which the free market anarchically provides (though the empirical arguments are, perforce, only touched on throughout the book).

First, I shall explain the chosen formulation of the libertarian conception of interpersonal liberty. This will be immanently criticized and then compared with typical libertarian alternatives. Drawing out the consequences of this novel formulation in a state of nature and purely abstractly further defends it as clear, consistent, and non-moral, and begins to show its comprehensive power. This is then tested by attempting to solve some problems that have been so usefully posed by two leading critics of libertarian philosophy: David Friedman and John Gray. This will probably deal with enough major issues in what is, in any case, the longest chapter.

Unless the context clearly indicates otherwise, no distinction will be made between 'liberty' and 'freedom', and 'libertarian' and 'liberal', and the various words having the same linguistic roots. As usual, any moral slant in quoted passages will be ignored or, occasionally, replied to merely hypothetically (for instance, the assertion that liberty undermines some value might be criticized without affirming that value).

3.1. Capturing the Conception[69]

'Liberty', in its most general sense, signifies the absence of some sort of constraint on something. The topic here is interpersonal liberty: the absence of initiated constraints on people by other people; or, more precisely, people interacting voluntarily without constraining, interfering with, or imposing upon each other – except to prevent or redress initiated constraining, interfering, or imposing.[70] As 'imposing' seems the most general of these terms, I shall stick with that as long as it withstands criticism. Positively initiating an imposition on another is to be contrasted here with merely withholding assistance, or with defense or redress (so not just anything that anyone else might do could be described as 'imposing'). This sense of 'liberty' is supposed to be the opposite of subjection and oppression: it is individual sovereignty. It is about the voluntary interaction of persons rather than selfish individualism, as its detractors sometimes misrepresent it. This is the liberty of libertarianism,[71] classical liberalism, and much – though not all – common sense. As far as I can tell, no one has hitherto provided an adequate account of liberty in this sense. This failure is particularly striking and ironic among those calling themselves 'libertarians'. I shall attempt a clear, or at least clearer, way of expressing this idea that is capable of dealing with various problems.

There are many different ways in which people might impose on each other. I want to cover as many relevant types of imposition as possible. Subjective *cost*, as opposed to *benefit*, seems to catch this broad meaning and so will be used until refuted. A 'subjective cost' is, roughly, a loss of what one wants; a 'benefit' is a gain. The ideas of cost and benefit here obviously relate to the person's unimposed desires: those not manipulated by initiating force (physical power) or fraud – as these are themselves imposed costs. This rules out, among other things, conceptions of 'positive liberty' that really involve paternalism. So I can now define 'interpersonal liberty' as 'people not having a subjective cost initiated and imposed on them by other people'. Or, for short, 'liberty is the absence of imposed cost'.[72] (I shall also sometimes write 'impose' instead of 'impose a cost'.)

I am not concerned with words or the 'essence' of the concept of liberty. I have no argument with those who prefer to restrict the use of 'liberty' to some other sense, such as the 'absence of any constraint on movement'. The chosen formula is intended to capture what libertarians and classical liberals require for practical purposes; it need not be necessary and sufficient for all logically possible situations.[73] As it does seem to capture the relevant sense of 'liberty' it seems reasonable to use that word, but the use of that word does not affect the substance of the theory; another word could do the same work.

One important contrast with this sense of 'liberty' is 'liberty' as a mere zero-sum game whereby any loss in my interpersonal power must be exactly balanced by an increase in the power of others: if I lose the interpersonal power to exercise free speech, then this must mean that others gain the power to keep me quiet. This position is even reached by the libertarian philosopher Hillel Steiner (1983). Such 'liberty' cannot be protected or promoted *for* all (specific powers can be, but not power as such); it can only be fought over *by* all. People sometimes seek 'liberty' in a way that entails this 'power' sense, to the detriment of people's liberty and welfare as more normally understood. Classical liberals, such as Herbert Spencer, sometimes write of *equal* liberty and thereby seem committed to this zero-sum view;[74] but equality, like democracy (see 3.6.d), is one of the various inconsistent accretions to classical liberal thought. There are, of course, many other uses of 'liberty' that it would often make much more sense to replace with 'ability', 'autonomy', 'opportunity', 'choice', 'want-satisfaction', 'moral action', 'license',[75] 'self-realization' or any number of other things; but it would be a distraction to illustrate and discuss such examples here.

A fuller understanding of this formula will emerge through its criticism and application, but there are a few things we can note immediately about it. Such liberty admits of degrees: we can say that someone has liberty to the extent that a cost is not imposed on him; and in any mutual clash of imposed costs the libertarian *policy* formula (which I shall focus on shortly) will be to *minimize* any imposed costs.

The idea of not imposing a cost is obviously something like J. S. Mill's problematic principle of not causing harm (Mill [1859]).

In what follows, 'imposed cost' – though somewhat complex –
should not prove as radically indeterminate as 'causing harm'.
Some people, particularly economists, might think that 'harm'
would be more accurate, and that this step is regrettable because of the difficulty in economics of getting people to see that
costs consist of the foregone opportunities of decision-makers.
The problem with 'harm' is that, in plain English, 'harm' (or
'damage') is fairly objective: so it must be libertarian to harm (or
damage) people *with their permission*. It might seem that I could
still define unlibertarian acts in terms of *imposed* harms. But
that will not work either because *preventing a harm* to someone
against his will is also imposing on him. These problems are
solved by using '(subjective) cost' instead. Then, however, I am
unsure which of two things to say – but one of these must be
right and either will do: 1) the 'cost' I am using *is* an opportunity
cost (so there is no inconsistency with economics), but it must
also be *imposed* to be unlibertarian; or 2) this is a different sense
of 'cost', but there is no more reason to fret about the essence of
'cost' being misunderstood thereby than there is for philosophers
of science to worry about 'induction' being used differently in
mathematics, electro-magnetics, and ceremonies.

The non-moral and causal contrast between imposing a cost
and, merely, withholding a benefit I also suppose can clarify and
replace the intuitive contrast behind the act-omission distinction:[76] for there is not a consistent, objective, and causal difference between the results of mere action and inaction.[77] So active
and passive impositions will not require separate treatment.

I am interested only in what costs people impose on real persons (I am not considering other animals here, though it is possible for them to cause and suffer imposed costs). An imposed
cost is always on a person as a continuing agent. A mere statement of the present facts can never demonstrate that any cost
has been imposed. The previous interactions among the agents
have to be known. This might look like what Robert Nozick calls
a historical principle rather than a patterned principle (1974,
153–60), but it is not a moral principle, it is a conceptual point.
Analogously, shooting someone dead could be an accident,
euthanasia, execution, self-defense, and so on, depending on the
historical circumstances and intentions: none of these descrip-
tions is necessarily about morals. Someone could accept this
formulation of liberty while thinking it to be a bad thing in prac-

tice. He could not do this if the theory were inherently moral (for example, 'the absence of immoral constraints'). There is something that this conception of interpersonal liberty is, and whether it is morally desirable is a separate issue.

It should be noted that no particular system of property is necessarily entailed by this view of liberty. Neither is it logically necessary that such liberty maximizes welfare (in the sense of want-satisfaction). However, this does not show that these things are purely 'empirical' matters, and so must be left entirely to the social scientists. We already have much of the requisite social scientific evidence. The task is to establish links between such evidence and the conceptions being defended. There are logical relationships among these conceptions and the evidence that are not obvious and which need defending. There are some putative logical relationships that are mistaken and which need criticizing.

This may now seem rather obscure and unlike the view of liberty we are attempting to capture. But this view of liberty should be visible throughout the chapter as the formula is applied. Rather than say more to elucidate 'imposition', 'cost', or 'minimizing' separately (which would risk degenerating into a fruitless attempt to 'justify' a mere form of words), further clarification will now be attempted by way of considering fundamental criticisms of the libertarian policy formula of 'minimizing imposed costs'.

Throughout, I shall be trying to work out the genuine implications of this conception. Other people might well see many of my interpretations as mere personal intuitions that are biased in the direction of the compatibility thesis. But as I have so much basic ground to cover to develop the general theory, and cannot possibly guess which points will prove the most controversial and for what reasons, I am obliged to wait until any specific points are helpfully made in criticism of this book. However, I shall occasionally contrast my account with some relevant libertarian alternative interpretations, particularly those expounded by Nozick and Rothbard as their libertarian theories are two of the most thorough and sophisticated that I know of.

3.2. Four Fundamental Criticisms of Minimizing Imposed Cost

The idea that observing such liberty entails 'minimizing imposed costs' is immediately open to various criticisms. We shall look at four fundamental criticisms: strictly interpreted, this would logically imply genocide in practice; it is impractically unclear and moralized; it could entail mob rule of some kind; it clashes with the Pareto criterion.

a. Libertarian Genocide?

If I am the only person in the universe then no persons are having effects on each other. There can be no loss of interpersonal freedom; no interpersonal imposed cost. My interpersonal freedom is perfect. As soon as another person exists we can have effects on each other. If unconsented-to effects make either one of us less want-satisfied then the other person imposes a cost: there is no longer perfect liberty with respect to other people. It might seem that perfect liberty is only certain to be achieved in a universe with at most one person in it. In fact the more people that there are, the more that liberty will be lessened as more costs are bound to be imposed. So if such liberty is literally to be taken as a goal to be maximized, then we need to aim at minimizing the population. In fact this theory apparently entails that genocide, if successful, would be a relatively small imposed cost compared to the costs that are bound to occur if the species continues indefinitely (even in terms of only the greater numbers of future murders that would otherwise have occurred given enough time). Therefore this is an ultimately implausible account of liberty in the sense I am seeking and one that cannot be compatible with maximizing welfare.[78]

One response might seem to be to say that this criticism overlooks the opposite aspect of the case: if preventing future impositions on potential people is to count as stopping imposed costs, then imposing[79] the prevention of the births of potential people – who would otherwise have had worthwhile lives – would seem to impose a still greater cost. So far-fetched philosophical criticisms designed to test whether a theory is ultimately plausible will sometimes require similarly far-fetched answers; this reply should not be taken to imply that potential persons would feature in everyday calculations of what is libertarian. That being said, it is far from clear to me that the formula implies that we should count potential people.[80] That is not how I would interpret it. But then this also applies to the original criticism and so undermines it. In neither case is genocide entailed. However, even if there were some mere logical possibility that would make the formula ultimately implausible, that need not prevent it from being plausible for all practical purposes – which is what I am really seeking.

b. Impractically Unclear and Moralized?

Does the subjective nature of cost with this conception of libertarian liberty not make cost assessments impractically unclear? In many cases cost is ranked *intra*personally. The individual alone determines what he finds to be a greater or lesser cost to him. Only, when there is a clash of interests with two persons being a cost to each other might *inter*personal comparisons of imposed cost be required (or simply the external assessment of an imposed cost if the claim is on one side only). Should the people involved come to an agreement about a solution then there is no longer an imposition in any case so, again, no problem of objectivity arises. If the parties involved disagree about what is a satisfactory solution to such imposed cost claims, then there *is* a problem about assessing cost interpersonally, or externally (general interpersonal utility comparisons are given an intuitive defense at 4.2). But observing liberty merely entails minimizing overall imposed costs rather than, as with the theory of welfare, what maximizes benefits. This restricts such assessments considerably. Rough and ready assessments of imposed costs of the 'reasonable man' variety are all that are occasionally needed (where 'reasonable' cannot be interpreted in a way that clearly conflicts with minimizing impositions). Legal systems currently use just such assessments in some cases to decide welfare effects. In neither case does this mean that they become hopelessly vague and relativistic. It is logically possible that they could do so, but they do not seem to do so in practice. Arguments about degrees of imposed cost (damages) are usually about the reality of the feelings of the people involved (and the history and validity of any agreements, and so forth) rather than any philosophical objection to the incommensurability or inherent un-measurability of the feelings of different parties. Such philo-sophical criticisms are not usually a *practical* problem.

It should not be surprising or inherently objectionable that a theory of interpersonal liberty must make some reference to in-terpersonal comparisons, or external assessments, of the values of the agents. Does this not entail that the theory is value-laden in some moral sense? Not at all. To think that person A is more of an imposed cost to person B than vice versa does not entail that anything ought to be done about it. Is this interpretation of interpersonal liberty to be understood to mean that people are to be counted as *equal* in comparisons of imposed cost (the same in-tensity of cost to two people means that they are equally im-posed on)? Yes, other things being equal. Again, does this not make it an inherently moral notion of liberty? No: this is a for-mula that anyone could use without thereby affirming the value of it or even thinking that liberty is correctly understood. This is analogous with welfare economics where the definition of wel-fare, once given, can be used by anyone regardless of whether he thinks that welfare ought to be promoted or whether he thinks the definition really captures the notion of welfare. It is cer-tainly possible to interpret 'interpersonal liberty' in an inher-ently moralized way (for instance, as suggested earlier, 'the ab-sence of immoral constraints'),[81] but it is not necessary and that is not what has been done here.

c. Mob Rule?

Suppose that many people find one particular person a cost to them all by his very existence. There is something about that person which he cannot change but which others find objection-able in some way. Given my formula, he seems to be infringing the liberty of others by his very existence. What is more, given enough people who find him objectionable enough it would seem to follow that the minimizing-imposed-cost policy could be that they kill him to stop his nuisance value to them. Some might feel that this is obviously illiberal, and so this interpretation of liber-tarian liberty is implausible. To see what is wrong with this criticism we have to make it more specific. It should clarify mat-ters to take some examples for examination: a typhoid carrier, a critic of religion, and libertarian utility monsters.

i. *A Typhoid Carrier*

A typhoid carrier is unaffected by the disease but, let us suppose, cannot help giving it to others.[82] There is obviously a great cost imposed on others if they die because of the proximity of this person. There is also a *small* cost imposed on him if he is forced not to use areas where he might infect people. No matter how much he suffers thereby, the cost *imposed* on him is not very great given that the real attraction is the people and the valuable items they have created: he is not having a *cost imposed* on him merely by being *denied the benefit* of their immediate company and artefacts (and he could still enjoy various types of communication and many artefacts outside society). The *cost imposed* on him by keeping him away from people *who wish to avoid him* is only how much he would have enjoyed the same area if it were uninhabited and uncultivated. This is clearly insignificant, and easily compensated for, compared to the imposed cost to others if he does not stay away. Requiring him to stay away from people must be the liberal solution.

I have not yet mentioned imprisoning the carrier. That would clearly be a restriction of his liberty in one common sense. However, it will still not be an (initiated) *imposed* cost if it is done in self-defense (or in defense of other persons than oneself, of course) because of the carrier's attempts to impose his deadly presence on others. And because such 'preventive restraint' does not impose a cost, there is no libertarian requirement for a detention centre 'luxurious enough to compensate someone for the disadvantages of being prohibited from living among others in the wider society', as Nozick argues (1974, 144). The imprisonment of those who are no serious threat to others is, of course, utterly different: this clearly imposes a cost and there would be little need for it in a libertarian society, which would probably aim at swift and proportional retribution or restitution (see 3.5.b below).

Now assume, however fantastic it may seem, that the carrier is so infectious that people could catch the disease from him wherever he might be. The carrier would then be bound to impose a cost on others so great that it would be liberal to kill him if that is the only way to stop his being the cause of others catching, and dying from, the disease. It is illiberal to live when doing so can be done only at the unconsenting and uncompensatable expense of other people. The cost imposed on the carrier is uncompensatable now, but it is only a minute fraction of that imposed on the others if he were to live. Though much more drastic and unfortunate, killing him must, on balance, be the liberal solution. So this fantasy case fits the vague account given above, but it should not intuitively seem merely intolerantly illiberal (nor does it seem likely, and perhaps there are no realistic analogs).

ii. *A Critic of Religion*

Criticizing a religion is quite a different type of case. Salman Rushdie, a novelist, is supposed to have greatly offended many millions of Muslims by criticizing, or satirizing, their religion. Surely he has imposed a cost on Muslims, or why are they so angry? Perhaps his presence is now so great a cost to so many Muslims that those offended have an imposed-cost-minimizing claim to take his life. But that is not compatible with our usual intuitions about the libertarian conception of liberty (and the plausibility of the 'absence of imposed cost' – and its policy implications – as capturing the libertarian conception of liberty is what we are examining here).

A first thing to note is that people more or less control their emotional responses to *mere opinions* – especially in the long term. The angry Muslims more or less chose to react angrily. What is more, it even looked as though they enjoyed their anger to some extent (righteous indignation can be great fun, as every protester knows) for they showed little sign of attempting to curb it, quite the reverse in fact, on news programs at the time. Of course there is often an *element* of uncontrollable emotional response to a mere opinion. We then choose whether to ignore, suppress, criticize, or exaggerate this. This is well known, and it is why it makes sense to tell people who are angry to control themselves. Are we also, therefore, to expect a raped woman or mutilated victim simply to control their feelings as a solution to what has happened to them? No, because we *cannot* choose to be so indifferent to such personal, physical attacks (though some self-control is possible), and because they are *direct* – not accidental – impositions: to prevent them is only to defend oneself, or someone else, and not at all to initiate an imposition on the attackers. These are not at all the same as caring about the possibility that someone somewhere is telling people things you disapprove of.

I do not need to deny that having others criticize their religion *is* an imposed cost to the Muslims to some degree (they are forced to become less want-satisfied by the unconsented-to effects of others). But there are general consequences of admitting, and institutionalizing, the principle that taking offense at a voluntary communication – or any voluntary activity – can become a justification for imposing restrictions on people. Any serious consideration of the universalized effects must reveal a system that would itself be a huge cost-imposition. It would undermine any toleration and stoke up mutual hatred all round. Non-Islamic people could similarly choose to work themselves into a frenzy about the opinions expressed by certain Islamic leaders. By the same argument, they would then have a claim to the deaths of those leaders. If generalized, this policy would mean that no one must express any opinion to anyone else which too many others might disvalue. No one would be able to speak his mind and be safe in such a world. Seriously to attempt to prevent such 'imposed costs' would require a horrific thought-police with extraordinary powers, and people informing on their neighbors. All this would be a tremendous imposed cost to everyone in terms of personal safety, voluntary communication, and the discovery of truth by debate. This clearly cannot minimize cost-imposition as much as does toleration of mere voluntary communication.[83]

Some people might accept that these arguments show that free speech would in general minimize imposed costs, but still think there are a few important exceptions that nearly everyone feels terribly strongly about. There may be some confusion here about 'free speech' or, more generally, voluntary communication. Properly understood, voluntary communication is only among people who wish to communicate and on property where the owner allows this (to import, for a moment, the private property conclusion I derive later). No one can be allowed to leaflet, advertise, mail, broadcast, pester, harangue, or in any way bother people with anything that is proscribed by any private property rules (and in an anarcho-libertarian society there will not be any 'public' property, in the statist sense, for people to fight over po-

litically). People will only come across any 'upsetting' material
by allowing it or choosing to go where it is allowed. No matter
how offensive they then find it to be, it will not be *imposed* on
them; and so they can have no libertarian complaint. For instance, suppose that the owners of a motorway allow billboards
with advertising that offends you (though they are unlikely to
allow anything that would generally offend their potential customers). If you choose to use the motorway, you can hardly complain that the advertising is imposed on you. It is, rather, part of
a package of costs and benefits that you freely agree to by using
the motorway.

It might still be suggested that it must always remain possible that people could be more upset about something that others
do *purely* privately than those others would be upset to be prevented from doing it. Without a concrete example, however, this
seems a mere logical possibility – at least on a large scale. It is
not necessary to refute mere logical possibilities when defending
the theory of liberty as practical for libertarian purposes and
this book's compatibility thesis. Even if it does occur occasionally, I do not see how it could be prevented by a practical rule
without greater side-effect impositions.

It should be noticed that this is not to offer a *moral* defense of
voluntary communication on these grounds, as Mill [1859] in
part does, but solely to argue about what observing this conception of liberty *entails* in certain circumstances. Also, people who
publicly express their disapproval of a person or shun him for
his views or behavior are not thereby imposing a serious cost on
him. They are mainly denying him the benefits of their approval
and society. On this view of liberty, Mill was quite wrong to see
such things as illiberal.[84]

As a significant related issue, what are we to say about someone in some hierarchical position who orders those beneath him
to commit murder but takes no physical part in the act himself?
Such an order would normally be understood as illiberal, but exactly how is this imposing a cost rather than merely exercising
free speech? The answer is that there need be no great difference between murder using an inanimate weapon and murder
using another person as a weapon, albeit a willing one who
might himself also be culpable. This is intentionally causing a
murder to happen in both cases, though not actually doing it
oneself in the ordering case. It is not merely exercising free
speech with other members of the public if I tell my followers,

henchmen, or secret-police to kill someone. I do not assert that the order is itself murder (come to that, neither is 'pulling a trigger') but that it does, at least, clearly impose a cost.[85]

Note that this brief section has not been an attempt to defend freedom of communication as such and generally. It has been concerned with specific criticisms of minimizing imposed costs and the compatibility thesis.

iii. *Libertarian Utility Monsters?*

It might still be objected that people are not always equal in their passions. A 'utility monster' type criticism is possible (for the utilitarian version see the end of 4.3). My conception of liberty does not allow people to impose costs on others (as they can, at least, in principle, with utilitarianism; though as far as I can see, and argue in the next chapter, observing liberty maximizes welfare in practice). But the more-passionate people can, apparently, still stop others doing what would otherwise be innocuous things, or possibly demand vast compensation if they do them. This sounds as though the passionate and uncivilized might thereby be restricting the liberty of the stoical and civilized. If this is true, then perhaps the given formulation of libertarian liberty is unacceptable.

First, there would not be any incentive to become uncontrollably passionate, as all that the theory of liberty entails is compensation (see 3.5.b). So people would not be better off by really being more passionate. It would only pay people to *pretend* to have had greater costs imposed on them by others than is really the case. That is often the case in the law courts now. A libertarian legal system could also take into account this possibility of fraud. Second, a society of passionate brutes demanding great compensation or blocking normal activities would undermine the efficient, long term, minimizing of imposed costs (or why have we not evolved to be more passionate?). So to avoid their multiplication is a sound libertarian reason not to give way to such people to the extent that they exist. As with preference utilitarianism (in the next chapter), the legal concept of the 'reasonable man' must limit such asserted impositions.[86]

I conjecture that all putative examples of the general 'mob rule' criticism under discussion fall, on closer inspection, into one of these three categories: 1) being unlikely but not illiberal after all; 2) not minimizing costs at all, at least in the wider repercussions; 3) not minimizing costs in the long term.

d. The Possibility of Paretian Liberal

The previous criticism has similarities with an influential one of Amartya Sen's. Sen has argued for 'The Impossibility of a Paretian Liberal' (1979). This short piece continues to have influence[87] and so seems worth addressing.[88] Sen holds that liberalism clashes with the, very minimal, Pareto criterion of welfare, whereby welfare increases if some are made better off while no others are made worse off. I shall be defending liberty and welfare as complementary, so a theoretical clash between liberalism and the Pareto criterion – normally interpreted[89] – would be a big problem for the compatibility thesis.

We can ignore Sen's theorems and go straight to his example. There are two individuals (1 and 2) and three alternatives (x, y, and z). 1 is a 'prude' who does not approve of some book. He most prefers that no one reads it (z); he next prefers that he (1) reads it rather than 'gullible' 2 (x); his last preference is that 2 reads it (y). 2 is amused at the thought of 1's reading the book and so his preferences are x, y, z. Sen then reasons that x is Pareto optimal but illiberal for 1 is 'forced' to read something he would rather not (in the terms of my formula, a cost is imposed on him). So 'given the Pareto principle and the principle of liberalism ... we seem to have an inconsistency of choice' (131).

First, in what sense is this outcome illiberal? If 1 prefers that he, rather than 2, reads the book then he is not literally 'forced' to read it. It is a cacophemism to use the idea of being 'forced' to do something when what is really meant is freely choosing the least bad option (which is only a pessimistic way of describing the best option). In reality 1 and 2 must, it seems, be merely striking a bargain over what is to be done with the book given the allowable options. Ex hypothesi, neither uses force, or imposes, on the other.

It seems that Sen's view of 'liberalism' is misconceived. It is perverse to have a view of 'liberalism' that means that people cannot have opinions about what others do in private and attempt peacefully to persuade them to accept certain options – as we now see is effectively entailed by Sen's definitions (128–9). Mill argued for the idea that public opinion can limit private liberty in this way [1859]. As Mill is certainly in the liberal tradition of thought it is not unusual for people to regard this view as part of liberalism. But if it is part of liberalism then liberalism clashes with liberty. If liberalism is supposed to include full respect for liberty then liberalism in Mill's sense is inherently inconsistent. It is not the conjunction of Mill's liberalism and the Pareto principle that generates the inconsistency.

Consistent 'liberalism' must mean simply observing liberty in the sense of not *imposing* costs on people. It is hard to see how person 2's mere failure to be the sort of person 1 approves of is much of an imposition (and it would surely be a greater imposition on 2 if he were really forced to change to please 1). When the disapproved-of person meets the other halfway, as in the bargain they would strike, that could only *lessen* any imposition anyway. That cannot be the *start* of the imposition, as Sen apparently implies.

Filling in some realistic details, it might look as though the person, not mentioned, producing the book is really imposing a cost on 1, the 'prude'. But, as with the previous criticism, the forcible censoring of private communications is surely a greater imposition on the parties suffering the censorship than it is for others merely to know that some people, somewhere, are thinking things of which they disapprove.

Sen is not alone in having confused definitions in this area. Even many libertarians do not do much better. To illustrate the point, we shall look at only two of the best known libertarians, Murray Rothbard and David Friedman, on 'coercion' and 'liberty'. Rothbard is a typical libertarian in his propertarian definitions. David Friedman attempts to avoid this but without much more success. I shall also comment on Friedman's account of the basic philosophical problem.

3.3. Libertarians on 'Coercion' and 'Liberty'

'Coercion' is a word that is often used by libertarians in discussing and defining liberty. The standard English meaning concerns the use of force on people. The *Concise Oxford Dictionary* is hardly eccentric to tell us that 'coercion' means 'controlling of voluntary agent or action by force; government by force'. This meaning seems plain enough. But libertarians often employ tendentious definitions of 'coercion', and of 'liberty' as defined in terms of 'coercion'. They are using the word 'coercion' in a loose, analogous, or metaphorical sense.[90] One reason for objecting to this practice, apart from the fact that it is confusing, is that it sometimes implicitly uses the undesirable aspect that real coercion often has to blacken the activities more loosely being called 'coercive'. This is an example of the fallacy of equivocation.

Rothbard (1982, chapter 28) seems to want to make coercion inherently unlibertarian by defining it as 'the *invasive* use of physical violence or threat thereof against someone else's person *or (just) property*' (219, emphases added). But, in the ordinary usage of the word – and my preferred usage – 'coercion' is not necessary for the violation of property (whether 'just' or not): theft and fraud violate private property without being coercive because they do not use force against the individual himself. And plain 'coercion' is not necessarily an *invasion* of 'liberty' in the libertarian sense: boxers give prior consent to the possibility of coercion in the ring; coercion can be used to protect one's liberty rather than to invade someone else's (to eject an intruder from your house is to coerce him).

David Friedman comes closer to the idea of force when he states that 'someone who forcibly prevents me from using my property as I want, when I am not using it to violate his right to use his property, is coercing me' ([1973] 1989, xviii). But even if the person had *in self-defense* forcibly prevented Friedman's use of his property that would still, in plain English, be coercion. Coercion does not cease to be coercion simply because it is used in self-defense.

If we want an antonym for 'liberty' then 'coercion' is not a good choice. Attacks on individual liberty are better described as 'unlibertarian' or 'illiberal'.

Liberty or freedom, according to Rothbard,

> is a condition in which a person's ownership rights in his own body and his legitimate material property are *not* invaded, are not aggressed against ... . Freedom and unrestricted property right go hand in hand. (1978, 41)

The trouble with this typical libertarian definition of freedom is that it is not specific enough: it is quite unclear what *exactly* constitutes, and why, 'legitimate' property and being 'aggressed against'. It is not enough to insist that 'freedom and unrestricted property right go hand in hand' for this does not tell us *which* system of property, out of infinite possibilities, is to be unrestricted (even common property is a system of property). We know that Rothbard intends to mean the system that arises from homesteading and the market because he tells us this. But he never gives any clear conceptual account of 'freedom' that shows how this system realizes freedom. This enables those who are unsympathetic to the workings of the market to dismiss his economic and historical arguments more easily than they otherwise might.

David Friedman sees many of the philosophical problems of defining libertarianism in terms of property rights and gives a useful list of them (1989, chs 41 and 42). He gives an economic approach to these problems and concludes that economic analysis of law can answer questions about what the law ought to be that I cannot answer – that I believe cannot be answered – on the basis of libertarian principles' (199). Here I give the basic problem that Friedman cites with an immediate response as to where it might be going wrong. Only during the general development of the theory of liberty, and especially afterwards in dealing with the rest of his list, shall I attempt to give the principled answers that Friedman believes to be impossible. (The point made about the meaning of 'coercion' will not be repeated though it occurs in two quoted passages.)

> In order to define coercion, we need a concept of property ... some way of saying what is mine and what is yours. The usual libertarian solution includes property rights in land. I have an absolute right to do what I want on my land, provided that I refrain from interfering with your similar right on your land. (168)

Friedman then points out that turning on a light or striking a match can send photons onto the property of others, so, given absolute property rights, one cannot even do such trivial things without the permission of everyone affected. It is obvious that 'under these circumstances, my "ownership" of my property is not worth very much' (168). He also considers effects that are

small in probability instead of size and suggests that 'if doing
something to someone is coercive, then so is an action that has
some probability of doing that something to him' (169). And this
is so no matter how small the probability, if property rights are
absolute. So as flying a plane always involves some chance of
crashing 'I must get permission from everyone living within a
thousand miles of my starting point' (169).

This therefore seems to be the wrong approach (which is
Friedman's point, of course). Libertarianism is being interpreted
in terms of property without any clear account of how property
is relevant to liberty. Surely a libertarian needs to give a more
abstract account of liberty first and then show how property is
related to this account. If this were done then it might well appear that the absolute control of property really conflicts with
the goal of liberty. It might be true that my liberty is slightly
lessened by the immediate effects on me of some actions taken
on neighboring property. But this might still allow me to have
more liberty overall if, likewise, I am free to take actions on my
land, with similar effects on my neighbor. Neither the fanciful,
photon-excluding definition of property nor the more realistic
definition, tolerating minor neighborhood effects such as stray
photons, yields perfect liberty. Libertarianism need not pursue
perfect liberty in cases where, as a matter of self-evident and
ineluctable fact, perfect liberty is entirely unattainable. In such
cases, libertarianism may consistently demand just that social
arrangement which will yield the maximum liberty that is practically feasible.

Friedman rejects the idea that the libertarian principle can
be made coherent by ignoring violations that do 'no significant
damage' because this is 'judging legal rules by their consequences' (169). This is not a valid reason: surely it is consistent
with libertarianism to judge legal rules by their 'consequences
for liberty' (in the sense of 'effects on liberty': I do not mean 'libertarian consequentialism'). Looking at consequences as such
cannot be the real objection. He obviously thinks of the consequences in only utilitarian terms. The problem is that he *cannot*
look at the consequences for liberty expressed more generally
because he has no explicit conception of liberty (though his book
is ostensibly about freedom and he calls himself a libertarian)
independent of property rules.

Friedman's examples do show that there are serious faults

with the purely propertarian definition of libertarianism. They do not show that *all* 'simple statements of libertarian rights' (by implication this includes our non-moral formulae) 'taken literally lead to problems of this sort' (169). That assertion is not a logical consequence of Friedman's examples but a bold conjecture. I hope to show that it is a false one. In order to do this convincingly, it is first necessary to abandon any analysis of contemporary society and apply the pure formulae to a state of nature.

3.4. Observing Liberty in a State of Nature

The definition of liberty does not refer to property. In order to see how property rules are entailed by maximizing liberty (or minimizing imposed costs, which is the same thing) we need to start with the simplest of cases and then gradually build up to more complicated ones. The convention of starting in a 'state of nature' is used to do this. It hardly matters to the argument, but I regard this derivation as similar to Locke's [1690] though clearer, more explicitly about liberty, and shorn of any moral or theological aspects.

Being in a very simplified state of nature, much of what follows involves unrealistic problems. By looking at such cases we understand various important things about the conception of liberty we are examining. It is an independent conception of liberty: it is not a covert definition in terms of private property and the free market, and it does not have to rely on legal, moral, or non-derivable social conventions[91] (though more familiar examples can illuminate the problems). It is comprehensive: it makes sense in all manner of extreme cases, even outside of advanced industrial society. It is clear: it allows us to arrive at reasonably unambiguous answers. It is consistent: it does not imply conflicting intuitions that cannot be reconciled. It is non-moral: it is an objective formulation that does not tacitly appeal to any conception of the right or the good. This general state-of-nature approach can itself throw light on the correct application of liberty in more sophisticated circumstances when dealing with later problems. It also helps us to understand more clearly the contingent relationship to liberty of more normal circumstances. There will be no attempt to build up to a realistic picture of society, but the relationship to real examples (especially with respect to the compatibility thesis) will often be pointed out as the argument progresses.

That this derivation may sometimes have the air of amateurish jurisprudence is to be expected, for this is an attempt to apply a novel formulation of liberty instead of some well-established legal principle (there are many difficult cases, and I am far from convinced that I have always applied this formulation correctly).[92] This derivation will naturally have similarities with various other libertarian accounts; but the relation to the given definition of liberty will usually distinguish it, and the conclusions will sometimes be quite different from any previous libertarian ones.

First, I attempt to derive property implications from assuming liberty and also attempt to show that no moral or other principles are required.

a. Self-Ownership and Property Derived Non-Morally

We have both been washed ashore on an unowned island of frugal resources. I assume that nothing is yet owned, including ourselves. I then assume that liberty is to be observed (that is, not infringed).

Now, to withhold a benefit, or good, to which one has given rise – without thereby imposing on others or agreeing to give it to them – makes others no worse off. It cannot, therefore, impose a cost (except in the insignificant, and reciprocal, sense of using any resources that another person might otherwise have used). And the benefit, or good, that one first and most directly gives rise to, merely by existing, is one's own body. So to decline to allow that body to be used by others is merely to withhold a benefit. By contrast, to use another's body against his wishes clearly imposes a cost on him. Therefore, the control of one's body (self-ownership) immediately follows if liberty is to be observed.[93]

If I am a complete misanthrope I might detest the idea of sharing the island. I want you as far away as possible. You dislike me for disliking you and so would prefer to be alone as well. Each finds the other to be an imposed cost. If we are to respect each other's liberty as far as possible, we shall attempt to keep out of each other's way.

There is only one natural water supply on the island. If neither of us likes having to share it then each of us is less free as a result of the other's existence; each imposes a cost on the other. But for either of us forcibly to deny the other use of such water would constitute a much greater imposed cost on the other: forcing him to die of thirst. Suppose, instead of being already available, the water had been produced by the digging of a well. Then whoever created the well could find the use of it without his permission to be a cost to him. He was not thereby causing a cost to anyone else, provided that the other person had other places where he could dig a well at least as easily.[94] Others' benefits impose no cost on us except insofar as we feel unavoidably covetous or envious. But people are usually largely responsible for such feelings themselves by choosing to inspect and dwell upon others' fortunes instead of going about their own business; and sometimes they deliberately cultivate such feelings. I assume that any mature person must regard covetousness and envy as largely self-inflicted costs.[95] However, even if we allow that these are not self-inflicted, it would surely be more of an overall imposition of cost on those involved, at least in the long term, forcibly to transfer or destroy goods, or disfigure attractive faces, on the basis of them: such actions would, as in the 'libertarian utility monsters' criticism above, impose more costs all round (few are unenvied by some people for some things at some time; even if it is only for being younger or taller) and even create the conditions for the genetic evolution of ever more of the unchosen destructive feelings.[96]

So to the extent that I exclusively possess an essential natural resource which you would otherwise have found and had the use of, I am imposing a cost on you (you are worse off than you would have been thanks to me alone, and you did not agree to the change); that is, curtailing your liberty. But when other wells are equally possible (not harder to locate or inconveniently situated, and so on), then even if you lack the wit or the strength to dig your own well, you would be lessening my liberty (imposing a cost on me) if you were, against my wishes, to use the well I have dug. I do not *impose* a cost on you by merely creating the well and denying you access. Therefore I have not lessened your liberty and I can *libertarianly* control, or own, the well.[97] (Though if I had explicitly given you some of the water, I would be lessening your liberty if I later seized it against your wishes. Liberty entails that such water is no longer mine. For I impose a cost on you by taking from you against your will what you have acquired, and continue to possess, without imposing a cost on me.[98])

It might be entailed by some *other* definition of 'liberty' that forcing the creator of the water supply to share does increase overall liberty. Or it might be that there are sound welfare or moral arguments for enforced sharing in this fantasy case (this is not intended to be the *realistic* picture where welfare and liberty overlap). But that enforced sharing of such a created supply is not libertarian clearly follows from the definition of liberty used here without mention of rights or morals. And this means that liberty (as defined), *if* maximized in this situation (I do not say that it ought to be), entails that the creator of the well *owns* the water supply: liberty entails property (for to have the use and control of something is to own it de facto).

It might be thought that ownership, or property, is either a legal or moral notion: that one can own something only to the extent that one either has legal rights or moral rights to the control of that thing. But legal and moral ownership are not exhaustive categories of ownership: one can also simply say what the application of some rule for acquiring control (or ownership) entails without implying that there are (or that there are not) valid legal or moral rights to have such a system set up. If there is to be liberty, as defined, in this situation (it matters not how it comes about) then the creator of the water supply shall 'own' the water in the sense that it logically follows that he shall have de facto control of it (others shall not control it, for whatever reason) – or liberty could not be existing as supposed. Law or morals do not need to be mentioned.

It might help to set out the important parts of the above general argument more simply:

1) Interpersonal liberty exists to the extent that people do not impose costs on each other.
2) I make object X without imposing a cost on you.[99]
3) If I deny you the use of X, I merely deny you a benefit.
4) If you use X against my wishes, you impose a cost on me.
5) If liberty exists (how, or whether it ought to, is immaterial), then you do not use X against my wishes.
6) What you do not use against my wishes I have control over.

7) What I have control over I own in a de facto sense.
8) If liberty exists then I own X.

Therefore, the mere existence of interpersonal liberty in appropriate circumstances, without the need to invoke law or morality (or any kind of agreement), entails the existence of libertarian private property (as usual, my point is conceptual and not advocatory).[100]

From this we can also see an important sense in which liberty can be said to internalize externalities. In economics, an 'externality' is said to occur where, *within any given system of property*, the costs or benefits to which any person's property gives rise spill over to affect other people's property. This means either that some property owners can cause unagreed costs to other property owners, or that some property owners cannot withhold some benefits they cause from other property owners. Such externalities are generally seen as undermining economically efficient (that is, waste-minimizing) behavior.[101] Externalities are said to be 'internalized' if this spillover can be prevented (though not all externalities can be efficiently internalized). However, as we have seen, it is possible to take a prepropertarian approach to 'externalities' such that only those initial property rights will be allowed which minimize spillover costs and benefits occurring among persons as such. Prima facie, this will be even more economically efficient than the general concept of internalizing externalities with respect to some arbitrary property system. Thus libertarianism, as defined, necessarily implies internalizing certain externalities (as far as this is practical), namely the costs and benefits to which persons give rise.[102] The idea that libertarianism internalizes illiberal externalities as such, in this even more economically efficient way, will be mentioned in several arguments that follow (and will be implicit in many more).[103] Note that the absence of such internalizing of externalities tends to occur when no one has any private property rights with respect to some, potential, resource. This means that no one has a personal incentive to produce, conserve, or develop it because others can simply take the benefits. On the contrary, everyone has an incentive destructively to consume it before others do the same. This general phenomenon has become known as the 'tragedy of the commons' (Hardin 1968).

Though agreements are not necessary for libertarian prop-

erty to make conceptual sense, certain agreements will have
radical effects on such property. So far in this chapter, I have
mentioned contracts only in notes. As contracts are important
and will be needed in what follows, it seems best to deal with
them explicitly now. This will be done by approaching them
through the related, as we shall see, but more basic topics of
honesty and promises. If this section is not quite a 'state of nature' approach in the usual sense, then it at least remains an abstract application of the conception of liberty. None of these arguments are, of course, intended to be 'proofs' (and even if they
were they would still remain conjectural[104]). Many readers are
bound to think of significant criticisms that I have not anticipated.

b. Honesty, Promises, and Contracts

Is it illiberal, unlibertarian, to deceive? It will be illiberal only if
there is an imposed cost. An analogy might illuminate the problem. If I give you a glass of water that you have asked for, then I
do not impose a cost on you. If I knowingly put any extra substance into the water that you would object to, then I am imposing a cost on you (if you would not object even if you knew,
then there is no imposition; for instance, if the substance is a
water-purifying tablet where this is needed for safety). If the
water is impure unbeknown to me, then that would be mere bad
luck on your part; I would not have imposed merely by aiding
you in your choice to drink (unless, perhaps, there were some
significant negligence on my part). It might be suggested that
there is 'negligence' on your part if you are carelessly trusting,
and so there is no imposition from me. But trusting me, however
foolishly, can hardly turn *whatever* terrible thing I then knowingly do to you into your mere bad luck.

By analogy, I do not impose a cost on you if I give you information that you have asked for. If I deliberately put any false-
hoods, that you would object to, into the information then I am
imposing on you (if you would not object then there is no imposition; for instance, if I deceive in order to keep secret a surprise
party that is planned for you). If the information that I give is
false in any way that I do not know of, then that is mere bad
luck on your part; I do not impose on you by merely giving you
my, requested, honest opinion even if it is mistaken (unless,

perhaps, I am negligent in some significant way). It might be different if it comes with a guarantee of some sort, but then I am not '*merely* giving you my honest opinion'. (I can think of various complications in both cases, but the general principle seems clear enough.)

It would only be illiberal to give a gift that is known not to be what we represent it to be, whether that be pure water or pure truth, if this trick imposes a cost on the recipient: if he would be worse off (that is, have less of what he values) as a result of *that aspect of* our unconsented-to behavior towards him. (It cannot be liberal simply because he benefits overall by his association with us. Benefits freely given cannot then be set against costs.)

It is usually better to avoid such fraud *if* we wish to avoid being illiberal. As most people would rather be told nothing than convinced by a deception it is almost always at least slightly illiberal successfully to deceive people. And if we deliberately tell someone that a particular fungus, that he would not otherwise have eaten, is edible when we know it to be deadly, and he consequently eats it and dies, then we have obviously imposed an extreme cost on him. This is, or at least approaches, murder, and so is quite illiberal by any standards.

So, to deceive someone – or even to attempt it and fail – is usually to impose on him at least slightly (though a deception might be liberal if one does it in liberal self-defense, or defense of another). If such illiberal deeds are to be rectified, we shall have to compensate others (or suffer retribution[105]) for the costs imposed on them (this is not to suggest that it would be practical to enforce this in trivial cases). But others have no inherent libertarian claim that we reveal anything to them, even on a matter where they find out we have previously deceived them (unless this is the only adequate rectification). One does not impose a cost on others *merely* by not giving them the benefit of information.

Is it illiberal to break a promise? People often alter their plans in expectation of having promises kept that were made to them. If I promise to meet you somewhere or to give you something and you are inconvenienced by my, possibly intentionally, breaking my promise then it seems to me that I must have imposed a cost on you. Are you not a joint contributor to your own subsequent inconvenience? There is certainly a causal contribution from you, but I do not see how that stops it from being an imposed cost. If someone is mugged while out for a walk, then in one sense he causally contributed to the mugging. But that does not stop the mugging being entirely an imposed cost. Even if someone has not altered his plans significantly he might feel let down by a broken promise and so would be worse off than if there had been no promise made to him. So breaking promises is almost always at least slightly illiberal. And if we promise to help someone to learn to swim and when he is in deep water we intentionally leave him there to drown, then we have obviously imposed an extreme cost on him. Again, this is, or at least approaches, murder.[106] (In these examples the extreme cases seem to be unambiguously imposed costs; so the real challenge for a critic is to say why the more moderate examples are qualitatively, rather than quantitatively, different.)

What about a promise made by someone we know to be unreliable? Presumably we would only act on such a promise when the gain seemed worth the risk, and we might take reasonable precautions. But the promiser still imposes on us to some extent if he lets us down. After all, we always accept some risk in dealing with other people, but that does not in itself imply that whatever they do cannot be imposing a cost on us. It might seem that one could make a promise but stipulate, or imply, that the other person relied on it entirely at his own risk, and so there is no imposed cost if the promise is broken. I do not see how this really could be a promise, as a promise seems to entail giving the other person *some* claim against us, if only a claim to an apology, if we let him down.

If we want to rectify the imposition of our broken promise, is it enough that we give someone compensation equal to the value of what he has lost, if possible, or does he have a libertarian claim to the thing promised (or its value to him)? The promisee was not *given* the property claim to the thing promised. He was only *promised*, given an assurance, that he *would be* given it. We have let him down but he is imposed on only to the extent of the inconvenience (where this is not due to his own negligence). This being understood, it is libertarianly sufficient that such broken promises, as with deceptions, are compensated for to the extent of the imposed inconvenience we cause others by not keeping them. (Again, this is not to suggest that it would usually be practical to enforce compensation.)

The situation is quite different with contracts.[107] We can distinguish between gift contracts (as distinct from promises) and exchange contracts. Assuming that liberty is to be observed (for whatever reason or by whatever means), only explicit gifts of future property claims are likely to give others the claim to that property at some future time. Such gifts will usually need to be recorded, possibly in formal circumstances. It seems that this is likely to be understood because of the possibility of unserious statements of such property transfer. And this popular understanding, or convention, will mean that mere spoken statements will not count.

If we explicitly state and record that we give away our future claim to X, then the act of gift is thereby done. This is not merely promising at time T0 that we shall give someone the claim to X at time T1; we actually give him the property claim to X at T1 now (at T0). Unless the other person imposes a cost on us that requires compensation, we must surrender X at T1 – for it shall then no longer be ours.

With exchange contracts we are obliged to keep our side of the bargain only if the other person keeps his. If he does, then not to give up what we have, under the circumstances, ceded a claim to is to impose a cost on the new owner of that thing as surely as if we had stolen it from him. It is also generally advisable, for practical reasons, to record such claims. But in the absence of any convention to the contrary, a spoken agreement would seem binding where there is clear understanding of the obligations of each side (proving that this is so is another matter) because unserious statements of such agreements are less likely.

The other person always has a libertarian claim to what we explicitly contract to give him (provided that he keeps his side of the contract, if any, and that we have acquired our property by libertarian means). It would be illiberal to insist that he instead accept compensation merely for any inconvenience. The thing in question is not our libertarian property but his. It counts for nothing that we might happen physically to possess it.

Rothbard considers that contractual specific performance and contractual slavery cannot be libertarianly possible because he thinks that this requires the person to 'alienate his *will*', and that this is logically impossible' (1982, 135). There is confusion over 'alienate' here. It is true that we cannot alienate our wills in the sense of making them cease to be *our attributes*, but that does not entail that we cannot alienate those attributes in the sense of making them cease to be *our property*. Rothbard is conflating what is necessarily my attribute with what is necessarily owned by me. If his argument were valid, then no non-human animal could be owned either, for such animals also have wills that cannot be 'alienated' in Rothbard's conflated sense. I can see no realistic reason that people would want to contract into slavery (the history of slavery is the history of state-imposed coercion or complicity, even in much poorer times and places). But to disallow explicit contracts of specific performance might more plausibly destroy some mutually beneficial trades. In most practical circumstances, however, I would expect people to prefer contractually agreed damages.

The contractual inheritance rule of entail is also quite libertarian (contra Rothbard 1982, 144) provided that we specify to whom or how the property is to be dispersed in the event of the inheritor's breaking the conditions of accepting his inheritance. Not to allow this, interferes with the liberty – or, slightly less oddly, libertarian interests – of the dead person. Such libertarian interests can be understood in the way that preference utilitarianism can allow want-satisfaction interests to extend beyond one's temporal as well as spatial limits (see 4.3). We impose a cost on someone by breaking a contract with him (withholding what he has a claim to) though he could never discover it. There does not seem to be a significant difference between whether this is because he is not physically there or not temporally there. This might sound more acceptable with other examples, such as a dead person's property claims to be buried in the way he contracted for when alive (all such claims obviously to be made on his behalf, rather as the claims of a merely unconscious living person must be). Perhaps this is one of the more unusual extensions of the idea of interpersonal liberty, but I am not attempting to stay within the confines of the commonsense view of such liberty. It would be odd if the rigorous application of the formulae did not turn up some radical consequences. I see no practical problem with this implication, and I suppose that most people who advocate libertarian liberty would want to affirm it.

Therefore, forcing someone to stick to an honest contract or to pay the due compensation is not imposing a cost on him at all. It might look like the imposition of a cost, but so might (if you do not understand the circumstances) the recovery of any debt from a debtor or goods from a thief.

Having said all this, however, I should emphasize that the general culture of an area can vary what it is reasonable to understand will count as a contract, and possibly to a considerable degree in some extreme cases.

We are now able to return to the state of nature proper and use this account in dealing with a variety of problems.

c. Rectifying Libertarian Clashes

You build a hut in a clearing. What are the libertarian consequences? It always depends on the background circumstances. If we interpret the Lockean proviso ([1690] 1966, 130) as meaning that we must leave 'enough and as good' *of what people would otherwise have had* (so that they are no worse off) then it is roughly correct[108] (though it will rarely curb activity in the normal world,[109] where the discovery of, say, a new oil field would typically leave everyone with more and cheaper oil than they would otherwise have had). If the trees you felled were plentiful and the clearing you choose as good as many others, then you would probably not have imposed a cost on me and so not lessened my liberty. But you would now have a continuing strong interest, we may reasonably suppose, in the hut that you have constructed. Therefore I would be significantly lessening your liberty (imposing a large cost on you) if I were now to take the wood you have used in your hut, or create a footpath through the area that entails knocking down your hut. By so doing I would be interfering with your valued creation and thereby lessening your liberty rather than defending my own liberty. Under the circumstances you libertarianly own the hut and the site it is on.

If there were very limited wood available or you had chosen the only suitable site for the hut, assuming that I wanted to build on that site, then you would be imposing a significant cost on me. I would be much worse off thanks to you, and without my having consented to the change. I would have a libertarian claim to a share of the hut myself, though we might negotiate some other arrangement. The imposition of cost is not all one way here, and some compromise is needed to maximize liberty. It might be thought that liberty is being consequentially rather than deontologically observed if there is to be a trade-off in such clashes. That would be an error. Minimizing the imposition of costs in an ineluctable clash is not *itself* violating individual liberty at all: it is respecting it as far as possible under the circumstances.

The island floods and your hut is on the highest and only dry ground. Would I be infringing your liberty by occupying it against your will? Again, this depends on our desires and the history of our interactions. If I had merely ignored your hut in the past then, come the flood, you would be imposing a great cost on me if you denied me access to the only dry area when I had never contracted with you not to go there. I would have gone there anyway if no hut had been built. I would be imposing a relatively trivial cost on you by using the high ground to save myself. So minimizing imposed costs (that is, observing liberty as far as possible) allows me to do this (and libertarianism does not entail *absolute* property rights, as Friedman was supposing in section 3.3 above). Though if I had contracted, not merely promised, never to enter the hut without your permission, then I would have constrained myself voluntarily. You would not be imposing a cost on me by denying me access.

Suppose that we live on separate halves of the island. Is any action I take on my half to be disallowed if it affects you on your half in a way you dislike? It may be that what I do to some extent imposes a cost on you but that to prevent me from doing it would be imposing an even greater cost on me. If we are to avoid imposing costs on each other as far as possible (that is, to observe each other's interpersonal freedom as far as possible) then the person who is imposed on less must give way to the activity, but the person doing it must pay some compensation for the nuisance. Again, the notion of an imposed cost has an unavoidable subjective element that may make the calculation more debatable but which seems to make theoretical sense.

For example, suppose that the smoke from my fires sometimes unavoidably blows your way but your smoke never blows my way. It is, we assume for argument's sake, a greater imposed cost on me to prevent me from lighting fires for warmth and cooking than it would be an imposed cost on you if you to have to suffer some occasional smoke drifting onto your land that you do not care to smell (the legal criterion of the 'reasonable man' will have to be applied to the practicalities of real disputes about degrees of imposition). However, *to the extent that they are unavoidable*, other people are also an imposed cost to any compensator. I could have had my fire without paying any compensation if it were not for you. To have to pay you compensation when I cannot easily avoid you imposes a cost on me. It would be a mistake to think that the imposition is all one way in this case just because you suffer the smoke. And so, still assuming an equally unavoidable clash here, by both losing equally the imposed cost is probably minimized, for two reasons: 1. A shared loss usually results in less total disutility (due to increasing marginal disutility, which is the obverse of diminishing marginal utility); 2. The feeling of unfairness, being itself an extra imposed cost, might on its own be sufficient to prevent imposing unequally on one party in such a clash (I am not acknowledging 'fairness' as an independent criterion; I merely observe the effect on utility of subjectively perceived unfairness).

Therefore, if we are to minimize our imposed costs on each other, you must allow the smoke (the lesser imposition) provided that I pay compensation to you that is half of what full compensation would be if it were a one-way imposition – as it would have been if I could have just as easily have built my fire elsewhere but chose not to do so. So, assuming equal unavoidability, if allowing my fire imposes a cost of ten ducats on you and preventing my fire imposes a cost of one hundred ducats on me, then the fire must be allowed and I must pay you five ducats.[110] More generally, the amount owed will be proportional to any difference in the unavoidability: the more costlessly that an imposer could go elsewhere, the more nearly he must pay the full one-way compensation. (In reality, new impositions are likely to be mainly one-way as newcomers *choose* to move into an area with *well-established and costly-to-adjust* practices. If one chooses to move next to a farm, then one is not imposed on by the smell. And one would be imposing on the farmer if one were, say, to play very loud music that disturbed his animals.) We have with the smoke problem another example of libertarian property rights not being absolute.

Similarly, the idea that *risks* of invasion of property must be absolutely proscribed does not follow from the conception of libertarian practice as minimizing the imposition of costs. For we must not ignore the cost imposed on a person who is prevented from doing some activity he could have done but for our presence. In the interests of minimizing interference with others'

lives (imposed costs), risks must be allowed provided that they
are the lesser imposition and the potentially damaged party receives compensation that is half the cost to him of a one-way risk
imposition (again assuming, what might not be the case, that
other people are unavoidable and that sharing will reduce the
overall imposition because of similar increasing marginal disu-
tilities). Who bears the transfer costs for compensation? To the
extent that each party is an unavoidable cost to the other (and
this can always admit of different degrees on either side), these
must also be shared in the same proportion.

In the case of flying a plane with a minuscule chance of
crashing on third parties (one of Friedman's examples in 3.3
above), we need not seek the permission of potential victims. The
imposed cost of the risk to them is less than the imposed cost on
people if they were to be prevented from flying. What is more,
the risk will typically be so small over even many years that the
administrative costs of paying compensation for it would impose
an even greater cost on the owner of the aircraft, so nothing
need be paid unless there is an accident (and then only to those
directly involved, or their estates). This goes some way to solv-
ing Friedman's problem of how the regulation of risks to others'
property can follow from a libertarian principle.[111]

Is it a problem for the assessment of clashes in imposed costs
that some things apparently cannot be privately owned? It is
hard to see how the Earth's ozone layer could be privately
owned. Let us assume, however debatable the scientific evidence
remains, that human activity is causing serious damage to the
ozone layer. The libertarian view must be that, as this obviously
imposes a great cost on people, it must be curtailed. Private
ownership of the ozone layer is not necessary. It is sufficient that
some people rely on a resource that no one has a unique claim to
for damage to that resource to impose a cost on them. However,
to prevent every possible cause of damage to the ozone layer
would be to impose a great cost on people as well: it would prevent many activities essential to life as most people choose to
live it, and even prevent anywhere near as large a population
from living. So where is the level that minimizes imposed costs?
Without clear ownership, this will be a particularly complex
technical and judicial matter that will probably also be controversial (though tradable 'ozone pollution' rights, allocated by

private courts, might be one way to introduce some market efficiency here). However, that level will not be arbitrary in principle precisely because we do have a libertarian policy formula of minimizing imposed cost.

We now look at the theoretical libertarian problems arising from the arrival of later people, both in the sense of newcomers and of new and future generations.

d. Newcomers and Future Generations

If I had been washed ashore on the small and poorly resourced island (where productive division of labor is hardly practical) before you, then this need not much alter the situation. I would be using things that I did not create and which would have been there for you to use had I not been there. When you arrive by equally unchosen means, we are an imposed cost to each other in terms of scant natural resources, however they are shared. Being at liberty as far as possible entails that such costs be minimized. Because of the diminishing marginal utility of goods, which we value equally, and as we had no prior contract, I must (if liberty is to be observed) allow you about half of all the natural resources. I need not, of course, part with any benefits I am wholly responsible for, such as fish I might have caught and preserved. We cannot help imposing costs on (restricting the liberty of) each other, but minimizing these costs at least maximizes liberty. There is no libertarian claim to equal shares as such; it just works out that way in this strange context: sparse natural resources on a tiny island, equally valued by people without prior contracts, who did not choose to go or remain there. Again, none of this is due to defining liberty in terms of moral rights, or to asserting the equal moral right to liberty (or utility, or anything else). It is simply that this is what is entailed if the liberty policy formula is to be observed. I am not commending it here.

If a third man is washed ashore under similar circumstances, then we must similarly share what natural resources are available if we are to observe liberty. The fact that the earlier two occupants might have an agreement as to the division of the island cannot be binding on him. The third man would have had the island to himself had we not been there, and he did not choose to come there. Our presence is an imposed cost on him, at least as regards the scant natural resources, which therefore lessens his interpersonal liberty. He similarly lessens our liberty, of course, so all must share *if* we are to minimize the interpersonal imposition of costs.

What if the third man were saved from drowning by me? Would the saved man have the same libertarian property claims? It might seem that because he could no longer truly state that he would have had the island to himself but for the two earlier persons (and that it was not his choice to come there), he would have no libertarian claim to any part of the island unless it is freely given to him. But this does not follow. If I save a man's life without first making a contract with him, then I have simply given him a gift of help. It is irrelevant that I might be worse off later as a result of my charity. Charity gives us no libertarian claim on the people we benefit. It would still be imposing a cost on him to deny him a share of the island.

It might still seem a mistake that my saving someone must also result in your losing a third of your libertarian share of the island. It might be thought that here I impose on you and that only I, the person doing the saving, must (if liberty is to be observed) give up my land or somehow give you compensation. But until we know who there is and their history of associations we cannot know who has a libertarian claim to what. In each case we have had to suppose a background of historical facts before we were able to adjudicate the claims. Suppose, back in everyday society, I save a man off the coast of Britain and he turns out to be your long-lost brother and co-inheritor. As a result of his being saved you lose half your substantial inherited wealth (as this was left to both brothers). You have no libertarian claim to created wealth that you did not produce except on the conditions that it was given to you. So you might be worse off as a result of the rescue, if you do not value your brother very highly, but you have not had a cost imposed on you because you have merely been denied a benefit to which you now have no libertarian claim.

A strange but libertarian contract is possible: I could agree to save the drowning man on condition that he gives me his libertarian share of the island (that is, what observing liberty entails in the circumstances is his share; not mentioning moral or legal claims). This would mean that he ends up with nothing while I keep both the third of my half of the island, that I would otherwise have had to give to him, and gain a third of the other half that you have. This will sound more plausibly the correct libertarian solution if we again analogously suppose the saving of your long-lost brother but add that I make it a condition that he gives me his fortune, so that you will thereby lose half of the inheritance to me.

Suppose that the third person is a woman whom we (two men) both desire, but she prefers you as a lover. If it were not for you I would have more of what I value – her. Does it follow from the definition of liberty, as people not imposing costs on each other, that you interfere with my liberty? No: it was never open to me to have this woman as a lover if she did not wish it, as that would be imposing a cost on her. Therefore it is no interpersonal imposed cost on me for her to withhold her benefits. If she changes her mind and leaves you then I have imposed no cost on you either. She cannot become your property (without her contractual consent at least) however much you invest in her or rely on her, for that would impose a cost on her, another person, and that is not compatible with interpersonal liberty. *Unowned* resources can become yours because you impose no (significant[112]) cost on anyone by controlling them, unless you are uncontractually monopolizing an essential natural resource. Uncontractually monopolizing the sole natural water supply by obstructing my access does impose a cost on me. But 'monopolizing' the sole *self-owning* woman by being *chosen by her* cannot impose a cost on me.

There might still be a suspicion, among heterosexual males at least, that because I am so obviously worse off as a result of your having the sole woman there must be an imposed cost here. I am indeed worse off because of you, but consider two analogous cases. I would be worse off if you murdered a friend of mine. The benefits that accrue to me as a result of his existence would then stop (just as they would have if he and I had fallen out over something). But nothing that I could have libertarianly owned (controlled without imposing costs on others) would have been taken from or denied me. The murdered person would have had his life taken from him, and that is the only imposed cost in the libertarian sense. Similarly, a business competitor does not impose a cost on us by winning away all our customers. We could never, non-contractually, own custom without imposing a cost on the customers, and so we merely lose the benefit of their custom rather than have a cost imposed on us.

Suppose that you have a child by this woman. Perhaps we should first ask what liberty entails that a dependent child has a claim to with respect to his parents. Normally, only what his parents give him. There was no prior contract. Almost everything that a parent gives a child is a gift that observing interpersonal liberty does not entail. This means that a parent does not impose on the child by mere neglect unless the child suffers so much that it would have been better for him not to have been born (which I guess is only likely if the child dies young having suffered more than he has enjoyed), for that would be an imposed cost on the child. However, it would impose a cost on the child if the parents were to prevent him from leaving them to go to better care elsewhere, or for them to prevent others from entering their property to rescue him from their neglect. To take a child who is not being neglected or seriously maltreated would usually impose a cost on both the parents (who otherwise have a prima facie libertarian claim to the benefit they have caused: the chance of raising the child) and the child (who does not want to leave).[113]

Now on the island, is the child in a position analogous with someone who is washed ashore or charitably saved and so has a libertarian claim to a share of the island's natural resources? In these unusual circumstances, the child who is no longer in need of support from his parents has the same libertarian claim to natural resources as the saved man (while he was being supported he was ipso facto not being prevented from using natural resources but simply failing to use them). The inhabitants did not create the island or choose to occupy it, and so they would be imposing a cost on anyone in a similar position if they denied him access to a share.

This gives rise to an apparent paradox. Assume for the moment that the couple are alone on the island and that no one else will arrive. If they have irreplaceably and unnecessarily destroyed many scarce natural resources, and not created new resources of at least equal value, then they can be said to impose a cost on anyone who would later use those resources. But those people can include their own children. The children can have a libertarian claim for damages against the parents. The children's lives were gifts, but being independent they now have a claim to enough and as good natural resources or created resources of equal value (if interpersonal liberty is to be observed).

The paradox is that the couple are only guilty of an illiberal destruction of what they did not create if they procreate. The parents' gift of life to the children is necessary to make their previous waste illiberal. Can giving a benefit really give rise to an imposed cost to the beneficiary?

One possible answer is to say that the couple always were illiberal in their destruction because one of the natural resources they inherited, and are libertarianly bound to leave enough and as good of, is a similar human life. In other words, there is a duty to reproduce. For it looks somewhat inconsistent to hold that it is illiberal to consume irreplaceably all natural resources *except* the natural resource of life as a person. But this solution is at least as troublesome as the problem that it seeks to solve. For the idea of a duty to reproduce must be counter-intuitive to those who normally value liberty in the sense of the opposite of authoritarianism. And exactly whom do you impose a cost on by not reproducing? I do not think that this is the correct solution.

The correct answer must be to accept the 'paradox' and explain it thus: the parents are in a situation analogous with me saving the life of my long-lost brother who then is in a position to sue me, despite my good deed, if I have squandered his share of his inheritance (this having been left to both of us if we are alive). And that does not sound paradoxical, though it does sound just as ungrateful. So the parents are indeed only illiberal if they needlessly consume all the island's resources, without creating at least equal wealth, and then have children who have to go without these resources.

It also seems that observing liberty implies that the family can gradually take over the island by reproducing. The single man will slowly lose libertarian claims to his land. (It would be different if he had, say, saved the land from complete erosion: the land would not then have been there for the new people to claim and they would be imposing on him if they took it.) Again, I would hold that this outcome is, strictly speaking, the correct libertarian one in these unusual circumstances. It might be at odds with welfare, but I am not defending liberty as compatible with welfare in all logically possible circumstances.

I explained at the very start of this section the theoretical reasons that these unusual circumstances were chosen. It can hardly be overemphasised just how different are these island circumstances from normal ones. On the island there is involuntary immigration and overpopulation, a profound shortage of land and natural resources, with no significant investment in them, and destruction by their use. Contrary to popular doom-mongering, in reality the situation is the complete opposite. Land, in particular, is not especially scarce; only land worked on, or land near valuable markets. Newcomers are willing immigrants who seek the fruits of industry and civilization not mere living space, or they would move to uncultivated land miles from anywhere (much uncultivated remote land is available for next to nothing). Thanks to the market and the new technologies it gives rise to, virtually all resources are getting increasingly plentiful and cheaper (despite an increasing demand for them) – *apart from labour*, the relative scarcity of which explains people's rising incomes (Julian Simon 1981). Where there is some resource destruction, damage, or diminution this is typically due to short-sighted political policies and the lack of libertarian property rights, in such things as endangered species and rain forests (Stroup and Baden 1983). Many resources are chiefly the result of investment (including the important investment of search costs). This turns them into commodities at little expense to anyone else, and usually greatly to their benefit (as their shunning of natural resources in favor of commodities indicates). Such investment means, of course, that it would be an imposed cost to take these non-impositionally acquired items from their owners without their consent (though this may not be true where market competition and industry has been pushed aside by a state monopoly or state restrictions).

Therefore no radical libertarian conclusions follow concerning the curtailment of consumption or population, or the conserva-tion or distribution of land or other natural resources. In prac-tice, the libertarian position is almost always to respect priority and private arrangements, provided that any property was liber-tarianly acquired. How do we know that people have acquired their property in a libertarian manner? In the absence of clear evidence to the contrary, people will have to be presumed to have done so. This is libertarian given that any other policy is likely to result in insecurity and violence that would be disas-trous to liberty (and, of course, welfare). We might expect the eventual libertarian rectification of many cases, such as dispos-sessed aboriginals (Waldron 1992) and land seized by the state (if only by dispersing the illiberally acquired property by lottery). But this is not the place to discuss particular claims.

I conclude this section with another venture into the realm of abstract application rather than anything that is clearly a state of nature. In this case the subject is intellectual property. Important though intellectual property is in the modern world, this subsection is fairly discrete and I shall not need to apply it to anything that comes later.

e. Intellectual Property

i. *A General Defense*

Intellectual property is an important issue for a theory of liberty. There has been no mention of it in the island example, but that is not because this topic is a matter of social convention. The observance of my conception of (libertarian) liberty has fairly clear implications as regards intellectual property, without reference to the actual laws or customs of any particular society (though it will be easier to discuss liberty here by supposing some abstract libertarian society with private property, private courts, and so on). Intellectual property is a vast and complicated area that poses problems different from, though often analogous with, those of physical property. All that will be attempted here is to show very briefly and approximately how the libertarian formulae apply.

Strictly speaking, copyrights and patents (along with other forms of intellectual property such as trademarks, and so forth) propertize intellectual innovations that are on a continuum between the two extremes of being non-independently innovatable and independently innovatable. That is the key distinction. The scope of intellectual property I have in mind is far wider than traditionally understood, and might include ownership of one's image, rights of publicity, and so on. However, I will stick to the traditional areas of patents and copyrights here, as my sources do, and will not go into the more novel, and more controversial, areas.

Copyrights and patents appear to be similar in that they allow private ownership in (the expression of[114]) ideas (or memes[115], to distinguish them more clearly from the realm of consciousness). There is much disagreement in the libertarian literature about whether, and why, one must recognize neither one, or one, or both of copyrights and patents. To attempt to take account of that literature comprehensively could expand this theoretical sketch into something too long for present purposes. I therefore relate this account only to a few other libertarian writers (in the next subsection). I argue very generally here that, from both libertarian and welfarist viewpoints, copyrights and patents have to be recognized. We first tackle copyright and the general arguments for intellectual property.

The people who create the ideas embodied in books, music scores, and so forth, often produce goods that would not otherwise exist.[116] Thus they impose no cost on others by their creations. People who use others' intellectual products without permission (perhaps asserting that 'ideas cannot be owned') are imposing a cost on those others as surely as they would be if they were to use their physical products without permission (perhaps asserting that 'physical resources cannot be owned'). If liberty is to be observed, the creators must be regarded as having ownership of the use of that resource. Neither do the creators impose a cost on others by passing their ownership on to their descendants, or anyone else. If someone builds a fine house (using libertarianly acquired resources) and that house is inherited by his descendants, then it would be an imposed cost to force the descendants to hand it over to anyone else no matter how much time had elapsed. A copyright protects an intellectual edifice that seems to be in an analogous position.

It is a useful thing from a welfarist viewpoint that such creations can be owned, for otherwise we should have a case of the 'tragedy of the commons' (Hardin 1968) in the realm of memes. Lack of intellectual private property means that people will have no personal incentive to produce, conserve, or develop a meme and every incentive destructively to consume it (however odd this might sound here).

It is more clear that this will limit the incentive to produce memes. People will often not invest in the creation or discovery of ideas if they cannot be sure of keeping some rewards from the benefits they cause thereby. If people had no control over the (expressions of the) intellectual products that they took some time and energy to come by, create, or cultivate (without imposing costs on others), then the incentive to produce new intellectual products would be reduced to a considerable extent (or a lot of resources might be expended by industry on keeping secrets). Of course, many people do choose to give their ideas freely: perhaps because they enjoy discussing ideas, or they are altruistic, or they value status or popularity more than cash, or they need the general idea to catch on before it has any commercial value. But if people had *no chance* to sell the fruits of their efforts in the intellectual realm, then many efforts would surely not be made.

However, it might seem that *after* an idea is produced it is effectively indestructible and one person's use of it cannot impede another's use. So how can already existing or known memes be conserved, developed, or destructively consumed? At least one example of each seems possible. A meme can be conserved to the extent that it is not lost by being forgotten because no one can reap the benefits from keeping it remembered and used. It can be developed in the sense that it can be intellectually added to or modified (even the translation of a book, for instance). This is clearly another aspect of production that requires the same incentives. Maybe it cannot be destructively consumed in a way that is destructive of the meme itself. But to the extent that it is a resource that was produced for sale, and profits from such sale are limited, unrestricted use will destructively 'consume' *this* use of the good. That is, the use of selling ideas as goods – which one might have invested resources in producing solely for such a purpose – can certainly be used up (immediately, if intellectual property is abolished).

In the interests of overall welfare, need there be a time limit on copyright or would it be in perpetuity? We might often have more consumption in the short term when a copyright expires – as we might if any private property were generally dispersed – but the long-term effects are probably different. If works are allocated to the public domain then the incentive to promote, keep alive, or revive some of them could well be destroyed. If others might step in as soon as one had paid for the revival of a thing, it might be uneconomic to initiate the revival in the first place. As long as there is some owner it would be possible to buy it from him in order to exploit it. If there is no traceable owner, and no act of donation to the public domain,[117] then the property might libertarianly be held to be owned by whoever first invests in it by using it in any way (as it would be imposing a cost on him for others to reap the rewards of his investment, given that he was not thereby imposing on them in any way[118]).

Inventions present extra problems, which is why they merit a separate category, but these are soluble in a non-arbitrary fashion that is compatible with liberty and welfare.[119] With copyrights, nobody re-invents so much as a complete poem or a song (though sometimes similar phrases, tunes, and so forth), let alone an entire novel or symphony. The main problem with minor or major inventions is that, unlike almost all copyrightable material, if one person had not come up with a particular invention then others might have done so.[120] Does the first person have the libertarian property claim to the patent in perpetuity as with copyright? In almost all cases, no.

If someone arrives at an idea that would otherwise probably[121] have been arrived at by another person in, for instance, about a year (the probability and time being impartially determined by professional assessors paid for by the contending parties or their insurance companies), then he can have a full libertarian patent for only about a year (the kind or amount of investment involved is irrelevant to any claim). If independent invention were effectively simultaneous, then both parties would simply jointly own the full rights immediately.[122] This is based on the idea that we are to follow the libertarian, and (long term) welfarist, rule of internalizing prepropertarian externalities as far as is practical (see end 3.4.a). To allow the individual to keep a longer patent would clearly be to allow him to exploit the discovery for longer than he is causally responsible for. His monopoly would then impose costs on others: on those who would have come up with the same idea[123] and possibly on consumers who are denied the lower prices that competition would have brought.[124]

At the end of a full patent the idea can gradually enter the public domain, in proportion to the likely speed of independent invention and competition by others (it need not be a sudden cut off).[125] There are bound to be hard cases when it comes to deciding the length of time that a full patent needs to run, and its period of decline, but approximations are far better than nothing. They are also better than some fixed period. Fixed periods are bound to give some, potential, inventions illiberally short patents and others illiberally long ones. A fixed period will also not be enough to encourage some welfare-enhancing research and development, but too long for a relatively unimaginative item or for one likely to be soon independently invented. Patent decisions need not be final: any judgement could be challenged in the private arbitration agencies or courts at any future time if new evidence were to come to light.

Intellectual property is still a relatively new and misunderstood notion, but then so, perhaps, was physical property at one time in man's history. There is a tremendous increase in liberty and welfare when private physical property is understood and allowed. There is an analogous increase in liberty and welfare with private intellectual property.

ii. *Some Criticisms from Libertarians*

It might usefully essay, elucidate, and elaborate the above sketch to respond very briefly to a few criticisms, and interesting issues, concerning intellectual property raised by libertarians, many of whom are opposed to it. I will draw on writings by Wendy McElroy (1985, 1998) and Tom Palmer (1989, 1990). There will be some occasional repetition where it seems desirable to emphasize an important point which is generally overlooked or misunderstood.

Wendy McElroy (1985) takes the view that ideas are in the mind, and so cannot be owned by others. She tells us that the idea 'is part of the producer' and that to claim ownership of what is publicly aired is 'slavery' once it is in another's head. I cannot see how ideas in the relevant sense are usefully regarded as being in the mind, especially as we cannot always remember them fully. It seems better to embrace Popper's version of Plato's theory of forms. In Popper's case this is what he calls World Three: roughly, the realm of all theories and concepts, or memes (World One is matter; World Two is mind or consciousness). With 'ideas', McElroy is right that you cannot 'alienate the information' in the sense that it remains in your head if you understand it. But you can alienate, some or all, control of the use of the meme – and that just is transferring ownership. To claim to own *that* is not to claim property in oneself or in another. It is merely begging the question to assert that there cannot be property in what is 'intangible' (some material property is fairly intangible anyway, for instance the 'airwaves' for broadcasting on).

If a book is sold on the condition that its purchasers are bound not to copy it in any way then that would seem to be contractually binding, as McElroy writes. We can allow that this contract applies to anyone who borrows, finds, or even steals the physical book. Perhaps it can even be broadcast with a similar contractual offer proscribing recording, and so forth (if understood as a general convention, this need not even be spelt out). McElroy's position is thus very similar to Rothbard's on contractual copyright.[126] However, contract alone cannot do all that is libertarianly required here. For if someone with a such a contract merely passes the information in the book (not the physical book itself) to a third party, then that third party cannot be said to be contractually bound in even the most tacit sense of contract. Though the contract breaker might be sued, the third party is completely free to reproduce the information without any contractual violation on his part. If we are to stop this, we require ownership of intellectual objects or memes. This is not so odd, for neither is there a contract to recognise physical property or self-ownership. In any case, how can contracts stop us resorting to owned intellectual entities given that they are themselves a kind of owned intellectual entity (if not in quite the same sense)? But all these types of property can be defended if the general culture is libertarian.

Consistency does not require that we observe the various absurdities of trivial copyright ownership that McElroy lists. There are limitations on copyright due to general practicality, de minimis non curat lex (that the law does not bother with trivialities), tacit contractual use of what is commonly owned (language, for example), whether ownership was ever claimed in the first place, likely independent invention of many sentences, and so forth. There are similar types of limitations on physical property. For instance, the aforementioned de minimis (for practical reasons) hardly means that physical property is thereby incoherent.

To take one of her examples, it must be mistaken for McElroy to think that intellectual property entails that she could copyright her name. She cannot because that is already in the public domain. It is theoretically possible (that is, possible in principle) under my system, that she could copyright a completely new name that would never otherwise have been independently invented. However, it is probably impractical to enforce this on a world scale. How does that make a nonsense of cases where it is practical? It is impractical to leave a pile of money unattended in the street (if one seriously intends to collect it from there later).

Are advocates of money committed to that possibility? Of course not. So the relevant reply to her problematic cases would seem to be along the lines of hard cases making bad law.

As some libertarians do, McElroy calls copyright a 'state privilege'. Well, if there is a libertarian case for it then libertarian free-market courts will uphold it. That the absence of full copyright would hardly 'destroy' literature, as she observes, does not amount to much. Surely the profits from writing, though possibly rising, are not usually 'immense' due to copyright (at least compared to many other high-profit activities). Why is a libertarian criticizing 'immense' profits anyway?

Reading through McElroy's articles, a libertarian argument for intellectual property occurs to me. Suppose there were some kind of strange aspect of human nature that psychologically prevented people from using ideas without their creator's permission (until likely independent creation, at least). The creator would hardly be imposing on anyone if he declined to give his permission. Other people have lost nothing they had a libertarian claim to. Such mere withholding of a benefit is quite libertarian. Therefore, it is *in principle* libertarian to control the use of (or own) one's ideas even though others understand them and would like to use them. All further argument is merely about the practicalities of protecting this in reality and whether these might sometimes impose greater costs than they protect from imposition.

Benjamin Tucker is cited on the utility of physical property (though David Hume, for one, explained the utility of physical property before Tucker). Contra Tucker (McElroy 1998, 5), good ideas are also scarce and intellectual property increases their production by internalizing illiberal externalities. Admittedly, intellectual property does create immediate scarcity in restricting its use, but then this is in a somewhat similar way to that in which physical property creates immediate scarcity: by propertizing land, and so forth, to which all previously had common access. In both cases the long-term effect is to avoid a tragedy of the commons and ensure that all receive more utility.

To what extent, asks McElroy, do we discover or create ideas? (6) It is not clear to me how far we create memetic entities and how far we discover them. In a sense, solutions to problems are often objective (such as the solution to some equation) and waiting to be found. In another sense, we have to create possible solutions and test them. I cannot see that anything relevant turns on the issue here though. Whatever we discover or create we have a full libertarian claim over for as long as likely independent discovery or creation (in the case of physical property it will, as argued, usually impose least to recognize permanent ownership for first propertizers).

McElroy appears to agree with Tucker that, in her words, 'only the labor of production can imbue the producer with a monopoly over the specific things produced.'(6) By this she means that only our labor gives us monopoly property rights over the specific *physical* things we produce. The labor theory of ownership seems as barren as the labor theory of value. Labor as such does not matter much (though we usually impose more if what we take causes people to have to work harder). In fact labor is an evil, so the less of it the better (if it were not an evil we would not have to be paid to do it). But if we must speak in terms of labor, why should you not be able to sell what your intellectual labor is responsible for discovering or creating? Why is it libertarian to seize this benefit instead of paying the producer as with a producer of physical property?

To (re)discover or create an idea *when it is explained to us* is, contra McElroy, different from being the source of it just because that is not to discover or create a potential benefit for others but to be *in receipt* of just such a benefit. That is the relevant difference that J. W. Lloyd does not appear to see when he is quoted saying 'Everything that I understand I discover, just as much as the first man who understood it and discovered it.' (6) And the 'idea' remains a specific entity in the memetic realm; we only use the mental realm to perceive it.

Tom Palmer (1989) is strong on history and empiricism. Despite Palmer's brief acknowledgement of their irrelevance (at the end of his section II), there seems to be a genetic fallacy (that a thing is essentially what it once was) or guilt by association in looking at the historical origins of patents. There is conceptual confusion anyway. I can agree with aspects of Palmer's criticisms of state patents. But patents in my system do not initiate impositions on people, as arbitrary state monopolies do, they merely internalize some of the illiberal externalities. And as patents of this type often compete with similar patents it is not clear that they are 'monopolies' in any serious sense. That is a bit like saying that a particular film star has a monopoly because there is no one else exactly like him.

Although intellectual property did not in fact develop 'spontaneously', as Palmer emphasizes, without state intervention maybe it would have done so (in a libertarian culture, at least). In any case, a prepropertarian theory of liberty is a better way to determine whether intellectual property is libertarian. I cannot see the 'privilege' in intellectual property when it offers universal protection to anyone who creates it. Special state grants of monopoly are real privileges just because they are not about universal principles. All accusations about intellectual property being statist (280, for instance) simply beg the question of whether it is conceptually libertarian and so would be defended by private, libertarian legal systems. Palmer keeps writing of preferring market competition (around 297), but what he really prefers here is piracy if intellectual property is, in fact, libertarian.

One person's unconstrained use of an idea clearly *does* diminish another's use (contra 275) if the creator cannot now use the idea to *sell for profit* (which can be the chief purpose in creating both intellectual property and physical property). Why ignore this real and crucially important kind of use? The creator might still be able to use the idea in *other* ways to his heart's content. Similarly, a farmer might still have more potatoes than he can eat if some are stolen. Or someone who invented a way of synthesizing a food from thin air might effectively have an unlimited supply if even 99% of the food were confiscated. However, in each case the producer's use (for sale) of his own product would have been restricted.

Palmer sees that innovations are scarce in the 'dynamic sense' (1989, 276 n50): there will be fewer new examples produced if there is less incentive to produce them. But he does not see that innovations are also scarce in the 'static sense': there is only one memetic entity that is each meme. Many people can come to use it but they are merely using the same one thing; they are not, contra Palmer, replicating the theory itself. There is, for instance, only one theory of DNA. To understand it is not to produce a second theory. Memes are thus economically scarce in these two crucial senses: they are unique and their use for sale is finite.

Intellectual property, we are told (281), conflicts with physical property and self-ownership. However, all forms of ownership constrain other forms of ownership. It is no more a valid argument against intellectual property that it restricts some things one can do with one's person and physical property than it is that physical property limits what we can do with our bodies. If I may not walk onto your land without your permission, for instance, that does not mean that I do not own my body. Neither does it if I cannot play your music without your permission.

There will certainly be ideal objects produced without intellectual property, as Palmer writes (287). But will they be protected in a libertarian way and in optimal welfare amounts? They will with my version of intellectual property because it internalizes illiberal externalities. Similarly, Jack Hirshleifer's view is, approvingly, cited that being able to be first in the field with an innovation means that 'the gains thus achievable eliminate any a priori anticipation of underinvestment in the generation of new technological knowledge' (298 n107). Well, only (libertarian) intellectual property internalizes illiberal externalities in principle (thus avoiding *completely* the tragedy of the commons). And that is a powerful aprioristic argument that it is therefore best for productivity. This is certainly used to defend the productivity of physical property. So the fact that some strong incentives remain without intellectual property is a weak reply to this a priori argument for keeping them all.

If intellectual property is sometimes clearly not very useful (as Palmer suggests, 300 ff.) then people will, presumably, not bother registering and defending it in such cases. Where it is useful, they will. The former cannot undermine the latter. Intellectual property is libertarian in any case. I do not have to defend the view that intellectual property must be useful and enforced in all circumstances. Palmer does have to defend the, prima facie more dubious, view that it is never useful and ought never to be enforced.

Contra Palmer (296 n104) and his quotation of S. C. Littlechild ('abolishing patent protection would encourage the early exploitation and improvement by competitors of those innovations made by others'), competitors can simply *pay* to use a patented idea out of their projected profits if they are reasonably likely to be so great. Why would some bank not lend them the money? And this can be done without undermining the incentive to produce new intellectual property and without interfering with the producer's liberty. And, of course, problems with general areas of patent blocking new developments (302) would be overridden by the likely-independent-invention aspect of my system. If other people would have come up with something similar eventually then this must imply that patents lose their exclusivity in proportion to the likely speed of independent innovation.

Shakespeare's plays, Palmer suggests, might have been inferior if he could not have taken plots, and so forth, without permission (302). My guess is that the market price for rights to certain aspects of others' works could not have been so very high. And how can we be sure that Shakespeare's plays would not have been even better if the authors, or other owners, would not sell to him (so obliging him to be more original)? This example is with the benefit of (dubious) hindsight, in any case. That breaking a rule, here intellectual property, might occasionally have some desirable consequences hardly shows that it ought to be abandoned as a rule.

I see no great challenge to the idea that intellectual property (in my system, that is) is both libertarian and preference utilitarian, because of sufficiently analogous arguments to those that defend physical property. We will now return to the rest of David Friedman's general philosophical problems for an account of liberty, and see whether convincing solutions are possible.

3.5. More Philosophical Problems

This section tackles more of the problems David Friedman has posed for a theory of liberty. Some idea has already been given of what liberty entails as regards the original acquisition of property and where others' property affects, or risks affecting, our property. Here the problems include how to rectify illiberal acts, and libertarianism's relationship to consequentialism and economics. First we need to look more closely at the exclusive acquisition of land.

a. Exclusive Land Acquisition

Friedman argues that Locke's account of the acquisition of land by mixing one's labor, and the libertarian idea of claiming land or marking its boundaries, cannot explain how 'if land starts out belonging equally to everyone' people can be completely excluded rather than merely denied the increased value. He can see why private property 'makes us better off – but it is very much harder to derive property rights in land from some a priori theory of natural rights' (1989, 170–1).

First, from a libertarian viewpoint, land must start out belonging to no one rather than 'equally to everyone' (or 'in common', as Locke put it) or we could do nothing at all to land without the consent of everyone else. We do not necessarily need to 'mix labor' with unowned land in order to have some libertarian property claim to it. We can use land without investing labor in it. If it is already right for our purposes as it is, then it would be perverse to say that we have to change it to make it ours. If, in a state of nature, we want pasture for cattle then we might need do no more than have the cattle in a suitable spot.[127] If others then try to use the same land, they will usually be imposing more of a cost on us than we do on them by requiring them to go elsewhere.[128] However, if our use is not often and clear then others might eventually come to establish stronger libertarian property claims by their greater use of the resource.

General libertarian ownership has already been derived. Here we focus on the libertarian reasons that *normally* allow us to exclude others *entirely* from the land we occupy (there are exceptions in extremis, as we saw in the previous section). These reasons include the following: (1) avoiding being personally interrupted, followed, spied on, and pestered when not in public places[129] (if such things are explicitly allowed even there); (2) people are likely to have no good reason to wander around our land – they put us in fear whatever their intentions; (3) they may well do some damage, if only by wear and tear, to what we have invested in; (4) they would probably have little reason to walk there unless we had produced something of interest (if they are enjoying our gardens then they are gaining from our investment without our agreement and, as this is not a public place, thereby stealing the use of it); (5) people usually want their own exclusive ownership respected and need to reciprocate as the price for that. In short, *exclusive* land ownership, for reasons of security and privacy, is *usually* a relatively trivial imposed cost on people and its absence is a great one.

All these facts are contingent on the nature of the world and human beings. In a desert world of natural nomads it might be the lesser imposition to require people not to settle any oasis rather than to require all the nomads always to avoid an oasis settlement. In our world the lesser imposition is usually to require any travellers to avoid private land. It is a restriction on freedom (an imposed cost that people cause each other) that we cannot just walk where we like; it would usually be a much greater restriction if we had to allow anyone to walk on our land and into our very homes whenever they chose to do so.

However, claims to property that are derived from observing liberty are not absolute. The earlier case of the hut on the hill during the flood is one such example (3.4.c), but a classic libertarian problem might make the case clearer. The problem assumes that libertarianism absolutely proscribes trespass. It then assumes that someone buys up all the property surrounding some innocent person. Apparently that person can now be held as a prisoner on his own property by a purely libertarian principle. Surely there is something mistaken about the 'libertarian' principle if such an illiberal consequence is derivable. There is something mistaken about this principle: it is not inherently libertarian. When liberty clashes with private property, then private property claims must be set aside in the interests of liberty (if liberty is to be observed). It is obviously a terrible imposition on an innocent person to imprison him in this way. Relative to this, it is a small imposition to walk across someone's land though the owner would rather people did not do so. So liberty normally entails reasonable property rights of access. When liberties clash, when we get in the way of each other's voluntary projects, the lesser imposition (insofar as this can reasonably be determined[130]) is usually to be preferred on the grounds of liberty; though, as in the smoke-pollution example (3.4.c), some compensation might be obligatory. (However, the greater imposition is quite libertarian if the parties agree on compensation.) This is thus radically different from Rothbard's 'solution' that one 'find some friends, or at least purchase allies' to help one escape (Rothbard 1977, 50).[131]

We see that we do have an 'a priori theory' that can tell us in principle what constitutes the libertarian acquisition of land and how exclusive it can be, but it does not entail 'natural rights'. All this remains a sketch, however; a consideration of the literature on Locke's theory, in particular, would undoubtedly throw up a wealth of detail.

b. Restitution, Retribution, and Evidence[132]

Next, Friedman poses questions about rectifying illiberal acts.
'In order to prevent theft, you must be able to take back more
than was stolen. But how much more?' (1989, 171). And 'how in
principle do libertarian moral principles tell you what degree of
proof should be necessary for conviction and punishment?' (171).
The brief answer in each case is that, first, any (non-
impositional) contractual arrangements would automatically be
libertarian and, second, in the absence of such contractual arrangements the correct method is to implement whatever procedure minimizes the imposition of costs. The application of this
libertarian formula does require much clarification and elaboration but I think I can give the bare bones of the account fairly
clearly. However, my interpretation has some fairly radical and
novel aspects that are likely to make it controversial even among
libertarians. We shall look at the general collection of issues
here: torts, crimes, restitution, retribution, and evidence.

Libertarians typically object to the state's dealing with law
and order for several general reasons: it is inefficient; it is carried out at the taxpayers' expense; it punishes 'victimless
crimes'.[133] Exactly what the observance of liberty implies with
respect to the treatment of tortfeasors and criminals is more
controversial among libertarians. A general theory of libertarian
restitution[134] and retribution is mainly what is attempted here.
However, this general theory alone raises some practical problems that require some immediate response if the theory is to
appear at all plausible. The main assumption is the hypothetical
one that *if* liberty is to be observed as far as possible, then the
imposition of a cost on (that is, the infraction of the liberty of)
another person calls for libertarian rectification[135] of some kind,
as far as possible. What follows attempts both to defend and derive the consequences of this assumption. I also assume that the
internalizing of illiberal externalities which this conception of
liberty entails, is the best long-term strategy for maximizing
welfare (in the sense of want-satisfaction); so I deal with any apparent problems with this that are peculiar to libertarian rectification. I assume throughout, to avoid unnecessary complications, that people have an initial libertarian claim to their persons and property (that is, that there is no imposition on others

involved in these claims) before any impositions occur. I shall first outline how I interpret the general libertarian account and then look at two important problem areas.

i. *'Torts' and 'Crimes'*

At present, a 'tort' is, roughly, a 'wrong, or harm, that is actionable in law for restitution'. A 'crime' is, roughly, an 'act punishable by law'. I propose stipulatively to define these in ways that I shall argue are libertarian (though not standardly so). My stipulative definitions of 'tort' and 'crime' are utterly different from the usual legal ones; but the conceptual links to the originals terms, and the libertarian purpose behind this translation, should become clear. A 'tort' becomes an 'imposed cost, for which restitution is due', and a 'crime' becomes a 'foreseen imposed cost, for which retribution or "retributive restitution"[136] is due'. Unlike the present system, all 'crimes' (in my sense) entail financial restitution (if that is preferred to physical retribution by the victim or his assigns). So it will be convenient to break the discussion into what I shall call 'non-criminal torts' (concerning unforeseen impositions) and 'crimes'. I hope this will not be too confusing.

First, the case of *unforeseen* impositions, which I call 'non-criminal torts', that the imposer admits to (to fail to reveal such a tort, such as after a car accident without witnesses, is itself to go beyond a mere tort and become a 'crime'). Although such torts are unforeseen, there must always be an element of *imposition*: a *pure* accident would not be tortious (such as falling on someone as a result of a freak gust of wind blowing one over a bridge: it was completely unforeseeable). Such pure accidents are highly rare. The imposing factor in non-criminal torts is usually an element of negligence (though it could be engaging in a normally safe activity, such as flying, that just happens to damage others). And there is a continuum of increasing negligence between non-criminal torts and crimes that passes through criminal negligence.[137] If liberty is to exist, then (to the extent that it is a one-sided non-criminal tort without contributory negligence on the part of the injured party) it will normally suffice that the injured party receive restitution amounting to the *value* of the damage (including any indignity that might be caused by being imposed on negligently) plus any other costs involved. I write 'value' because it is not necessary, and might not be possible, somehow to make things physically as good as they were. The imposition is ultimately psychological (but in flouting our preferences when we are not imposing on others thereby, not in being mental states of disutility) and that is what has to be rectified. In fact, even though no accident ensues, 'merely' risky activities (which might, after all, be significant risks of severe damage) are tortious to the extent of the *imposed risk* (which is, roughly, how much one would have to be paid ex ante to bear such a risk).[138] Not to allow the enforcement of restitution for non-criminal torts is effectively to allow people mistakenly to impose costs on others. That cannot be libertarian.

Second, consider where the imposition is clearly foreseen (though it can be foreseen and yet be an unintended and unwanted by-product of some chosen activity – such as continuing to sell goods after one has discovered them to be unsafe). The foreseen imposition is a 'crime', in the only libertarian sense of that word.[139] The imposing party has effectively treated another's person or goods as though they were his own. If liberty is to be observed, then as far as possible the imposer must give his victim the choice of financial restitution (now including an extra amount for the side-effects of its being foreseen: the indignity, and so on) *or* an equally-valued (to the imposer) claim against the imposer's person or goods. Unless the criminal also gives the choice of such equally-valued claims against his person or goods, we are left with the view that financial restitution can always be sufficient for maximum rectification.[140] This would inadequately reflect the crucial distinction between what I have called 'non-criminal torts' and 'crimes': between mistakenly imposing and wittingly imposing. Wittingly imposing gives rise to a qualitatively different kind of imposed cost, because its foreseen and usually deliberate nature often gives rise to indignity and even fear. In fact, one imposes such a cost even if one unsuccessfully attempts a crime, analogously with those torts that impose a 'mere' risk.[141] Suppose that someone tries to shoot you dead but misses. Surely the very attempt is an imposed cost: it is your life and you disvalue attempts to end it without your permission (whether you discover them or not, given that costs relate to preferences and not to mental end-states). To attempt murder but fail due to a pure accident means that one creates a claim to a similar attempt against oneself (that is, with a statistically similar chance of success) by one's victim or his assigns.[142] If exercised, that is almost certainly to cede one's life to the victim.[143] To allow the enforcement of *only*, even if punitive, financial restitution for crimes is effectively to allow people to pay money to impose foreseeable costs on others; to allow the compulsory purchase of crimes. That cannot be libertarian.

So assuming the enforcement of liberty and no attempt to evade capture, which I deal with later, for you knowingly to take or damage another's *goods* is to create the claim that he take or damage your goods up to the same value. Knowingly to damage, violate, or use another's *person* is to create the claim that your victim have some physical damage, violation, or use done to you up to the pain, inconvenience, and indignity that you imposed. This is the libertarian and civilizing rule of lex talionis, the law of retaliation.[144] More precisely and libertarianly interpreted, lex talionis does not imply 'an eye for an eye' but rather 'an equal imposition for an imposition': the loss of a blind eye or the eye of a person soon to die of cancer, and so on, is not of equal disvalue to the loss of the typical eye (it seems that the ancient Jews may well have interpreted lex talionis this way).[145] To calculate the disvalue it is necessary to have an approximate interpersonal comparison of disutility (see 4.2), probably comparing the likely values of 'reasonable men'.[146]

With foreseen damage to goods and persons, the imposition-rectifying claims – if exercised by the new owner or his assigns – will amount to libertarian retribution or punishment (whether or not there is an attendant intention to cause suffering). This is so even though the claims might all be taken in the form of money for the imposed damage, including the indignity and fear, or money negotiated not to perform an appropriate retributive act (if that is a greater sum). Both the latter financial settlements will still amount to retribution because the option of personal retribution exists (so the criminal cannot simply choose to 'buy crime') and because the criminal pays a greater sum than with a non-criminal tort merely for the foreseen aspect (to the extent that this causes indignity, fear, and so forth). In the case of their goods, I guess that many people would opt for a financial settlement that added the imposed cost of any indignity suffered owing to the foreseen, and perhaps deliberate, nature of the imposition. In the case of their persons, I guess that many people would want at least some personal retribution: partly to symbolize the greater disapproval of the act and partly out of vengeance.

Full financial restitution is often not possible in extreme cases, such as murder or maiming, in the sense that the victim would almost always be better off if it had not happened. But receiving as much financial restitution as possible, with any balance as physical retribution, is clearly more libertarian than the victim's receiving anything less. And so is the victim's opting for full physical retribution and no financial restitution, or any ratio of the two, or simply letting the criminal go if that is what he or she prefers.[147] One cannot have full financial restitution *and* full physical retribution: that would be double counting the same imposed cost.[148]

Those who are tried without their agreement, by a court they have no contract to recognize, would clearly be having a cost imposed on them if the judgement went mistakenly against them. But if people contract in, then as long as the judicial procedure takes place as agreed, any outcome will ultimately be libertarian – at least in the sense that everyone has voluntarily accepted the system in the first place and thereby bound themselves.[149] An unavoidably imperfect libertarian system must take the chance of imposing on, or at least contractually convicting, some innocent people in order to deter even greater impositions on the innocent by criminals. This is certainly not using the innocent for 'libertarian consequentialist' reasons, any more than is engaging in many other activities with the risk of negative externalities, such as driving a car. It will be a regrettable mistake whenever a false judgement occurs. To please its customers any private system will probably offer compensation for loss, to the extent that this is possible, when errors are discovered. So it seems that all processes of prosecution are likely to be made very safe given the large restitution that would likely follow a mistake with even a contractual conviction, and given the contingency-fee lawyers who would therefore have a great incentive to expose such cases.

Although defending a separate conception of 'crime' – which many libertarians think is inherently statist or otherwise unlibertarian – I see no sound libertarian reason to defend any aprioristic distinction in standards of evidence for non-criminal tort and crime. The libertarian degree of evidence that would be necessary for both has to be whatever minimizes the infractions of freedom (imposed costs). However, if, as seems possible, it is *contingently* the case that mistaken criminal convictions impose far greater costs (or, if contractual, are at least less preference utilitarian) than mistakenly not convicting, and this gap is larger than the same one with non-criminal torts,[150] then it is contingently libertarian (or preference utilitarian, at least) to prefer higher standards of evidence for criminal convictions. The market is likely to take account of these contingencies: profits will reflect people's choices and views, as people can contract into their individually preferred systems of adjudication. Technology might also change the optimal (imposed-cost minimizing) standards for evidence.

We shall now look at two major problem areas with this general account: first briefly, as there are fewer purely conceptual or new issues here, the effect of differing levels of wealth; then the crucial idea of risk-multiplier rectification.

ii. *Can Wealth Levels Distort Rectification?*

Pure financial restitution is indeed rather like 'buying crime' by paying afterwards, or possibly even before: 'I am going to give you this large check and then break your nose, and there is nothing you can do about it except cash the check'. Given that someone has little money, it seems that it might sometimes be worth it for a rich man to impose on him and then pay mere financial restitution. But with libertarian retribution the criminal creates a claim against himself to treatment as severe as he imposed on his victim. With wealthy people this would typically be something that they are prepared to pay more to avoid than most people could afford. This means that the victim is put in a *better* position with wealthy criminals. He will often, if he wishes, be able to have some ratio of financial restitution *and* physical retribution without suffering financial hardship. Does this, then, discriminate against the wealthy? I do not see how. If they wish, the wealthy can decline to buy off the physical retribution and so fully suffer it, as the less wealthy might be obliged to do (or, perhaps, pay only the court-ordered 'retributive restitution' if the victim was bluffing).

What of the empirical charge that the rich will simply buy the best lawyers and thereby get away with crimes?[151] This is not the place to go into the details of the likely operation of free-market law and order,[152] but there seems no reason to suppose that in a free-market society lawyers will not often wish to take cases on the basis of contingency fees. And because of the possibility of making them pay much more to avoid retribution, it will generally be better to win against a rich person than a poor one. For those who worry that private institutions are inherently more open to corruption than state ones, consider private banks: they do not habitually steal or counterfeit money (despite inefficient state policing and punishment[153]), as those with even less understanding of the market might suppose – but the coercive state effectively does both. Competition in the provision of law and order, consumer scrutiny, full retribution or restitution, that a lawyer who knowingly defends a guilty person is guilty of fraud and liable to prosecution himself, that previous offenses may well be revealed in court and never wiped from the records, ... all will go to ensure higher standards than are currently found, or likely to be introduced, with the normal state monopoly in this area.

On the other hand, how will the impecunious pay restitution? I guess, as do many other libertarians, that it will usually be a case of the victim's insurance company paying the money to the victim and then attempting to recover the purchased debt from the tortfeasor or criminal. Such a debt could always be sold for immediate·restitution, even if there were no insurance. If a tortfeasor or criminal then has extreme debts and cannot easily work productively enough to pay them off, then the free market is bound to be inventive; and competition will increase the imposer's productivity while minimizing his cost. At the extreme, for instance, there is the possibility of selling his bodily organs or putting him to gladiatorial combat on pay-television. This might sound rather awful but then he will probably have done something rather awful to owe this much. Moreover, he is only really not being allowed to get away with imposing the cost of his actions on others. Those who seek damages in this way need not defend, intend, or use any theory of punishment. They can accurately assert that they are merely seeking libertarian rectification for what they are owed; although, as mentioned earlier, from the viewpoint of the criminal's experience he will *in effect* be being punished in libertarian proportion to his crime.

Generally, the libertarian system would be far more humane than the state system. In particular, the libertarian system would almost entirely avoid the current state system of long prison sentences for relatively petty offenses. Only a tiny minority, consisting of those who are a continuing threat to others in ways that cannot fully be compensated for, would bring long-term incarceration upon themselves (and maybe only then if electronic tagging is not adequate): mainly seriously violent criminals. Even for such criminals the incarceration itself, unless involved with some extra aspect of retribution, may be as pleasant as they can afford to pay for (for only the criminals themselves must bear the cost of what they have made necessary to protect liberty).[154]

iii. *Risk-Multiplier Rectification*

With most crimes it might even be wondered whether libertarian rectification could offer enough deterrence to maximize liberty and welfare. Surely it would often pay to commit a crime of, say, theft if one usually gets away with it and only faces little more than paying back what one stole. I cannot see by what clear libertarian principle one can simply add on all the costs of security devices, policing, and so on. For if this policy were taken seriously, then there would be no upper limit to passing on such costs for even the most trivial of offenses. There must come a point where the criminal himself is being imposed on by going beyond any claim against him he might have created by his own criminal behavior.[155] At this point the role of criminal and victim becomes reversed. But where is this point if it goes beyond any apparent damage done by the act itself? There is, it seems to me, a fully libertarian way of determining, at least in principle, the correct degree of restitution and retribution in such cases. This is where Mane Hajdin's (1987) gambling theory of crime comes in; though, contra Hajdin's interpretation, I apply it individualistically and also to retribution.

When one imposes a cost on another the full cost to him need not, despite superficial appearances, be merely the obvious damage done by the act itself (including indignity, anxiety, and so on), as Hajdin thinks (1987, 81). The full cost must also take account of the likelihood that the criminal might have got away with the crime. This is another kind of imposed risk. If a criminal imposes ten ducats worth of damage (including indignity, anxiety, and so on) with a one in ten chance of capture, then that is to impose a cost in excess of ten ducats in the sense that it would probably not pay the average victim to agree beforehand to such a risk unless he were sure of at least one hundred ducats if the thief were caught (real attitudes to risk would need to be empirically determined). So the full imposition, in monetary terms, is probably in excess of one hundred ducats. The full imposition is the sum one would have to be paid ex-ante to accept such a risk. For want of a better expression, I call this 'risk-multiplier rectification'. The precise amount will vary with the circumstances of the victim. Some 'reasonable man' interpretation of the imposition will have to be made to rule out inflated claims. Such proportionality is clearly related to liberty, in the sense of rectifying imposed costs, in a way that Rothbard's '*double* the extent of theft' is not.[156] Such doubling is an unlibertarian limit as far as I can see: it will occasionally be too much and very often too little for full libertarian rectification.

Several problems with risk-multiplier rectification readily spring to mind. I cannot begin to tackle anything like an exhaustive list. I shall deal with a few that strike me as the most pressing.

One problem concerns the likelihood of capturing the criminal. If determinism is true, then in a sense the criminal is either bound to be caught or bound to escape, and that cannot do the job required here.[157] If a purely subjective estimate of probability were allowed then that would be too indeterminate and subject to biased interpretations. It seems necessary to have some kind of statistical approach based on the number of such crimes where the criminal is caught. The criminal himself will typically be operating with some such statistical likelihood in mind. We cannot have the certainty of capture, but at least we can have the well-advertised certainty that crime will be a 'bad bet' for criminals (which is apparently not the case with many offenders facing only state punishments and capture rates).

Should other victims automatically receive a share of the risk-multiplier restitution? No: once *full* financial restitution (if that is preferred to any physical retribution) is paid to the individual victim, then there will be no 'extra money' for distribution to other victims of crime.[158] It is true that there are imposed externalities of crime that affect the general public; most obviously, the uninsured victims where the criminals escape rectification. As there is no proof that a convicted criminal also committed unsolved crimes, there is no libertarian reason that he should compensate those victims (even if he did not already owe, as he does owe, a libertarian debt for *all* the risk-multiplier to his actual proven victims or their assigns). However, such victims can minimize the imposition by insuring themselves. Uncompensatable crimes aside, all they will then suffer is roughly the price of the insurance and security measures. In this case the insurance company is then owed the risk-multiplier whenever the criminal is caught, for it will have bought the debt.[159] As it will use this money to pay its claims, this will spread the risk-multiplier money around to all insured victims in a similar way to that which Hajdin wants, though on a completely libertarian basis. But I do not see how it can be libertarian or preference utilitarian (in practice, rather than as a mere logical possibility) to disallow people the free choice of not paying insurance (and thereby 1. saving money, or 2. losing from crime, or 3. gaining all the risk-multiplier for themselves).[160]

Are crimes not also against society? I admit that insurance and security measures are effectively an imposed cost by all criminals on all who pay for them. I do not see that this means that particular crimes are really against 'society'.[161] Considered in himself, the single criminal cannot constitute a significant enough threat to make his own share (of any such restitution due to *everyone*) a collectable amount. Nor should we overlook the probability that the criminal suffers very similar costs and concerns, regarding crimes against himself, to those which most people do. Therefore the vanishingly small amount we are considering here is, in any case, more or less cancelled out. Given that the captured criminal must pay the actual victims or their assigns the amount – or suffer the retribution – that fully internalizes illiberal externalities between them, I see no serious reason to doubt that this will be optimally libertarian and preference utilitarian. While crime exists, though, it will be impossible to have perfect libertarian rectification such that all victims are no worse off.[162]

What if, after any victim's choice of a restitution-retribution ratio, a dangerous criminal is still at large? If he is so likely to re-offend that this risk itself imposes more of a cost on the general public than his incarceration would impose on him, then we do not need to wait for the next victim: a class action for the imposed risk to the public might imprison him on libertarian grounds. It is somewhat like banning home-made nuclear devices, except that the person makes himself the danger. Until this risk disappears he has to be electronically tagged or, at the extreme, incarcerated or sent to some escape-proof wilderness. Despite appearances, this is *not* a punishment (if it were then alternative 'suffering' or restitution might replace it) but, rather, the denial of the benefits of free association due to being too great a danger to others. I guess that professional expertise will be required to calculate just how long incarceration or transportation needs to be.

Granted the risk-multiplier, might violent criminals be liable to suffer many times the physical imposition they are convicted of if that is what their victims choose? I do not see why not. After all, violent criminals will on average get away with similar crimes just that many times without being caught. Given the likely involvement of insurance companies, though, it seems that receiving money is going to be generally preferred to intentionally inflicting suffering.[163] Then is there a danger that great restitution or retribution could cause criminals to be more dangerous? Might a violent criminal with little to lose choose to 'destroy the evidence' – you? Or faced with such severe punishments, perhaps the jury – if it is a (private) jury system – will be reluctant to convict. I should say first that it would not be unlibertarian if, in order to stop worse crimes from being committed, people were to choose private judicial systems that limited their own libertarian claims to restitution or retribution. As admitted already, I am far from asserting that in practice illiberal externalities can be perfectly internalized even using libertarian principles with respect to 'crime'. On the other hand, it might well become apparent from market competition that full risk-multiplier rectification is an effective incentive for the criminal to avoid such crimes, or to turn himself in so that he can avoid the risk-multiplier (plus any interest that would be owed on the overall debt), or at least to avoid doing more imposing than a crime 'requires'. So the chosen judicial systems, whatever they are, are likely to be both libertarian and preference utilitarian as far as possible.

We should also consider the opposite problem: will there be optimal libertarian and preference-utilitarian deterrence by restitution and retribution where there is *no* attempt to escape?

That is, where there is no risk-multiplier can lex talionis be enough? Might someone regularly commit some crime but always turn himself in afterwards in order to minimize what he then owes? As stated earlier, anyone who is a serious threat to others in a way for which they cannot be fully compensated would be liable to long-term incarceration, or at least electronic tagging. Where the threat is a mere nuisance or against (not too expensive) physical property, there is no real problem. With *full* libertarian restitution people need not worry about such things because, ex hypothesi, they will not lose out. Having said this, it is hard to see why anyone would have an incentive to commit such criminal acts regularly. Full restitution and retribution would mean that the eventual expense to the criminal would almost certainly be far greater than his initial gain: crime is typically a negative-sum game whereby the criminal destroys more welfare than he personally gains.

Finally, what of the occasional possibility that a criminal might make considerable money from his crimes by, for instance, selling his story to a newspaper? Might crime not thereby become a paying proposition that will be encouraged rather than deterred? If the crime is a very serious one, then full libertarian restitution might consume all the money made in this way (no amount of money will usually be enough to compensate for murder). The criminal might even libertarianly be forced to sell his story for this very purpose. With lesser crimes, if people have been *fully* compensated then it is not clear what libertarian grievance people would have or why this should be a problem. However, to make public intimate details of an identifiable person's life that one has come by illegitimately (for instance, the details of some crime someone has suffered because one was oneself the criminal responsible) would itself constitute an imposition; and one would be liable to further restitution or retribution (subject to any risk-multiplier, of course). Even an unwitting publisher would be liably imposing by publishing such details. So I see no serious objection to the libertarian approach here either.

I am keenly aware that if this theory of libertarian rectification is even approximately right, then there are myriad questions that have not been addressed. If it is not even approximately right, then I look forward to its refutation and hope thereby that clearly perceiving its errors may still help to discover the libertarian approach.

I have argued that with libertarian rectification there is no need to resort to consequentialism to maximize liberty or welfare. Friedman next poses some explicit consequentialist problems for libertarian principles.

c. Consequentialism and Economics

David Friedman offers the criticism that 'the usual statements of libertarian principles imply conclusions that almost nobody, libertarian or otherwise, believes in' (1989, 171–2). A madman is about to shoot at a crowd. The owner of the only rifle available for shooting the madman, which is all that could stop him, would not allow us to borrow it. Libertarian theory, as Friedman understands it, implies that people have no claim to take the rifle, even for this purpose. Friedman says it is desirable to take the rifle and shoot the madman. He suggests that to 'do whatever minimizes the total amount of coercion' can be 'not only consistent with libertarian principle but required by it' (175). He then gives what he feels to be a counterexample: it seems 'wrong' to steal a hundred-dollar rifle to prevent only two hundred dollars from being stolen (where he is assuming that 'coercion' – illiberalism – is measured by the value of what is stolen).

Insofar as Friedman is suggesting that it is at least conceptually coherent to respect liberty consequentially, this seems valid if not realistic (to avoid such consequentialism being endlessly used as an excuse for illiberalism, it is probably more liberal to ban it completely and require libertarian rectification for any loss imposed even in any rare, genuine cases). His intuition that it would clearly be 'wrong' in relatively trivial cases, can be answered along the lines of one of Hare's defenses of utilitarianism (see 4.3). We are tacitly aware of the impracticality of a consequential rule that allows such small differences to sanction theft. It would clearly be open to abuse and have all kinds of illiberal side-effects. I suppose that Friedman's intuitions are formed and constrained by such factors.

He continues by suggesting that neither does this 'coercion'-minimizing approach help when 'we must choose between a small cost in coercion and an enormous cost in something else' (175). He feels it right to steal a hundred dollars worth of equipment if by so doing he can save the world from a natural catastrophe. Obviously this cannot be justified as minimizing total 'coercion' (infractions of interpersonal liberty). Our response to such questions shows that 'we do not really believe in single simple values' (176). The libertarian 'claim that we put individual rights above everything else is, for most of us, false' (176).

This example does offer a genuinely competing principle. Friedman thereby demonstrates that liberty is not plausibly the supreme value, come what may, even to 'libertarians'. Again, there is no need to deny this. What is being attempted here is a reconciliation of liberty, welfare, and anarchy in normal practice. It is admitted that they can diverge in theory. As long as one accepts the principle of liberty in everyday applications, one can concede both of Friedman's thought-experiment points and still sensibly call oneself a 'deontological libertarian' – though of the 'practical' rather than the 'though the heavens fall' variety.[164]

We are then given an example that is particularly interesting as regards the reconciliation of liberty and welfare. Friedman wants to give some weight to happiness but rejects utilitarianism because he can also construct situations where he feels strongly that the utilitarian solution is the wrong one. He cites the well known fantasy example of the sheriff in the small town who is only able to prevent a riot, in which three or four are going to be lynched, if he frames and hangs an innocent man.

The interesting point here is that not only utilitarianism but also libertarianism, interpreted consequentially (if, at least for the sake of argument, we can allow that not to be a contradiction in terms), apparently entails that it is better to hang the innocent man: four lynchings are, other things being equal, four times the imposed cost of one such hanging. Friedman's response might again be explained as applying strong practical intuitions to a highly unusual but relatively unextreme case. He seems to corroborate this view when he admits that, in the extreme case, he might frame the man to save a million lives. Yet if we seek to protect liberty *or* utility as far as possible, and if there really are no countervailing long-term side-effects, then we must choose that only one is hanged rather than two. To feel otherwise can only be to have strong intuitions that have their origins in the practical hazards of such a policy. And my view is that those practical hazards are so great that it cannot really be preference utilitarian or libertarian to allow individuals to judge the consequences in particular cases.

Let me spell out what I take to be the relevance of consequentialism here. If (my argument is hypothetical not advocatory) we are to have as much liberty as possible, then it seems necessary that we prefer a situation where there is less apparent overall imposition on individuals – whatever else thereby occurs. In other words, promoting liberty as such, just like promoting utility as such, must theoretically be consequentialist. Any limit on the consequential promotion of liberty shows that there must be another end than liberty. I do not mean to argue that the acceptance of just any principle (such as, 'everyone should take exercise') must entail maximizing it. Neither do I argue that every formulation of a libertarian-type principle entails maximizing liberty. But there is something inconsistent about holding X as an overriding principle, and then rejecting an option that leads to greater observance of X: some other principle must be trumping X, so X cannot be overriding.[165] However, whether or not this reasoning is valid, one can validly assume 'libertarian consequentialism' for the sake of argument in order to show that it leads back to 'deontological libertarianism' as the best way of maximizing liberty in practice. And it does so for very similar long-term economizing and moral-hazard reasons to those that also cause the assumption of preference-utilitarian welfare to lead to deontological libertarianism.

It will be useful to finish this section by mentioning Friedman's loose account of libertarianism and the role of economics with respect to it. He concludes that libertarianism is 'the attempt to apply certain economic and ethical insights to a very complicated world' (176). It is clearer to say that libertarianism is the view that *people should have liberty* (one could even think this for misanthropic reasons). Economic, ethical, otherwise philosophical, and any other types of insight can only be used to explicate and defend this view. Friedman later asserts that the superior development of economics to moral philosophy means that 'economics is not only a better way of persuading others. It is also a better way of finding out what I myself am in favor of' (182). And he holds that, as quoted at the start, 'economic analysis of law can answer questions about what the law ought to be that I cannot answer – that I believe cannot be answered – on the basis of libertarian principles' (199).

Important though economics is, it must now be clear that economics cannot be an alternative to the libertarian principle for it can only be one tool for examining it. Philosophy is necessary to show what interpersonal liberty is and what it *generally* entails in all areas, including that of law. Economics can only then fill in more of the details and show the preference-utilitarian advantages of liberty (though philosophy is also necessary to explain and defend that utility). I do not doubt that the view of liberty developed here requires much defense, correction, and elaboration. But without the libertarian principle and its philosophical elaboration there can be *no general libertarian framework at all* for economics to work on. There can only be a utilitarian defense of the free market. This only escapes taking liberty as a principle by taking utility as a principle, as Friedman implicitly does. So utility is what Friedman's book must be about (apart from those sections, added in the second edition and replied to here, criticizing the principle of liberty). However, as liberty and utility coincide in practice, this causes Friedman's book to be full of libertarian conclusions despite his utilitarian approach.

David Friedman is one of the more sympathetic critics of the philosophical problems with liberty. John Gray is one of the more antipathetic critics. Gray will now provide us with some complementary fundamental criticisms of libertarianism, which take us to the end of the chapter.

3.6. Refutations of Illiberalism

There is no end of opponents of liberalism whom I might choose here, but John Gray is a political theorist who is currently one of the main critics of this ideology. In his *Liberalisms*, Gray has performed the extremely valuable task of analysing various conceptions and foundations of liberty and liberalism, declaring them all to be indeterminate and incoherent (1989, vii). Many of Gray's arguments in that book seem sound. I respond only to those main interesting arguments that are at odds with the compatibility thesis, and which have not been dealt with yet. Gray's essays overlap in many areas. Consequently, this section

of my book needs to be read as a whole to yield a more comprehensive answer to any apparently single issue Gray raises; in
fact my entire book is needed to fill in many further details. We
begin with Gray's discussions of 'restrictivism' and the liberal
principle. Then we look at his interpretation of Isaiah Berlin's
'free-slave paradox', as I call it. Next, there is a new problem
with the determinateness of liberalism in circumstances of initial acquisition. Gray has also endorsed Karl Popper's comparison of critical rationalism with liberal democracy, though without adding much to it; so I offer a free-standing analysis of this
important topic. Finally, we return to Gray's arguments for a
new justificationist and post-liberal political theorizing.

a. Conflationists and the Libertarian Principle

In arguments about liberty Gray objects to 'restrictivists': those
who think that 'disputes about the nature of freedom may be resolved conclusively and to the satisfaction of all reasonable stu-
dents of the subject'. Various approaches include the 'stipulative
definition of freedom backed up by weighty arguments about its
operational utility', and an appeal to ordinary usage or that of
classic texts. In all cases what 'restrictivists have in common ...
is a rejection of the claim that freedom is what has been called
an *essentially contested concept*' (Gray 1989, 45). Gray tells us of
typical secondary positions: viewing freedom as 'a *descriptive*
concept' without evaluative aspects; tending to 'affirm that rational consensus on the proper uses of the concept of freedom
can be reached in the absence of any prior agreement on broader
issues in social and political theory' (45); and being 'disposed to
reject the claim that metaphysical views about the self and its
powers are germane to disputes about the nature of social freedom' (46). Gray concludes that,

> Restrictivist theses about freedom demonstrably endorse na-
> ïve and superseded positions in the philosophy of mind and
> action and in the theory of our knowledge of the social world.
> (46)

The view of liberty in this book is undoubtedly what Gray
would label 'restrictivist'. Gray is offering a persuasive definition
of 'restrictivism' (in this case, designed to persuade us against

it). Because it is so sweeping in its assertions, his definition cannot be criticized in detail here. A fuller reply must include my other responses to Gray and also other parts of this book that don't directly engage his criticisms. However, it seems necessary to comment on this definition to some extent lest it appear to have some of the persuasive force that is intended for it.

Though this book offers a 'restrictivist' account of freedom it is not suggested that this account is obvious, or without problems in practical applications, or likely to achieve a rational consensus (at least in the near future). Also, to aim at resolving a debate conclusively, and thinking that others ought to agree, is quite consistent with the idea that one might be mistaken and being certain that the debate will continue indefinitely. Gray seems to be incorrectly implying that people who offer bold, comprehensive solutions must thereby be dogmatic and naive. This book has indeed attempted to refine the ordinary usage of interpersonal 'liberty' to make that usage consistent and clear, so that problem cases can be dealt with decisively. But even if what is called 'liberty' here is not, as intended, a refinement of that usage but something quite new, the assertion that it solves the problems it is applied to is a separate issue, compared with which the 'essence' of some common usage is trivial and irrelevant.

In some sense all concepts are open to being contested because everything is ultimately conjectural, as Popper has conjectured – without refutation as far as I can see. But concepts such as truth and freedom are here conjectured to be less contestable than morals. It is at least partly because Gray thinks that freedom presupposes a moral position that he thinks it is 'essentially contestable'. If this is not the case, as this book has argued, then freedom can be a descriptive concept and the contestability is at least much weaker. This means that 'agreement on broader issues in social and political theory', to show that this conception is moral when applied, is not necessary. And to think that 'views about the self and its powers', in any detail at least, are relevant to an understanding of interpersonal freedom is as confused as thinking that problems in epistemology affect the metaphysical concept of truth (as in the mistaken idea that unless you can give an account of how to discover truth you cannot make sense of the idea of truth). So Gray also partly thinks that the 'restric-

tivist' position is naive because he is himself conflating the issue
of interpersonal freedom with what it means to be a person. In
fact his conclusion, indented above, seems to show that he may
be conflating a variety of metaphysical, epistemological, and sociological issues (but we cannot profitably guess at what these
all are).

It must, therefore, be at least as fair to respond to Gray's
charge of 'restrictivism' by charging him with 'conflationism'
with respect to the liberal conception of interpersonal freedom. A
conflationist is someone who thinks that disputes about the nature of such freedom are beyond path-breaking solutions. Conflationists stipulatively define freedom as essentially contestable
(as though this were unusual) and back up their arguments by
appeals to authority, observing the lack of a rational consensus,
and accusations of naivety. They mistakenly insist that freedom
is a value-laden idea that requires prior agreement on broader
issues in social and political theory and metaphysical views
about the self and its powers. Conflationist theses about freedom
demonstrably endorse a philosophically muddled approach to
freedom that insists on dragging in tendentious theories of mind
and action and our knowledge of the social world. Perhaps more
important than all this, conflationist theories of liberty are invariably pretexts for overriding interpersonal liberty in favor of
some other goal while claiming to respect liberty.

In a later essay, Gray even dismisses as hopeless the liberal
quest for a 'single aboriginal right' (or, by implication, any single
principle). He suggests, in particular, that there is no derivable
connection between initial self-ownership and initial acquisition
in Nozick or Locke (147–8). This is a crucial criticism with respect to the theory of liberty defended here. This book does not
take a rights-based approach to liberty but, nevertheless, the
principle of liberty is supposed to be a single one that has clear
implications without ancillary principles. It seems worthwhile to
reply to Gray by briefly recapitulating and clarifying the general
account that has been developed so far.

Initial self-ownership follows quite easily from the idea of interpersonal liberty as persons not imposing costs on each other.
If I use only myself I do not usually impose a (significant, non-
reciprocal) cost on anyone else. If someone else were to use me
without my permission he would usually be imposing a (signifi-

cant, non-reciprocal) cost on me. So observing liberty usually entails that I have the use of myself, and that simply is self-ownership. Therefore self-ownership is not itself part of the principle of interpersonal liberty, though it follows from observing liberty in virtually all practical circumstances. There are cases where it would be libertarian to deprive an individual of his self-ownership. For instance, where killing someone (for surely that is one way of depriving someone of self-ownership) is necessary to stop him from killing others. This shows that self-ownership is neither a separate libertarian principle nor necessarily entailed by, or part of, the libertarian principle (of minimizing the costs individuals impose on each other) in the sense of being one of its theorems. Initial acquisition then usually follows from self-ownership because to deprive a self-owner of the previously unowned resources he is using is normally simply to impose a cost on him, which exactly is to infringe his interpersonal liberty. But, again, this does not inevitably follow. It might not follow, for instance, if he had monopolized an essential natural resource. So here there is only one basic principle: interpersonal liberty as the absence of imposed cost. Only by observing this, as far as possible, is initial self-ownership normally derivable, and only given self-ownership and the use of previously unowned resources is initial acquisition normally derivable. (I cannot, of course, demonstrate that this principle is determinate in every logically possible case. I can only attempt to answer particular criticisms as they arise.)

With both Locke and Nozick, as various discussions and references have indicated, something like this single libertarian principle is implicit. Locke first argues that no one has any right to set himself above others (for God has given no sign that anyone has such a right). He then attempts to derive the consequences of this equality of men in terms of which social interactions are allowable. Everything about self-ownership and property acquisition, including Locke's proviso, follows from this idea of no one being above any other. In effect, he has roughly the same theory of liberty as the non-imposition of costs (though with a moral and theological backing). Most of Nozick's individual 'rights' are even more clearly derivable from observing this single libertarian principle.

Despite criticizing various conceptions of liberty and concluding that they are all to be rejected, Gray eventually rejects the very idea that developing a robust theory of liberty as such is the fundamental liberal problem. Instead, he calls '*the liberal problem* – the problem of finding fair terms of peaceful coexistence among persons with different conceptions of the good' (166). Perhaps this is the 'modern liberal' problem. It has nothing in particular to do with liberty; liberty is not even mentioned. This modern view of liberalism matters for it would seem to indicate that even if confronted with a coherent value-free account of a society that is based on liberty, Gray (and 'modern liberals') might deny that it is liberal on the basis that it is not a 'fair' system.

Gray goes on to give an alternative account of the nature of liberalism, suggesting that

> Oakeshott has isolated and identified the very kernel of 'liberalism', which is a mode of associations constituted by adherence to rules that are as non-instrumental – that is to say, as little substantive and as much procedural – as is attainable. (199)

First, there is not any obvious connection between this understanding of 'liberalism' and the previous account of 'the liberal problem'. Second, how far is this account coherent? The idea of aiming at non-instrumentality looks as impossible as pure impartiality. Social rules can only be impartial and non-instrumental with individuals if there is some abstract end, such as liberty, that these rules are partial and instrumental to upholding. Or does Gray mean that people should be allowed to carry on their lives with as little interference by others as possible? Well, that is just what the theory of liberty in this book is all about.

At the end of the same essay Gray states that the liberal doctrine 'implicitly presupposed, what contemporary cultural pluralism destroys or diminishes, a single cultural tradition as undergirding the institutions of civil society' (214). It is clear that liberalism as defended here does not implicitly presuppose 'a single cultural tradition'. Liberalism is compatible with any number of different cultures provided only that they are voluntary affairs that do not impose costs on others. Given the fairly uncontentious character of the particular definition of 'liberalism' I have just given (that people should be allowed to carry on their lives with as little interference by others as possible) it seems utterly mistaken for Gray to assert that cultural pluralism as such is incompatible with liberalism. On the contrary, as I argue in the final chapter, liberalism is likely to increase pluralism.

Now we turn to one of Gray's greatest conceptual conflations: his response to Isaiah Berlin's assessment of the liberal status of a contented slave.

b. The Free-Slave Paradox

Gray first explains the free-slave paradox, as I call it, as it is to be found in Isaiah Berlin's 'Two concepts of liberty' (1969). This is that if negative freedom means not having our desires frustrated by others, then we can control our desires to increase our freedom. But as Berlin later realized, this 'precludes our characterizing as unfree a wholly contented slave' (Gray 1989, 69). To avoid this paradox Berlin's new account of freedom depends not only on particular desires but important opportunities with respect to potential choices. And the absence of such freedom is due to 'the closing of such doors or failure to open them, as a result, intended or unintended of alterable human practices, of the operation of human agencies ... ' (69–70). After examining various criticisms of this position, Gray suggests that the problem of the 'contented slave' is better resolved by supplementing the notion of autonomy with an account of human nature (83). Accordingly, Gray holds that it is by having a substantive account of an autonomous human life that 'we override the avowals of the slave that he is content with his lot, and dismiss the claim that there could be a "truly contented" slave' (84). It will help to separate two issues here: What is the correct solution to the paradox? What is wrong with Berlin's and Gray's accounts?

The theory of interpersonal liberty defended in this book is a version of Berlin's original conception of negative liberty, as existing to the extent that (as Gray expresses it) one's 'desires are [not] frustrated by the interferences of others' (69). An 'interference' is understood by me as imposing costs on people. So if you were not to mind the thing that someone is doing to you, then there would usually be no imposition and so no loss of freedom. Here are two difficulties with the general idea that you can simply choose not to mind all impositions. First, people do not seem psychologically capable of simply choosing all their desires. Some tastes can be cultivated but it usually takes time and effort. Fundamental, possibly biological, values are much harder to alter. Second, suppose I could choose not to mind your causing me a loss of liberty by taking an apathy pill. Even if I judge it best to take an apathy pill after the imposition, that does not alter the fact that you have imposed on me, for I would rather not have needed to take the apathy pill. If the mere absence of a continuing objection by the person imposed on is sufficient to show that there is no loss of freedom, then we have an even more absurd paradox than that of the 'free slave': we have to say that a murdered man did not have his liberty infringed (was not imposed on) given that he does not now, for he cannot, resent his being murdered. Impositions must be looked at in the context of the continuing individual. A change or loss of desire does not necessarily mean that a past loss of freedom ceases to be a loss or need not be rectified, if liberty is to be respected.[166]

However, the main error in the free-slave paradox is really Berlin's conflation of different – but, in their way, equally unobjectionable – senses of 'freedom'. A slave is owned by someone else even if he does not at all mind being owned, perhaps because his master lets him do what he likes. In the same way, a prisoner is incarcerated even if he does not mind it. A slave and a prisoner are not free, whatever their feelings on the matter, in two clear senses of the term 'free' (two because a slave need not be in a prison and a prisoner need not be a slave). But suppose that – in an attempt to clarify Berlin's original conception of 'negative liberty' – we define 'interpersonal freedom' in a third important sense as 'the absence of imposed costs'. People who are spontaneously (that is, without imposition) content with, or have contracted into, or are duly punished by, slavery or imprisonment have not lost any of *this kind* of 'freedom' (for, ex hypothesi, there is no imposition of cost in these cases). So the idea that a slave need not have had his 'freedom' diminished only looks paradoxical if one runs together different senses of 'freedom'; in this case, 1) not being owned by another, and 2) not having costs imposed on one by others. Once these senses of 'freedom' are clearly distinguished, the paradox is seen to be based on a conflation. If we suppose his existence, the spontaneously and entirely contented slave is unfree in sense (1) but free in sense (2). This is the real solution to Berlin's paradox of the free slave. Nevertheless, it is desirable to go on to criticize Berlin's and Gray's putative solutions as they are mistaken in ways that are not unusual and which cloud the nature of interpersonal liberty.

Berlin's new account of liberty is roughly one equating it with valuable opportunities – though he does include the freedom to make mistaken choices – whether or not these are eventually taken. Presumably Berlin would see a society as more free to the extent that people have more of such opportunities. Berlin is now in an ironic position. In his original essay he told us, quoting Bishop Butler, that 'a thing is what it is and not some other thing' and that we cannot expect all valuable things to overlap just because we would like them to do so. With this new definition of liberty Berlin has apparently abandoned the value-free problem of finding a consistent formulation of negative liberty in favor of a definition that makes liberty very broad and inherently valuable to the individual: each individual is more or less bound to like the idea of his having as many valuable opportunities as possible. (Though given that a contented slave does not consciously value being freed, it must sometimes be others who are, illiberally, deciding which opportunities are valuable. But this still makes 'freedom' inherently and broadly valuable.)

Admittedly, 'liberty' as interpreted in this book is also desired by definition, but reasons have been given that it does capture the consistent formulation of negative (interpersonal) liberty, and it is not as hopelessly broad as Berlin's idea of liberty as the degree of valuable opportunities due to other people. It is part of our theory that maximum opportunity (for want-satisfaction) and maximum liberty are contingently highly congruent, but it is logically allowed that liberty could have destructive effects for such opportunity. Berlin has now so linked these concepts that he cannot even make sense of such a possibility. He has not given us a persuasive explanation of why valuable opportunities, due to others, and liberty are the same thing. So that linkage seems arbitrary or tendentious in just the way to which Berlin had originally objected in the first edition of his essay.

Gray has praised Berlin for his view that we should not expect all desirable things to be co-possible. In his attempt to solve the free-slave paradox, Gray ignores this advice even more that does Berlin. His solution is to deny that a slave can be truly contented. He is attempting to tie together concepts such that contentment is only possible within a range of autonomous human norms. But to deny that someone is contented or autonomous because he does not fit into our list of approved lifestyles is little more than an insult. It is mainly by fiat and an appeal to popular opinion that Gray attempts to deny that some fail to achieve these desirable things. It is revealing that Gray chooses to allow 'religious devotion' to be apparently unproblematic as a contented form of autonomous human life while denying this status to 'the cocaine addict' (84). This seems based more on Gray's conventional prejudices than anything else. It is at least possible that some religious devotees are vacant, miserable, and obedient while some cocaine addicts are fulfilled, joyous, and autonomous. The real error, however, remains the conflation of distinct concepts when 'a thing is what it is and not some other thing'.

Once more, why must the notion of autonomy be tied to any conception of human nature? What Gray calls the 'bare notion of autonomy' (83) just is autonomy, and he is trying to adulterate it. There need be nothing more peculiarly 'human' about 'human autonomy' than there is something peculiarly human about human death (because there are more general senses of 'liberty', I do refer to *interpersonal* liberty' but this involves no special theory of persons or human nature). Gray asserts that in the uses of 'autonomy' in moral and political contexts there is always some account of human nature (83–4). That is not the case in this book. We can distinguish intellectual autonomy from physical autonomy. Intellectual autonomy I take to be, roughly, about developing one's own moral and factual theories; no theory of human nature need be mentioned[167] (nor is such autonomy necessary for interpersonal liberty). One is physically autonomous to the extent that one is not controlled by others; no theory of human nature need be mentioned (nor is such autonomy necessary for interpersonal liberty: one can contract in to such control). Gray is offering another conflationist and persuasive definition instead of philosophical distinction and argument.

To contrast this mere conflation we shall look at a new problem for original acquisition, which seems to me to be one of Gray's best criticisms.

c. Ownership by Mere Reliance on Natural Resources

Gray outlines a specific problem of conflicting property rights:

> A family of fisher folk has since time immemorial trawled a given strip of coast. Now, because of industrial activity further along the coast, the catch which it had always brought in falls substantially. What are the fisher folk entitled to demand according to Lockean theory? ... in their applications in the state of nature they [Lockean principles] contain vast indeterminacies. The guidance they appear to offer in civil society is, for this reason, delusive, and we rely in reality on convention to settle boundary problems ... . (Gray 1989, 148)

Again, I have already given a general theory of libertarian acquisition but it would test the theory to tackle the specific problem that Gray poses. To get a grip on Gray's example it might help to start with a simpler case.

Suppose that another group of fisher folk were to come into the area and fish to the extent that the catch of the indigenous group fell substantially. For the new fisher folk simply to take a resource that the others were already relying on would normally be a great cost to the original group. It would normally be a small cost to the new group to require that they find some other place to fish or way of making a living and pay compensation for the initial imposition. Only if this is extremely difficult (perhaps due to some unusual circumstance such as a famine on the land and no fish elsewhere) would the new group have a libertarian claim to share the fishing (because there would not be any viable alternative way of making a living, and they would have been able to fish had the original group merely not been there). What counts as imposed costs can be influenced by what is happening in the wider society.

The case is similar with the new industrial activity.[168] Assuming no analog to the famine and fish scarcity (such as the uniqueness of the site for some essential production), the industrial activity must cease and compensation be paid or, if the more productive company can afford it (unlike the new fisher folk), the original fisher folk have to be compensated to roughly the value of their continuing losses (including any non-pecuniary ones).[169] This compensation could either continue for the duration of the effects of the industrial activity or be settled by a lump sum. It would usually be libertarian for the fisher folk to have the power of veto over the industrial activity up to the point that full compensation is paid to them. They cannot have an *absolute* power of veto if full compensation is possible, for they could then impose costs on the other group by using the veto to obstruct it capriciously or bid up the compensation beyond the level of any real imposed cost to themselves. Even if the original fisher folk are genuinely opposed to accepting poorer fishing for any amount of compensation, that might still be the lesser imposition if siting the industry elsewhere is highly expensive (the earlier discussion of clashing impositions, in 3.4.c, shows that the lesser imposition must be allowed with full compensation being proportional to any difference in the cost of avoidability).[170] Disputes about such things would best be adjudicated by private arbitrators. Exactly how these would operate is more of a practical than a philosophical problem.

However, while the *direct* libertarian property claim can be determined in this way, there is another issue. We might also wish to give weight to the first users' claims on the *indirect* libertarian basis that the stability of property is very important for avoiding cost-imposing conflicts and expense that would be caused by frequent challenges in relatively trivial cases.

So the general solution is that, in the mostly likely scenario, the traditional fisher folk do have a libertarian property claim in the fish (circumstances can certainly alter and considerably complicate this, but they do not thereby undermine the theoretical determinateness of the libertarian principle). If any convention is used which has a result that is different, and not freely agreed to (that is, without imposition) by the parties involved, then the outcome is illiberal. If liberty is to be observed then the claim to the fish is valid whether or not the law recognizes this. From a libertarian point of view it would be better if the law explicitly recognized this libertarian property claim in order to facilitate compensation or trade and to help to avoid unnecessary disputes or unintentional impositions.

This might not look like a Lockean position because the fisher folk do not do anything to the fish or the sea apart from rely on them (and they are different individual fish each time). But the fisher folk's use of the fish in this way imposes on no one significantly (given that there are 'enough and as good' other places and ways of making a living), while the new industrial activity is imposing a serious cost on them just as surely as it would if it were to involve taking the land on which the fisher folk had built their houses. I submit that this solution to the problem is within the spirit of Locke's general theory of equality of persons (that is, individual liberty). Locke was merely mistaken to think that labor-mixing could catch all the property acquisition that his theory required. However, even if this is stretching Locke's theory too far, the result holds as following from the theory of liberty defended here, and we see that Gray has not shown that all libertarian theories contain 'vast indeterminacies' in a state of nature.

Before we look at the final statement of Gray's views on the future of political philosophy, we should consider the relationship between critical rationalism and politics. This issue is quite important but Gray does not do much more here than nod approvingly in Popper's direction. So rather than answer Gray's points, as in the rest of this section, it seems better to criticize Popper directly. What follows might appear out of place just because it interrupts Gray's points, but it is clearly relevant to the critical-rationalist defense of the compatibility thesis and I cannot see where it could more felicitously be located.

d. Critical Rationalism and Libertarianism[171]

Gray agrees with Karl Popper's defense of liberal democracy: that it most closely approximates the conditions of scientific criticism. Gray apparently approves of the 'non-violent adversarial exchange of ideas' (22). This is not, however, quite what happens in a liberal democracy. As we shall see, this is an important area of disagreement for a variety of reasons.

What is my thesis? It is not that radical experimentation by the state, rather than liberal democracy, is more in accord with the spirit and logic of Popper's 'revolutionary' epistemology. It is the opposite criticism, that full anarchic libertarianism (individual liberty and the free market without any state interference) better fits Popper's epistemology and scientific method.

I think this thesis important because I accept Popper's epistemology and methodology, and I think that these are a useful part of the defense of libertarianism: the value of complete liberty is a bold conjecture that withstands criticism rather than a theory to be supported by any specific argument or set of arguments. And, in its turn, libertarianism is a useful part of the defense of Popper's epistemology and methodology: it illustrates their beneficial social applications. In one sense, Popper's picture of the best way to pursue truth is only a part of the more general picture of libertarianism. Popper advocates what can be called 'intellectual libertarianism'. I am here suggesting that his libertarianism should be extended to the realm of individual persons and businesses (as contractual organizations, but I do not mean to exclude other voluntary organizations). Popper writes that he seeks to put 'the finishing touches to Kant's own critical philosophy' ([1963] 1978, 27). I seek to put the finishing touches to Popper's own social philosophy.

Let us briefly recapitulate Popper's scientific epistemology and methodology.[172] As Hume showed, it is logically impossible to support a universal theory with evidence. All corroborating evidence, even if accurate, is an infinitely small proportion of what the theory predicts. But one counter-example shows a universal theory to be false. Thus the only rational way to pursue truth is to conjecture without supporting evidence and then deliberately to seek refutation. The bolder the conjecture (compatible with background knowledge), the greater the chance of capturing more truth.[173] A free scientific culture is more or less a libertarian anarchy: anyone can form a theory and test it, and the results can be accepted, further tested, rejected, or ignored by other individual scientists. Laypeople tend to hear mostly about theories on which there is a scientific consensus and so do not always perceive the diversity and competition in science.

There are similarities with the anarchic workings of individual liberty and the free market. Anyone can originate a practice or product. People have individually to choose to try such practices or buy such products. Social and individual practices are aimed at satisfaction. They increase immediate utility or at least are useful experimentation. A new product offered by the individual entrepreneur is analogous with the bold new theories of the individual scientist. Analogous with having scientific theories aimed at truth, consumer products are aimed to satisfy demand.[174]

By contrast, 'liberal democracies' illiberally ban and mandate various practices and products in a way that tends not to happen in science (unless the state intervenes). Unlibertarian regulation of social and personal practices decreases immediate utility or useful experimentation. Such policies as state subsidies to failing businesses and import restrictions that 'protect' domestic production are analogous with ad hoc defenses of a theory (here in the form of a product) instead of accepting the 'falsification' that is the absence of consumer demand.

If the scientific community were run democratically, then it would be as great a disaster for the discovery of truth as democracy is a disaster for the promotion of liberty and welfare. Michael Polanyi (1951) shows the deleterious effects on science of greater state regulation. Full blown democracy could only be more severe for science.

Popper sees that the people 'never rule themselves in any concrete, practical sense' ([1945] 1977, 1: 125). His understanding of 'democracy' is not rule by the people but rather a way of limiting bad rule, ultimately in order to preserve maximum equal 'freedom' – or so he asserts. But from a libertarian viewpoint, liberal democracy is a practical contradiction (at least, to the extent that 'liberal' means having respect for interpersonal liberty): the more liberty individuals have the less they can be ruled by 'the people' (or anyone else). A liberal democracy is a sort of substitute for all-out civil war. The winning side imposes its rules on the others by force and the threat of force. The taxation and regulation of people who are not imposing on anyone are themselves forms of aggressive imposition rather than peaceful persuasion. Popper insists that 'any kind of freedom is clearly impossible unless it is guaranteed by the state' ([1945] 1977, 1: 111). The possibility of competing private police and courts protecting persons and their property and of anarchic defense are beyond rational consideration for Popper.[175]

He writes that the question "'Who should rule?" ... begs for an authoritarian answer' ([1963] 1978, 25). Libertarians disagree. 'Each should rule himself: a sovereign individual' is a coherent non-authoritarian answer. Popper prefers to ask, 'How can we organise our political institutions so that bad or incompetent rulers ... cannot do too much damage?' ([1963] 1978, 25). But this clearly does presuppose the necessity for political authority over subjects. The very possibility of individual sovereignty, rather than the 'institutional control of the rulers', is also 'thereby eliminated without ever having been raised' ([1945] 1977, 1: 126). And with libertarianism, analogously with Popper's defense of good democratic institutions, the institution of individual sovereignty would ipso facto be maximally spread for safety.

I am interested only in what I call 'actually existing democracy' rather than some impossible ideal (just as people used to refer to 'actually existing socialism' – meaning regimes calling themselves 'socialist' – rather than some impossible ideal of socialism). I mention this because Popper often explicitly sees some unfortunate state of affairs but he fails to see that it is practically intrinsic to liberal democracy. In fact he goes so far as to assert that it is 'quite wrong to blame democracy for the political shortcomings of a democratic state. We should rather blame ourselves, that is to say, the citizens of a democratic state' ([1945] 1977, 1: 127). For Popper, democracy itself is apparently put beyond rational criticism. He does argue explicitly against the free market and in favor of what he calls 'protectionism', by the state, to defend freedom and welfare (for example, [1945] 1977, 1: 110–11). A comprehensive response to Popper would have to include a close analysis of such arguments. In this philosophical outline I shall have to refer the reader to the relevant social scientific literature for the evidence against such 'protectionism'.[176]

I shall now expand on and make slightly more precise the supposed similarities and dissimilarities in the following, somewhat schematic, list. I do not doubt that this list could be further extended, clarified, and elaborated. Points are grouped together with the same number for each (dis)similarity, for ease of comparison and criticism.

CR.: Critical rationalism (Popper's epistemology and methodology).

LL.: Liberty and laissez-faire (individual sovereignty and the free market).

LD.: Liberal democracy (actually existing liberal democracies rather than some impossible ideal).

CR.1. No one has the authority to establish whether a theory is true or to impose his theories on others.

LL.1. No one has the authority to establish whether a product or practice is desirable or to impose his products or practices on others.

LD.1. The state has the authority to establish and impose what it sees as desirable products and practices.

CR.2. We can be optimistic about attaining truth via free competition among theories.

LL.2. We can be optimistic about achieving welfare via free competition among products and practices.

LD.2. Political intervention is due to pessimism about achieving welfare via free competition among products and practices.

CR.3. Scientists perceive their individual problems.

LL.3. Persons and businesses perceive their individual problems.

LD.3. Governments claim to perceive collective problems for the country/nation/society/economy/public interest (all these almost invariably being euphemisms which disguise special interests).

CR.4. Scientists specialize in problems, not subjects with conventional boundaries.

LL.4. Persons and businesses specialize in their problems.

LD.4. Politicians are generalists without specialist skills – except in sophistry.

CR.5. Scientists seek interesting and substantial truths.

LL.5. Persons and businesses seek valuable and substantial practices and products.

LD.5. Politicians usually seek votes.

CR.6. Scientists should conjecture as boldly as they can imagine.

LL.6. Persons and businesses should conjecture as boldly as they can imagine.

LD.6. Politicians must usually consider cautious, small policy variations ('extremism' will lose more votes than it gains).

CR.7.   Paternalism or special interest cannot impose or restrict scientific conjecture and experimentation.

LL.7.   Paternalism or special interest cannot impose or restrict individual and business conjecture and experimentation.

LD.7.   Paternalism and special interest must impose or restrict individual and business conjecture and experimentation.

CR.8.   Error elimination is required: so seek falsification, not ad hoc defenses.

LL.8.   Error elimination is required: 'falsification' is obvious in less satisfaction or lower profits; coerced subsidies are not possible.

LD.8.   Error is unclear to politicians, except in terms of lost votes. So they deny error and subsidize mistakes.

CR.9.   After error elimination there is a new scientific problem situation.

LL.9.   After error elimination there is a new personal or business problem situation.

LD.9.   No clear new problem situation emerges, except that politicians have to buy more votes from somewhere, somehow.

CR.10.   This requires a new scientific theory.

LL.10.   This requires new practices and products.

LD.10.   Politicians usually seek a short-term botch without a clear theory, hence testing is difficult.[177]

CR.11.   The general social picture is of peaceful, polycentric competition among scientists about theories.

LL.11.   The general social picture is of peaceful, polycentric competition among individuals and businesses about practices and products.

LD.11.   The general social picture is of politically imposed privilege, predation, persecution, and Procrustean rules.

CR.12.   This is against holistic (society-wide) experiments because it is impossible to understand and test with so many variables or with unique situations.

LL.12.   This ensures individualism in understanding and testing personal or business problems.

LD.12. Politics is typically holistic about understanding and testing problems of 'society' and 'the economy'.[178]

CR.13. This is against the historicist theory that social sciences make long-term prophesies.

LL.13. This views unique individuals and the market catallaxy as unpredictable in the long term.

LD.13. Politicians often rely on historicist theories to defend both 'inexorable' change and 'unshakeable' tradition.

CR.14. This is against the historicist theory that universal (hence timeless) social scientific technology is impossible.

LL.14. This view embraces universal social scientific technology, especially from microeconomics.[179]

LD.14. Politicians often belittle social scientific advice, especially from (anti-political) microeconomics.[180]

Why does Popper not see that libertarianism is the better social application of his epistemology and methodology? I suggest three possible contributory factors: 1. Popper came to his political position from a socialist one and retained some sympathy for socialism. 2. He made no serious study of economics; he simply swallowed many popular anti-market prejudices.[181] 3. Popper thinks 'absolute freedom is impossible' ([1963] 1978, 345). Instead, following Kant, the 'liberal principle demands that the limitations to the freedom of each ... should be minimised and equalised as much as possible ...' ([1963] 1978, 351).

As (3) is the philosophical factor, let us focus on that. It is probably Popper's anti-essentialism that has caused him to avoid any explicit formulation of a theory of liberty that can be applied. But if we say, as I do, that a free person is someone who is not being imposed on by others (withholding a benefit, defending oneself, and enforcing a contract, restitution, or retribution cannot really be *imposing*), then it is possible to have a group of people who are completely free with respect to each other. And by such a conception of freedom it follows that state interference with non-invasive activities will be an assault on freedom.

When Popper was writing *The Open Society and its Enemies* he was contrasting the workings of liberal democracies such as Britain and the United States with totalitarian regimes of the kind with which they were at war. He considered the book to be his war effort. By such a contrast, liberal democracies are certainly more conducive to individual freedom and welfare, and I do not intend to contradict the general thesis for which Popper was arguing. But even if I were to agree with Winston Churchill that (liberal) democracy is the worst form of government apart from any other, I should wish to add that private-property anarchy is not as bad as liberal democracy.[182]

Hegel's 'principle of subjective freedom', that free speech allows people 'an irrelevant opportunity to give vent to their feelings' (as Popper interprets Hegel), seems quite realistic from a libertarian position. Popper's view that this is 'cynicism', that the ordinary man is substantially free because he can speak his mind about politics, is quite inadequate ([1945] 1977, 2: 310 n43, 2). The illusion that a liberal democracy constitutes a so-called free country is partially sustained by this trick, which Popper perpetuates instead of taking liberty seriously.

At the end of the addenda to *The Open Society and Its Enemies*, Popper states that fallibilism 'can show us that the role of thought is to carry out revolutions by means of critical debates rather than by means of violence and warfare ... This is why our Western civilisation is an essentially pluralistic one ...' ([1945] 1977, 2: 396). But what is politics finally backed up by if not aggressive violence? And what could be more pluralistic than respecting individual sovereignty instead? And this liberal democracy does not do.[183]

Like his one-time endorsement of classical liberalism, Gray's endorsement of Popper's epistemology was not to last. These two apostasies combine to form an even greater depth of confusion at the end of Gray's *Liberalisms*. This relationship is what we shall finally focus on in this chapter.

e. After Illiberalism and Justificationism

Gray reviews his objections to liberalism and looks to the future in the book's 'Postscript: after liberalism'. The postscript is particularly marked by an approach whereby Gray has abandoned Popper's critical rationalism, for he demands new and impossible proofs of the value of liberalism. I focus on his new approach here, but also tackle a few additional points in passing.

Liberalism, which in its application to personal conduct aims for toleration and even pluralism, is in its political demands an expression of intolerance, since it denies the evident truth that many very different forms of government may, each in its own way, contribute to an authentic mode of human well-being ... No liberal can accept (without thereby ceasing to be a liberal) that liberal practice expresses and embodies only one among many ranges of often conflicting and sometimes incommensurable varieties of human flourishing (239).

The only thing which consistent liberalism demands is liberty; the only thing it is intolerant of is assaults on liberty. Liberalism does not call for mere 'toleration'. Mere toleration cannot be practised: one needs to specify what is to be tolerated. What liberalism demands is toleration of individual liberty: the individual's doing what he likes (however much that seems disgusting or damaging) provided he is not interfering with (imposing costs on) others. Liberals have to be intolerant of politics because the state is, empirically, the greatest enemy of liberty. So there is no strange inconsistency in liberal toleration here. It is certainly true that different forms of government are compatible with some types of well-being for some people. The state does not destroy *all* wealth and welfare (especially for those who know how to use the state to their own advantage). If Gray is seriously asserting that many political systems are often at least as welfare-enhancing as liberal practices he needs to give an example rather than relying on the apparent implication that liberals are merely dogmatic.

Gray states that he has 'examined and found wanting all the major justificatory strategies in the project of constructing a liberal ideology' (240). He does not accept Popper's epistemological theory of critical rationalism. If he did, he would see that the liberal idea that it is desirable to respect individual liberty does not need to, and logically cannot, be justified. It can be a bold conjecture that remains plausible until it is refuted by criticism. Gray has only to show us one example of liberty failing (which it is logically possible to do), rather than complaining that we cannot prove universal success (which it is not logically possible to do). He is right to think that he has deflated various attempts to justify liberalism; he is mistaken to think that this means that liberalism has to be abandoned. It is true that liberalism cannot operate if no theory of liberty is coherent, but the theory in this book remains unrefuted by any of Gray's criticisms.

Gray complains of Mill's experiments in living that we do not have a 'criterion of success' and so 'how are we to know when the relevant evidence is before us? How are we to know when the experiment has been completed?' (243) *Liberally*, the individual is to decide. He is bound to use tentative conjecture to guide him. So any 'criterion of success' will be personal and conjectural. It would be illiberal to impose someone else's criterion. Critical rationalism shows us that it is impossible to guarantee any criterion. Gray's line of argument is continued by asking why we should allow 'freedom of action in respect of a form of life which experimentation has shown to be disastrous' (244). But who knows that some form of life is disastrous? Who can best judge but each individual for himself? Gray surely wants to decide for himself, as do I. If he has a reason to deny others the same liberty then he needs to state it for criticism. It is logically possible that if individuals are allowed to live as they please they will fail to learn from their own mistakes and others' mistakes concerning what increases welfare (though even that would not in itself show that paternalism would be an improvement in practice). Is this a real possibility? We are not told so. Apparently it is enough for Gray that there is no guarantee of success. He has no real evidence of failure to offer.

This justificationist mistake is repeated in the assertion of 'the fundamental insight that there is no pre-ordained harmony and no inevitable connection between human well-being and the promotion of truth' (248). The conjecture that there is a connection between these two (and that liberty is best for both) is but one bold conjecture that can be defended (and thereby provide a defense of liberty). It cannot be given unshakeable *support* and it cannot be offered as *support* (especially the main support) for liberty. So Gray is completely correct in his view that the 'epistemological route to the *justification* [emphasis added] of liberalism is a failure' (248). He fails to see that the epistemological route can nevertheless be held out as but one among many *defenses* of liberalism.

Gray links his criticism of the growth of knowledge with his earlier point about competing forms of life when he writes that knowledge is 'only one human good and may come into competition with others that are sometimes weightier' (248–9). He gives the example of 'the interest we have in reproducing our cultural traditions' (248). The epistemological strategy does not necessarily come into conflict with other goods than knowledge. It might just be that one can have more of many valuable things in a free society. It might be that there is no significant clash between knowledge and other human goods. Gray specifically suggests a clash between knowledge and cultural traditions. Unfortunately, he does not indicate the form such a clash might take. The growth of knowledge might well undermine such things as traditional religion, opinions, and authority *when these are based on error*. I see no reason to think it can be in people's interests to preserve such errors. Again, if Gray had real examples here instead of logical possibilities it might be that he could make a powerful point. In the absence of these we can only move on.

Eventually Gray gives us something *slightly* more substantial to criticize:

> The virtues of a courtier, of a warrior, or of a pious peasant, presuppose a social order which cannot coexist with a liberal society ... It may well be ... that a liberal order undermines important virtues, including virtues upon which that order itself depends. The hedonism characteristic of market societies may threaten the martial virtues that are indispensable to it, and individualism may weaken the familial virtues on which an individualist order rests. The connection between liberal freedom and the virtues is a contingent and sometimes a delusive one ... . (260–1)

Let us grant, for the sake of argument, that the occupations listed have their particular 'virtues' (and so in a way does that of a torturer, perhaps). The question is: Are they worth the loss of liberty that makes them possible? Either Gray thinks that a society with such things is genuinely preferable or at least as good (in which case he needs to tell people why they are mistaken if they think that liberty is better for these societies) or, more plausibly, he is merely complaining that a liberal society is not better in every imaginable way. But obviously this point can be conceded without impugning the general superiority of liberalism. (My intention here is not morally to defend liberty, but to point out the insubstantial nature of Gray's criticism.)

It is conceivable that the liberal order undermines the virtues on which it rests, but Gray's brief examples are not very challenging. Even if we assume that hedonism is dominant in market societies, it could be replied that good wages might motivate some poorer hedonists to go into the army, especially if war is unlikely at the time, while other richer hedonists pay to protect their continuing hedonism (mercenary armies are a historical fact). Like most people, Gray is also supposing that the state is preferable to anarchy here. In fact, the state is a war-machine: statesmen often gain status and political advantage from starting or entering wars and conflicts that other people's lives and taxes will pay for, so they are positively encouraged to do this. The state is also an Achilles's heel that invites aggression: capture it and you capture its territory and subjects.[184] Political terrorism would also make little sense without a state to implement any terrorist demands (non-political terrorism is a relatively small problem). Would it be worse to be an anarchy without such a troublemaker-cum-target? Instead of the immense destruction of people and property on both sides, would it not be better to offer a bounty to deal with any bellicose foreign statesmen personally? Putting this huge topic aside, it ought to be obvious that 'martial virtues', in themselves, are the chief enemy of liberal orders rather than anything that liberal orders can be based on.

How might individualism weaken family virtues? Allowing individuals their liberty has no such implication, and that is the only kind of individualism being defended here. That individuals have no *inherent* obligations to do things for the benefit of others does not entail that they will be selfish[185] or that they cannot bind themselves contractually, such as in marriage. On the contrary, it is the dependency state[186] that has undermined the family by playing the husband's role in 'one-parent families'.[187] The church and the state by their natures compete with the power of the family. In fact, the original aspirations of these institutions is typically to destroy family life if only they can. (Those who doubt these bold theses should read Mount 1982.) The market, by comparison, will considerably reinforce the family if it is only allowed to do so.[188]

What is wrong with a 'contingent' connection between liberty and the virtues? Gray again wants a logical guarantee that liberalism is the best system. This is too demanding. He has not, in any case, given a sound example of the 'delusive' nature of the connection. There is at least one necessary link between liberty and virtue: coerced virtue is not virtue at all.

As ever, much more could be said on all of these issues. I am undoubtedly too sweeping in my responses to Gray to convince those who are sympathetic to any of his points. But Gray is even more sweeping in his assertion of them. Detailed responses to Gray are difficult without detailed accounts of what seem, as usual, mere logical possibilities. I could seek out detailed forms of these arguments to reply to, but that considerable task would then prevent me from presenting an overall defense of the compatibility thesis, which is the object here and which seems more pressing. Also, there are many others, a few of whom I have mentioned, who have dealt with the details of the social scientific matters better than I could hope to do.

Gray continues:

The spurious universality of liberal principles is a consequence of the self-deception of liberal philosophy, which is bound to deny the particularistic character of all genuine moral and political reasoning. (262)

Insofar as liberalism is held morally it is held universally. Gray is asking the impossible if he wants moral sentiments to respect political border controls. People will naturally tend to have different moral and political views from the liberal to the extent that they live in illiberal societies. The liberal merely thinks these other societies would be better if they liberalized fully. Exactly which are the illiberal practices in such societies which Gray wants to recommend? He is evidently reluctant to offer any examples for criticism, but it is difficult to answer him more thoroughly until he becomes more specific.

Gray denies that there is 'anywhere in liberal theory a compelling demonstration of the priority of liberty over other political values' (261). Yet again, he wants a justification and a guarantee. But he also holds out the 'insight' that 'philosophy as a search for foundations' ought to be abandoned (263). So why is the lack of a 'compelling demonstration' a failing for liberalism? It looks as though Gray must embrace critical rationalism in political philosophy. Instead he thinks philosophy ought to be abandoned in favor of 'theorizing':

> In the wake of philosophy, the object of theorizing is the attainment of self-understanding as practitioners of the historically contingent and specific forms of life we inherit or adopt. (263)

It is as though Gray is confused by philosophy and so declares it to be a Philistine activity when used in the realm of politics. 'Theorizing' seems to be inherently conservative and to require the grasp of a particular culture rather than deeper philosophical issues. If Gray thinks that he can maintain a comfortable conservative and cultural approach to politics that rules out of court troublesome philosophy, then he is mistaken. He can only turn a blind eye to the subject that is bound to change the world in ways which those who decline to study it will fail to influence.

As we have seen, it is the epistemologically hopeless search for foundations or justifications that has led Gray to skepticism, cultural relativism, and conservatism. What he now wishes to preserve is not, as he suggests, 'the historical inheritance of liberal practice from the excesses of an inordinate liberal ideology' (264) but, rather, degenerate and incoherent 'modern liberalism' from consistent classical liberalism.

The title of Gray's final section is 'After liberalism: Pyrrhonism in politics'. The position taken in this book is 'After illiberalism: gnosticism in anarchy' – but with a conjectural gnosticism that seeks criticism, unlike Gray's new dogmatic Pyrrhonism. Before we can turn to a more explicit and philosophical defense of anarchy, we next have to consider welfare and its relationship to the foregoing account of liberty.

4. Welfare

4.0. Chapter Thesis

The conception of welfare used by preference utilitarians and many modern welfare economists is that of want-satisfaction. This is here understood as people having what they spontaneously want (that is, the want is not imposed in any way that is incompatible with libertarian liberty). This will be defended only as a plausible and practical conception of welfare, not as an ultimate good or a moral end. Maximizing such welfare, as with maximizing interpersonal liberty, requires contingently deontological libertarianism.[189] Also as in the previous chapter, of course, the free market is held to provide such liberty anarchically. Here though, as the very idea of such welfare is not quite so philosophically problematic, there is more discussion of the (non-moral) reconciliation of liberty, welfare, and anarchy. So this chapter defends the compatibility thesis more broadly.

First the relationship among welfare, liberty, and the market is outlined. Then, broad and approximate, interpersonal utility comparisons are defended. The conception of want-satisfaction welfare is clarified and criticisms considered. Some practical and economic implications of promoting such welfare are discussed. Finally, the key issue of welfare's relationship with private property is discussed in more detail.

Throughout this chapter the terms 'welfare', 'utility', 'utility-maximization', 'utilitarianism', and 'preference utilitarianism' refer to unimposed-want satisfaction – and should in principle be capable of translation into such 'want-satisfaction' terms or expressions – unless the context clearly distinguishes them.

4.1. Welfare, Liberty, and the Market Overviewed

This chapter defends, among other things, the idea of using want-satisfaction as a theory of welfare. This is interpreted here as meaning that people are systematically better off to the extent that they have what they spontaneously want; that is, without imposed engineering of these wants: desires based on fraud (say, by dishonest advertising[190]) or force (say, by threats of physical violence) are ruled out. By spontaneous, or unimposed, I certainly do not mean pre-social or extra-social. Wants stimulated or evoked by voluntary social interaction are quite spontaneous, or unimposed, in my sense. There is an obvious connection between want-satisfaction as a theory of welfare, as defended here, and as a theory of motivation, as defended in the rationality chapter. Many arguments in that chapter will be relevant to this one, and vice versa to some extent.

This theory is utilitarian in a broad sense, but the discussion concerns want-satisfaction as a plausible and practical view of welfare and the correct ways of implementing it rather than being a moral defense: for one can argue about what welfare is and how it is maximized without drawing moral conclusions; and one could accept want-satisfaction as a conception of human welfare but reject the idea that it is always, or even ever, desirable or right to promote it (if one has incompatible, or even explicitly antipathetic, values or morals). In much of what follows it might look as though preference utilitarianism (promoting want-satisfaction) is being morally defended. This is simply because many of the arguments used to defend preference utilitarianism as a plausible, practical view of welfare (and compatible with liberty and the market) just happen to be arguments that a moral defender could also use. Also, the critics usually have an advocatory moral aspect to their points which here has to be, but might not seem to be, ignored.

A major consideration, especially from a practical political viewpoint, is that most people consider overall want-satisfaction to be a plausible theory of welfare in their own cases. Derek Parfit is not unusual among philosophers in rejecting this as an account of welfare because he does not see how, even if fulfilled, desires for ends (such as the good health of a stranger I once met) not connected with my active projects 'makes *my* life go better' (1984, 494, emphasis added). But this seems to be due to the quoted form of words chosen to characterize such welfare. If, like most people, I want my overall welfare to be measured by my overall want-satisfaction, then it seems irrelevant for someone else to object that the link with what 'makes my life go better' *personally* is unclear to him. This is not a convincing reason to object to my preferring a conception of my overall welfare that includes such remote and even abstract aspects.[191]

The economic calculation argument (2.6) showed that with a large industrial society there is no general alternative to having a market system, even if a lot of state intervention occurs. But here I am defending a completely free market. By the 'free market' I mean the anarchic (or state-free) market. I do not mean a 'perfectly competitive' market.[192] The idea is that in the free market people have more of what they want than in any known alternative. This is because the free market produces better and cheaper products – including those conferring status[193] – while increasing the leisure time to enjoy them.

Liberty, as defended in the previous chapter, is held to be maximized with welfare in almost all realistic, especially market, circumstances. Many objections to this compatibility thesis are philosophical or merely presuppositional, and hence require philosophical analysis to expose them and refute them. We should note immediately that part of the overlap of welfare and liberty, as they have been defined, exists for conceptual, rather than practical, reasons. For if welfare only increases by having more of what is *spontaneously* wanted, then you cannot increase welfare by *imposing* desires: welfare necessarily requires liberty of desire. And if liberty only increases to the extent that people have *fewer* costs imposed on them (where 'costs' are also defined in terms of, thwarted, spontaneous desires, 3.1), then more liberty must – in itself – *increase* welfare: liberty is necessarily desired.[194]

Detailed discussion of welfare economics, as normally found in the relevant literature, will be avoided; for that usually involves one of two things that are inconsistent with the approach taken here: 1) simply presupposing that imposed redistribution can increase welfare and then trying to give mathematical analyses of the 'best' theoretical rules for such redistribution, or 2) dismissing interpersonal comparisons in favor of a Paretian approach. One of the biggest problems in this area is this very possibility of comparing different people's utilities. As the rest of this chapter assumes that this is broadly possible, partly for the sake of argument, this needs to be discussed next.

4.2. Interpersonal Utility Comparisons

Here there is a brief account and defense of interpersonal utility comparisons (IUCs). This is necessary to be able to argue that such welfare considerations do not entail illiberal interventionist policies (it also helps to defend the, much more limited, comparisons of imposed costs in the previous chapter). The account is not as long as its apparent importance might indicate that it should be, for two main reasons. 1) As was argued at 2.6, it is not possible to compare strengths of utility directly and in detail and so to construct anything like a comprehensive social welfare function, but general arguments can show that certain social rules are more likely to promote overall want-satisfaction. 2) As these rules are those respecting liberty and the free market, what follows in this chapter can be read as a hypothetical argument: granted that IUCs make a sort of sense – I admit it is only a sort of sense – and given preference utilitarianism as a welfare criterion, then liberty and the free market follow.

It ought first to be noted that standard economic theory does allow *intra*personal comparisons of utility. A person who is prepared to suffer the bother of moving his desk to change the view from his window is making an intrapersonal comparison of utility: he feels he will be more want-satisfied with the new view than he is with the present one, even allowing for the disutility of moving. What is more, standard economic theory also seems to allow that for welfare discussions IUCs may be possible in a loose, informal way but not with the scientific definiteness that it grants Pareto comparisons: where overall utility is deemed to have increased only if at least one person is better off and no one else is worse off.

It is accepted by most people that IUCs are possible to some degree. A clear case of a utility comparison between persons is where A values x (has some utility from it), and B is indifferent about x (has zero utility from it). It follows that A values x ('some') more than B does ('zero'). It then seems a small step to comparing a case where A strongly values x and B has only a small preference for x. And so forth. Whether utility is literally the same 'stuff' is unimportant in practice except in delicate cases. We rarely doubt that one person gets more disutility from a broken leg (in this case because of the pain, but I am not equating pain with disutility) than someone else does from a small scratch on the knee – in the normal case. But we can also make good sense of the idea that a macho football player might have utility due to pride at having broken his leg once in a game (though thereafter diminishing marginal utility might set in so rapidly that a second broken leg gives disutility), and a beautiful model might have great disutility because she now has a tiny scar on her previously perfect legs.

To save a friend from breaking his leg we would usually consider it a small price to sustain a scratch ourselves. Though standard economics with its Pareto criterion cannot make sense of empirical IUCs, it can still make sense of my choosing to sustain a scratch to prevent a friend's breaking his leg: I simply prefer that to the alternative *among my own wants.* But *I* would be making such an IUC; so such comparisons seem to make some intuitive sense.[195] And, as explained at 2.1, economics needs this sense to some extent if it is to determine which property systems better promote utility and liberty (understood as minimizing imposed costs). Nor can we seriously doubt that the average richer person gets less utility from an extra unit of income than does the average poorer one – so income and wealth redistribution might look welfare-enhancing *at first glance.*

To take a more libertarian example, by the Pareto criterion we cannot say that it is a welfare improvement to move from a society with rent control and a terrible accommodation shortage to one without rent control and a flourishing rented sector if even one tenant feels himself to be worse off. The Pareto criterion disallows the welfare evaluation of changes from any status quo in an existing society, including one with slavery, if even one person objects to the change – and there is usually a powerful lobby of special interests to object. So 'pro-market' economists who accept the Pareto criterion in place of any IUCs cannot, in practice, consistently advise changes from any non-market system of property rules unless every single person feels better off.

Making utility comparisons more precise does become progressively harder, but that problem is a separate issue. The point is that we cannot help making some IUCs. We do it all the time. If we did not then we would *never* forgo any benefit to ourselves on the grounds that others would appreciate it more. We would never help people for their own sakes for we would only be sure that we were losing but not know whether others were gaining more, gaining at all, or even losing as well. Provided that we can make some obvious comparisons, then we can often see whether welfare generally goes up or down with some practices rather than others even when there are some losers, as is normally the case. Merely making such comparisons cannot be inherently ethical (contra Rothbard 1956, 245), though advocating changes based on such comparisons might be.

This being said, the problems of IUCs can often be avoided in any direct way by focusing on the prices people are prepared to pay to achieve their goals. Other people's tastes can be so strange to us that we can wonder whether they really desire some of the things they get up to. One good indication that they do is seeing that these people seem to enjoy some of the same things that we do, but that they are also prepared to spend money on things which seem strange to us. Often it is the fact of someone's parting with his own money that convinces us of the reality and intensity of his desire. If this mechanism is disrupted then we often make poor guessers of his desires, for 'one man's meat is another man's poison'.

In order to explore the issues involved in all this, it is desirable to tackle a variety of significant and typical criticisms and alternative accounts. *Utilitarianism and Beyond* (Sen and Williams 1982) is a particularly useful collection for this chapter, and several essays from that source will be looked at. Preference utilitarianism or maximizing want-satisfaction is here a distinct welfare theory, but also a moral theory for R. M. Hare (whose essay is looked at next). It might seem that criticisms are sometimes mistakenly taken to apply to preference utilitarianism when they are really aimed at hedonistic utilitarianism (maximizing good feelings). However, Sen and Williams explicitly state that

It is such a reference to desires which – particularly when they are assimilated to interests – underlies the intuitive justification of utilitarianism ... . There is nothing peculiar about Hare's characterisation of utility as such, and in this respect he has provided new arguments for defending an old tradition rather than reformulating the content of utilitarianism. (Sen and Williams 1982, 11)

It is clear that they take themselves and others to be criticizing a general position that certainly includes preference utilitarianism. In any case, critics will be dealt with only insofar as they seem to be at odds with preference utilitarianism and with its compatibility with liberty and the free market.

Many of the points made about utilitarianism by those to be discussed are merely 'in principle': some such expression often being used to indicate what is logically possible or what seems likely given popular assumptions. As a result, many of my replies to these points will often comprise either 1) showing that such logical-possibility arguments can be stood on their heads with considerably more plausibility, or 2) giving some general theories or evidence to criticize the popular assumptions. These replies are not, of course, intended to be conclusive. Of necessity, this is mainly philosophical clarification that attempts to make the compatibility thesis clearer and more plausible at the abstract level, so that the relevant social scientific evidence can better be understood. It would be foolish to think that philosophy alone can settle such matters – but it would be equally foolish to think that the facts speak for themselves.

I shall now attempt to clarify the conception of unimposed-want satisfaction, as that is still more complicated than it might appear.

4.3. Clarifying Want-Satisfaction

R. M. Hare is one of the clearest exponents of preference utilitarianism, and this section will concentrate on one example: Hare 1982. Hare defends this as a moral theory, but his arguments are often just as relevant to defending it as a welfare theory. I diverge radically from his interpretations of how this theory applies to politics, as we shall see later (4.5.a). The main matter here is to clarify unimposed-want satisfaction by drawing on, or contrasting it with, Hare's general account. This clarification is necessary because preference utilitarianism is often misunderstood in two important ways, even by moral philosophers. First, people conflate hedonistic utilitarianism and preference utilitarianism (so much so, that when the distinction is made clear, they can deny that preference utilitarianism is utilitarianism at all). Second, people assume, and even insist, that utilitarianism is necessarily collectivistic in its policy implications, when it must logically be an empirical matter whether collectivism will increase utility overall – and I shall argue that it does not do so.

Hare writes that it is prudent 'to seek the satisfaction of desires which are important to me, even if I am not going to know whether they have been satisfied or not' (37). He gives the examples of wanting above all that one's children do not starve after one's death, and that a 'dying man's interests *are* harmed if promises are made to him and then broken, and ... mine are harmed if people are cheating me without my knowing it' (37).

One way in which it is prudent to aim at the satisfaction of such desires is that we shall be frustrated here and now if we cannot satisfy them. If you value, above all, leaving your children provided for after your own death, then you shall feel psychologically unsatisfied if you cannot *now* make the arrangements. But this is not the most important point here. More important is seeing that a person's *actual* interests (the interests he actually feels) are harmed to the extent that all that he wants – however remote or abstract – fails to come about, whether he knows it or not. Contra Kymlicka (1990, 26) the 'experience requirement', that it is what we feel that *solely* matters, thus drops out of preference utilitarianism at this stage and before any reference to 'informed preferences' (the preferences that we 'ought', in some sense, to have).

However, not all our wants are compatible. To make sense of them an observer might, *in principle*, be able to use superior knowledge to tidy up inconsistent desires and put them in order of intensity. In fact, Hare writes of respecting only 'perfectly prudent' (28) desires, so there is some doubt as to how far he wants to respect real desires and how far he wants to respect something more ideal (but the defense of *real* want-satisfaction is left to the discussion of Harsanyi, 4.5.b, who clearly wishes to go much further). Even so, our interests must be clearly related to *our* actual wants at some point – otherwise they will, instead, probably be related to someone else's wants concerning us.

It might still be thought, contra Hare, that at least when someone is dead that person cannot have his interests harmed; how can there be an interest without an existing valuer?[196] The answer is that not being present temporally is relevantly analogous with not being present spatially. We can care about some things that will happen outside our own time span as much as about some things that will occur outside our spatial region. If we can allow damage to the interests of a valuer who is never present at some *place* to observe it, then it seems we can allow damage to the interests of a valuer who is not present at some *time* to observe it.[197] From a preference utilitarian viewpoint, all goals are ranked in terms of welfare according to the strength of desire for them – not because of the psychological state their realization brings about (except insofar as that is included in a goal). We thereby get more of what we really want, however 'happy' some alternative might make us. Surely that is what we prefer as a measure of our own welfare. It seems that we necessarily prefer it, for even to prefer 'blissful ignorance' is simply to make that what one really wants.

Preference utilitarianism is, then, apparently very unlike hedonistic utilitarianism. With hedonistic utilitarianism, we must, if it were possible, brainwash people so that they have the wants that they will find the most enjoyable.[198] Preference utilitarianism requires that individual wants be satisfied; and it is often or usually the satisfaction of some external end that is wanted, not some psychological state. It might seem that we could still, in principle, brainwash people so that they have stronger preferences that can be more easily satisfied: that would consequentially result in more preference satisfaction than merely satisfying existing preferences. So it might appear that preference utilitarianism is as potentially illiberal, in this way, as the more hedonistic variety. However, as no one currently wants his wants engineered without his permission, and would not allow that as increasing his welfare, such brainwashing cannot get started. Satisfying the subsequent wants would not, by preference utilitarian welfare, be allowed to count as better than not engineering them in the first place.

We might also defend this position, as a practical and plausible view of welfare, by observing that our unimposed desires are not as arbitrary as they might seem to others. We are complicated individuals knowing ourselves best, and we cannot in fact have our motivations manipulated at will by others, or even by ourselves. Such manipulation of people's desires, even supposing it were possible, would obviously have great dangers. If it really were possible then it would probably be safest, from a preference-utilitarian viewpoint, for people to choose how they wished their own motives altered. They might well take advantage of this facility to some extent; for people do now sometimes object to their own desires, such as the desire to smoke, and try to cultivate different ones. But as this would still be promoting the satisfaction of an individual's spontaneous will, there is no illiberal imposition that anyone could object to as lowering his welfare.

Is this still utilitarianism? It is about giving people the things they aim at in proportion to the strength of their unimposed desires for them. That strength of desire is utility-as-a-motive (the psychological 'satisfaction' one feels when aiming at things), as discussed in the rationality chapter; it is not utility-as-a-goal (pristine utilitarianism's psychological satisfaction as an end-state). Though we cannot, qua preference utilitarians, interfere with people's actual desires or wants, we can still attempt to maximize goals by reference to interpersonal comparisons of utility-as-a-motive: if I find the thought of X (some particular state of reality) more satisfying (I want it more) than you find not-X satisfying, then it seems that, ceteris paribus, overall welfare is increased if X is the case. This is why it still makes sense, to Sen and Williams for instance, to call it 'utilitarianism' even though a psychological end-state is not aimed at. However, if some people think that pristine utilitarianism has been left too far behind, then we can simply drop that name and call it only 'maximizing unimposed-want satisfaction', or 'want-satisfaction' for short. (The divergence from pristine utilitarianism is a major theme throughout this chapter.)

Hare is right to see that rule-utilitarianism is compatible with act-utilitarianism (33), and so we do not have to choose between them. *Rule*-utilitarianism is the idea that the best way to maximize utility is to follow the rules that are best in the long term, for without such rules there would be chaos. *Act*-utilitarianism is the idea that it is best to do whatever act will maximize utility. The distinction seems to collapse in light of the observations that 1) if any rules are best for utility in the long-run, and we know them, then the best act to do now must be to obey them, and 2) if there is any reliable way of telling that a rule can be waived, and we know it, then that information can be put into a new rule. The practical interpretation in this book, though, is quite unlike Hare's: the best utilitarian act is to follow the utilitarian rule of not interfering with individual liberty. And, analogously, the best liberty-maximizing act is to follow the libertarian rule of not interfering with individual liberty even to attempt to increase liberty thereby (given that such 'libertarian consequentialism' is not a contradiction in terms). Neither of these propositions can be defended in comprehensive practical detail. They are, rather, explained and defended as more coherent and plausible positions than those of any of the critics dealt with, including Hare.

Hare makes an important point concerning the fantastic nature of 'fanatics of ... heroic stature' who might, from a preference-utilitarian viewpoint, justify extreme oppression of gentler persons. He gives the example of fanatical Nazis who desire 'not to have Jews around' (30), by which euphemism I assume Hare means killing all Jews (or at least exiling them). He is surely right that the Nazis could not, in reality, be fanatical enough to make that the preference-utilitarian policy, given the greater desire of Jews to live (or not be exiled). Though if there were a million Nazis and only one Jew we would need to appeal to the indirect consequences of allowing any sufficiently large majority to persecute a sufficiently small minority.[199] There are no objective 'utils', but it is sufficient for the practical purposes of this book that nearly all people would agree and that the conjecture remains unrefuted. Hare correctly sees that the critical force of this fantasy example 'depends on appealing to the ordinary man's judgement about a case with which ... his intuitions were not designed to deal' (30). This goes a long way towards explaining what is mistaken about many of the fantasy criticisms of preference utilitarianism. It cannot be a sound criticism of preference utilitarianism as a practical and plausible criterion of welfare that we do not have preference-utilitarian intuitions about certain bizarre thought-experiments. This is a version of the 'utility monsters' criticism of utilitarianism: that those with ordinary desires can be used by those with very powerful desires

– utility monsters. Less extreme examples do pose practical problems of when to give in to 'strong desirers' and, to conclude this section, these need to be dealt with.

Preference utilitarianism requires that stronger preferences trump weaker ones. If this were enforced then this might still seem to entail, in practice, some oppression (going well beyond the imposed-cost-minimizing variety discussed at 3.2.c.iii) by those who are *relatively* utility monsters: highly passionate people would often get what they want at the involuntary expense of normal people. Most of us would not accept preference utilitarianism as a criterion of welfare if this were so. To see the mistake here, consider the long-term consequences of allowing this. Utility monsters would increasingly spontaneously arise for perceived-incentive and, eventually, genetic reasons. A society with such beings in it would not have more preference satisfaction when all become like this (as they would be bound to: each must have such a personality or lose to those who do). There would be extreme frustration as one brute tries to 'out-want' another brute in order to get his way. The break-down of commerce and social dealings that would ensue, as people try to get things without trading for them or seeking the consent of others, would cause more frustration still. Given that outcome, it seems that any pandering to utility monsters must immediately partially undermine the productive system of incentives that exists with individual liberty and private property. So preference utilitarianism does not in practice require that the more passionate need get their own way. If any example of this would lead to such devastating escalation if generally allowed then it must not be given its full weight. The legal concept of the 'reasonable man', with reasonable levels of desire, seems applicable to stop this unutilitarian escalation.

What, for the sake of argument, if more powerful passions were to lead only to *satisfied* utility monsters (they could always have what they so passionately want)? The previous point was concerned with the practical problem (for preference utilitarianism) of whether, and how far, to give in to unusually strong preferences now. This new problem is another mere fantasy criticism. What the economic system and such beings would be like, and whether this outcome would be a plausible welfare improvement, is hard to judge. Even if one rejects want-satisfaction welfare in such a fantasy case, that is not a sound reason to abandon it as practical and plausible in reality.

Having gone some way, I hope, towards clarifying the relevant conception of welfare, we shall now consider some criticisms of it. As usual, I do not attempt a thorough account of the writers' positions, but adopt a more dialog-like style dealing with points most relevant to the compatibility thesis.

4.4. More Criticisms of Want-Satisfaction

There is no end to possible criticisms of want-satisfaction as a view of welfare, and my space is limited. But many criticisms were implicitly covered in the chapter on rationality. Here I choose only two more that are typical and that come at the issue from different angles. This should at least give a better feel for the nature of the conception. Amartya Sen and Bernard Williams focus mainly on what they call the 'severe informational constraints' of utilitarianism: that utilitarianism neglects so much that is important to the welfare considerations of real persons. John Rawls can be interpreted as being more interested in the idea that utilitarianism neglects the welfare of the worst-off in a way that it would not, in a sense, be rational to accept; though he also puts essentially the same point in moral language. These are forceful expressions of important and general kinds of criticism of utilitarianism by leading critics.

a. Informational Constraints and Utility

Amartya Sen and Bernard Williams object that utilitarianism, by considering only the quantity of utility when ranking outcomes, imposes 'severe informational constraints' (4). Now, it is true that any such final ranking will not mention anything apart from the amounts of likely utility. However, in the process of determining these outcomes all sorts of empirical issues must be considered in all their human detail. What information is neglected in this process? By definition, only the information that nobody gets any welfare gain or loss from: the information that nobody cares about. If anybody cares about it, or would if they knew about it, then it must be included in the preference-utilitarian calculation. If nobody cares about it then why does it matter from a welfare point of view? As it stands this criticism sounds like objecting to examination results on the basis that they do not tell us the details but, at most, how many points each candidate received. With utility or examinations, if we wish to criticize the outcome we shall need to examine the details. But ranking cannot be objectionable just because it does not mention these details.

Merely looking at overall welfare is supposed to take 'a remarkably narrow view of being a *person*'. Why? Because 'utilitarianism sees persons as locations of their respective utilities' (4). It does no such thing. To look at people's welfare is not to say that they are identical with where their welfare is located, nor to say what it means to be a person. They are quite unnecessarily reading metaphysical implications into a fairly simple welfare criterion.

Sen and Williams assert that persons 'do not count as individuals in this any more than individual petrol tanks do in the analysis of the national consumption of petroleum' (4). The petrol-tank analogy is quite inappropriate. Petrol tanks are mere instruments of storage for the use of people. People do not store welfare for others but have it themselves. And preference utilitarianism gives each individual equal weight as a person capable of welfare. If an individual were not capable of being better or worse off in terms of welfare then it is not clear why he ought to count in a welfare calculation: it would not matter to him what happened to him. To assign equal weight to the welfare of each person, other things being equal, (as preference utilitarianism does) seems to be one way to respect all persons equally. Not to do this seems to be to neglect some persons to the benefit of others.

Utilitarianism is depicted as a combination of 'welfarism, sum-ranking and consequentialism'. It is asserted that even the combination of welfarism and sum-ranking means that 'persons as persons have dropped fully out of the assessment of states of affairs' (5). Sen and Williams clearly imply that there is something wrong here. It is not clear what. The ten commandments proscribe and prescribe certain activities without reference to 'persons as persons' – at least they don't mention anyone by name (except God, perhaps) – or tell us anything about them 'as persons'. Is there something wrong with this 'impersonality'? As has been argued, all moral rules have an impersonal, or impartial, aspect (2.3.b). In fact it is sometimes held that a moral rule is more moral to the extent that it is more impartial. A big difference between preference utilitarianism and most deontological moral rules is that preference utilitarianism takes account of *more* facts about the welfare of persons. Popular deontological rules tend to protect welfare to some extent, but to the extent that they are inflexible they must neglect at least some aspects of at least some people's welfare. So we see that it is exactly such deontological rules that must impose 'severe informational constraints' if one is concerned with welfare.

For the utilitarian to judge actions it is held – by Sen and Williams – to be sufficient, but implied to be unsatisfactory, that 'the impersonal sum of utilities is known' (5). This is merely like saying that with a deontological rule it is sufficient to know only which of two alternatives observes the rule to know which is better. In both cases the only way we find out which really upholds our values is by investigation. In either case it is enough to be accurately informed which outcome measures up to our criteria in order to judge it, but we are unlikely to accept it without some observational testing.

The 'drastic obliteration of usable information' is supposed to result in the 'neglect of a person's attachments and ties' (5). How can this be? A person's attachments and ties will be taken into account by preference utilitarianism in proportion to the importance that the person himself places on them. How could preference utilitarianism neglect them? True, it does not grant intrinsic and sacred value to attachments and ties, but why should it?

They complain that utilitarianism regards 'attachment, ties, aims, plans, agency, etc., ... as worthless in themselves and valuable only to the extent of their effects on utility' (5–6). But if no value is placed on a thing, or derivable from some felt value, then how can it have a value? Values are about desires, what we *want* the world to be like; only facts are about what the world *is* like. Things do not have *objective* worth in themselves; utility is a measure of how much worth is placed on them by individuals. *However*, individuals can *subjectively* value these things as ends in themselves (to the extent that they do not seek to use them as mere tools for some other purpose), and preference utilitarianism respects that. It is not even generally utilitarianly desirable for people to put less weight on their own personal ties in favor of impartial interpersonal comparisons of personal ties. That is made unnecessary by the 'invisible hand' conclusions of the economists being philosophically defended in this book.

Sen and Williams assert that even if it is a necessary condition for something to be valuable that it be desired, it still does not follow that one ought to equate 'the importance of a thing with the *extent* of the desire for it or with the pleasure generated by it (i.e. utility being the measure of importance)' (6). Well, we have to equate the importance of a thing with *someone's* desire or value, or *potential* desire or value, or we have the paradox of desires or values existing without any desirers or valuers who ever hold them. And the only alternative to an impartial weighing is a partial one. Whose desires or values should we be partial to and why, given that overall welfare will fall as a result of this partiality? They do not say.

They see as a deeper objection that 'something can be valuable even if it is not desired by anyone' (6). But it is quite compatible with preference utilitarianism that there are things that are, at least potentially, valuable (things that would satisfy more unimposed desires) though they are not yet, or not directly, desired. The value of these things is due to the increase in want-satisfaction that they would bring about.

Apart from the above objections to utilitarianism, we are also told that a utilitarian society 'is not simply a society which happens to satisfy utilitarian requirements, but a society which is run in accordance with these requirements' (15). This echoes an earlier remark that utilitarianism is 'also a criterion of public action. It therefore must assume a public agent, some supreme body which chooses general states of affairs for society as a whole' (2). So though Sen and Williams see that *some* utilitarians 'see no need to assume a public agency' (3), they clearly do not really accept this possibility. It is worth stating this point clearly for the sake of the compatibility thesis: there is no reason that preference utilitarianism logically entails that societies must be controlled as a whole, let alone by a 'public' agent or body (where 'public' is probably intended as a euphemism for 'state'). If any kind of anarchy is better at achieving welfare than any known alternative then preference utilitarianism demands it. Preference utilitarianism cannot rule out anarchy on purely logical grounds.

b. 'Social Justice' versus Utility

John Rawls's theory of justice (Rawls [1972] 1983) will be sketched and then briefly responded to, concentrating on the areas that are relevant to general criticisms of preference utilitarianism and the compatibility thesis. I am not, of course, directly defending preference utilitarianism here as more moral than Rawls's conception of 'social justice'. Rather, I am maintaining that it has a more plausible conception of welfare for practical purposes – more people accept it – and it does not clash with liberty and the anarchy (as these terms are interpreted here). This will have to stand as a typical response to various incompatible theories of 'social justice'.

Rawls feels that sacrificing some people's welfare to maximize aggregate welfare is the objectionable aspect of utilitarianism (for example, 3–4). His theory is designed to produce more acceptable principles. He has a notion of 'primary goods' (basic desirable things, of which all will want as much as possible), which is held to imply a conception of a person that is compatible with there being many rational conceptions of the good – supposedly unlike utilitarianism. In his 'rational choice' formulation of his argument, Rawls offers us a hypothetical contract to choose the principles for distributing these primary goods. This is his 'original position' (17–22). In it individuals are self-interested and generally knowledgeable, but deprived of knowledge of their own attributes and their place in society. This set-up is supposed to ensure that fair principles are derived, as no arbitrary discrimination is possible. 'Rational choice' is assumed in order to ensure a concern with the worst-off: we want to make them as well-off as possible for we might be them. In his first statement of the two principles (60), Rawls argues that people will choose a lexical ordering with his conception of 'liberty' being enforced first; whereby 'each person is to have an equal right to the most extensive basic liberty compatible with a similar liberty for others'. There is also a more egalitarian-inspired idea in the second ('difference') principle that 'social and economic inequalities' must be 'reasonably expected to be to everyone's advantage'. I shall examine these points and only then give some consideration to the basic argument which underpins Rawls's whole enterprise.

Preference utilitarianism does not *in principle* entail the sacrifice of the individual, to which Rawls explicitly objects. That sacrifice is only required if overall welfare increases thereby (and this book denies that such sacrifice is compatible with long-term, practical, preference-utilitarian rules). Ironically, Rawls does advocate sacrifice of the individual, despite his protestations to the contrary, insofar as he allows for the involuntary use of some by others. If Tom and Sophie trade without imposing a cost on Harry and they are then forced to give a share to Harry, then their interests are sacrificed to Harry's (whether this is ever morally desirable is a separate issue). Rawls does defend such scenarios, and thereby advocates the very thing (the sacrifice of some people's interests for others) for which he rejects utilitarianism (albeit mistakenly).

Rawls is trying to argue at a very basic level: prior to our adoption of assumptions about what property rules ought to exist. He argues that people do not inherently own their talents, social advantages, and so on, and so they give up nothing to which they have a 'legitimate' claim. But such 'legitimacy' or otherwise can be ignored here. The point I am making is that the sacrifice, or imposition, is objective. To take from people what they have acquired and possess without their imposing on any other people, is objectively to use them for your own purposes (whether or not this might be morally desirable in some cases). It might be suggested that it is impossible to say what will count as an imposition until we first know who has a legitimate claim to what, and that this is just what Rawls is trying to determine. And once this is determined, then it follows that to withhold what another has a legitimate claim to, even if this includes the fruits of one's own natural abilities, is to impose on him. Such a view entails that sacrifices or impositions are entirely system-relative and never objective. I can accept that such system-relative impositions make some sense, but the objective sense still stands.

Consider a clear case. Assume that no valid property claims yet exist, even in one's own person. A man tries to rape a woman. That woman's interests would thereby be objectively sacrificed to the man's interests. If the woman tries to prevent the rape by, say, running away then she is objectively merely protecting herself, the body that she is, and not thereby sacrificing, or imposing on, the would-be rapist in any way. Merely to withhold a benefit one gives rise to – in this case the use of the body that one sustains – is not to *impose* a cost or sacrifice on anyone else (see the earlier discussion of self-ownership at 3.4.a). And what is true of our bodies is just as true of any external property we come to possess, as long as no imposition on (or sacrifice of) others is involved. The less obvious and more complicated argument about such external property was given in the previous chapter, and I shall not repeat it here.

We can also go on to ask whether preference utilitarianism necessarily has a single conception of the good, as Rawls states. It might seem to be definitionally true that preference utilitarians must hold that 'the good' is preferences being satisfied. But this is not so. Preference utilitarianism can consistently be interpreted as a modus vivendi (or more stable 'overlapping consensus'; see 5.2). Given that people are bound to clash as regards what they want, all may agree to give equal weight to the wants of each person. This does not mean that each must think others' wants matter as much as his own. It is sufficient that he thinks that according equal weight to individuals' wants is likely to achieve a more pleasant world for him than constant conflict. He will maximize his chances for achieving his own ends in this way. I shall not here go into the plausibility of the contingent arguments on this point (in which, of course, I see liberty as the rule to achieve this). It is sufficient that this is conceptually coherent. Thus preference utilitarianism does not have to be interpreted as a theory of the good. It is not that there then needs to be a single more fundamental theory of the good; everyone can have their own views on what is valuable.

We can set these points aside though and ask what outcome Rawls's thought-experiment would yield. If the people in the original position knew and understood their social science, as Rawls assumes they do, then it seems to me that they would opt for private-property anarchy. They would see that a political system is in practice bound to destroy liberty and welfare, sacrifice the interests of some to others, and make those at the bottom of the social system even worse off. Of course this is a contentious and contingent view,[200] but it should not be as contentious as Rawls's implicit assumption that we can know *a priori* (rather than contingently) that we shall be better off with politics. Rawls's conception of 'liberty' is inherently political (5.2). And the 'difference principle' that 'social and economic inequalities' must be 'reasonably expected to be to everyone's advantage' also disallows possible inequalities that raise the welfare of some without producing redistributable benefits – let alone redistributable to *'everyone's* advantage'. Everyone gains *overall* (and more than in any other system) by allowing inequalities that result from free markets, but it can only destroy this overall gain to require that *everyone* gain by *each instance* of market inequality – and Rawls is at least open to this extreme interpretation. Neither can it be trivial, in practice, that his rhetoric has an egalitarian slant: that would probably affect any real attempt to implement Rawls's theory. Having said this, however, the free market has no practical rival as regards promoting *prosperous* equality. The general free-market trend is clearly that of a growing and richer middle class. The state cannot hasten this process, as Rawls's second principle appears to suggest, without destroying wealth-creation and creating what are really privileges for certain special-interest groups.

Finally, let us consider Rawls's fundamental argument, of which his elaborate theory is largely a development. This is that a 'society'[201] that is not deliberately ordered by moral principles allows advantages of person and position that are 'arbitrary from a moral point of view' (for example, 72). In particular, if people do not *deserve* the things they possess or receive, then it is arbitrary that they should have a preferential claim to them. We can put aside the explicitly moral part of this argument and consider whether the consequences are arbitrary when it comes to maximizing welfare and liberty, including that of the worst-off groups. Again, if the classical liberal compatibility thesis is correct, then *anarchically ordered*[202] advantages of person and position are not arbitrary in this way. For if we look at the long-term results of forcibly interfering with personal and positional advantages that were acquired without imposing costs on others, then we see that both welfare and liberty are destroyed – especially those of the worst-off groups. So far from being obvious, as Rawls believes, it is a non sequitur to move from the idea that something is not 'deserved' to the view that therefore any existing claim to it is arbitrary. In other words, it is arbitrary to claim that allowing undeserved advantages must be arbitrary. And, a fortiori, to deny people a claim to what they receive without imposing on others because they do not 'deserve' it, will in practice be to destroy the very things that Rawls wants to promote.

This is already to begin to consider some of the more practical implications of maximizing utility. We should now examine some of these more directly.

4.5. Some Practical and Economic Implications

Hare is a prominent preference utilitarian. Examining some of his views on maximizing want-satisfaction should focus on the practical implications. We shall look again at his views on discrimination, then equality (in more detail, because it is so important), and preference-utilitarian rules. Another self-proclaimed preference utilitarian, John Harsanyi, provides some even more illiberal views on preference autonomy and free personal choice.

a. Discrimination and Equality

It was agreed earlier that R. M. Hare is right that no group of people could, in reality, be fanatical enough to make the murder of another group preference utilitarian (4.3). However, in his attempt to demonstrate the 'normality' of preference utilitarianism, Hare overlooks the mere wish not to mix with certain types of people (of whatever sort). Allowing this choice must in practice be preference utilitarian. For the desires of compulsory integrationists, of any sort, cannot plausibly outweigh the desires of those who merely wish to live in peaceful ways without mixing with some kinds of people. Compulsory integration is probably more destructive of welfare than is compulsory segregation: forcing people together when at least some of them would rather keep apart is more likely to result in conflict and even violence in many areas of life. And that is in addition to the general disutility of the initial and continuing imposition of compulsory integration.

This ought to be obvious but it is confused by various popular errors: 1) the fact that the streets are typically state-owned makes people think the choice can only be between compulsory segregation and compulsory integration; 2) people fail to see that freedom of association entails freedom *not* to associate; 3) people fail to see that 'property discrimination' (choosing who enters your property, including your business premises) is as much a part of freedom as 'personal discrimination' (choosing with whom you personally interact); 4) the prejudice that discrimination that one does not oneself engage in is somehow 'irrational' rather than due to ordinary personal preference or prudential calculation.

So we should make a crucial preference-utilitarian distinction between liberal discrimination (freedom of association) and imposed discrimination (persecution). Hare is right that imposed discrimination must be stopped if human welfare is to be maximized. But liberal discrimination must be allowed if human welfare is to be maximized. What exactly distinguishes *liberal* discrimination from *imposed* discrimination should be clear from the theory of liberty in the previous chapter. 'Discriminating', freely choosing to do, with what you acquire and possess libertarianly is always liberal.

Hare 'reassures' us about the preference-utilitarian consequences for equality. He offers 'two important utilitarian grounds for a fairly high degree of equality of actual goods (tempered ... by various advantages that are secured by moderate inequalities)'. First, diminishing marginal utility 'means that approaches towards equality will tend to increase total utility'. Second, 'inequalities tend to produce, at any rate in educated societies, envy, hatred, and malice'. So preference utilitarians do not need to 'fear the accusation that they could favour extreme inequalities of distribution in actual modern societies' (1982, 27). This is a clearly a major issue as regards the compatibility thesis. Here we focus on some general preference-utilitarian arguments for allowing extreme inequality. Later we consider whether equality even starts out as preference utilitarian (4.6.b).

Contra Hare, I would suggest that any 'extreme inequalities' that arise in the market are defensible on several welfare-maximizing grounds: 1) the necessity for some extreme monetary incentives; 2) the signalling function of extreme incomes; 3) many extreme wealth and income differences are due to past or continuing choices; 4) forcible transfers to the worst-off do not seem to reach their ostensible targets. I shall expand briefly on these points in order to make them more plausible rather than in an attempt, in so short a space, to provide a comprehensive refutation of Hare's view.

In what follows I generally have in mind taxation of people in the market sector. To the extent that people are in the state sector (or their incomes derive from the state, however indirectly), they do not, on balance, financially support the state. If their jobs were abolished the state would have more money, unlike with the genuinely contributing market sector. Their own 'taxes' are more like wasteful book-keeping exercises that could in principle simply be replaced by lower wages, were it not politically expedient that they be conflated with people in the market sector. But the distinction between the two groups of people remains clear enough. They are sometimes known as net taxpayers and net tax-recipients.[203]

1) *The necessity for some extreme monetary incentives.* All income-taxes lower monetary rewards for the jobs taxed and at the margin make work less attractive than leisure or non-market activities.[204] With progressive taxation, people will be that much less likely to do the most highly paid jobs (I focus on work but similar arguments apply to all market incomes).[205] If equality is a supreme end then perhaps this does not matter much. However, if the highest marginal tax-rates deter people from taking the most highly paid jobs, the rewards to which ultimately reflect their considerable contribution to consumer satisfaction, such taxation may substantially destroy welfare.[206] The key point, more generally, is that taxes, especially – but not only – high marginal rates of income-tax, will deter some activities which are, prima facie, welfare-increasing.

Having said this, it seems that the market does make incomes from work more equal than they would be if people were paid their marginal revenue product in pecuniary terms. Within enterprises of all kinds, the more productive tend to subsidize the less productive so that they tolerate their lower status. It is often possible to choose among firms according to one's preference for status or additional income (and taxation makes status relatively more attractive at the margin in a way that can only reduce welfare). All this is completely voluntary (taxation aside), and taking into account non-pecuniary costs and benefits is simply good economics.[207] It should also be noted that charitable gifts are quite different from forcible tax transfers: being *voluntary*, they do not affect incentives. In fact, preventing them would reduce incentives.

2) *The signalling function of extreme incomes.* Another aspect

of levelling incomes is that information is destroyed: even if someone wants to produce what is most desired – regardless of the effects on his own income – he will not be able to find out what this is if the price signals of some incomes have been destroyed by taxation. The informational content of price signals is the central part of the economic calculation argument against disrupting them (see 2.6). This is a particular theme of Hayek's, for example his 1948.

3) *Many extreme wealth and income differences are due to past or continuing choices.* In many cases the wealth and income differences among people are a hopelessly crude indication of how want-satisfying their lives are. Within any particular market-society, to the extent that the market is free, people have roughly the material standards that they choose to earn (state barriers to trade and migration lower welfare within societies while maintaining material differences among societies). Most people prefer more leisure, lack of stress, an enjoyable job, and so forth. But almost anyone could choose to earn a modest fortune by hard work. Common observation shows that long hours in a business producing popular family items is the most certain way of achieving material riches. The exceptions to this general rule within a society tend to be due to the state's aggressively initiating and maintaining material differences by enforcing restrictive practices or straight transfers to the wealthier.[208]

4) *Forcible transfers to the worst-off do not seem to reach their ostensible targets.* Coercive redistribution from rich to poor is not practical in any case. The evidence suggests that the ill-educated poor are typically manipulated into a worse position by the better-educated and better-off (see for example, LeGrand 1982). It is not obvious that coercive transfers from the relatively few at the very top could, in any case, add much additional income per person if divided among the rest (Norman Barry 1981, ch. 3). And the money is also largely wasted in the redistributive bureaucracy itself and the overclass of state 'carers' (social workers, probation officers, and so on).

There is, then, at least a plausible case that the level of inequality has to be left to the market if welfare is not to be lowered.[209] The 'envy, hatred and malice' in the presence of inequality[210] are, contra Hare, certainly not part of 'educated societies' but, rather, due to *lack* of education[211] (insofar as they are not simply misanthropic) about the liberal nature and welfare benefits of the free market. Theories that hold the rich businessman to be rich at the expense of the poor are part of the problem. The idea of winners and losers in a zero-sum game is held to be commonsense arithmetic. The positive-sum gain of trade is a real insight of economics that the public has yet fully to appreciate. The same is true of the market's tendency to focus on the demands of the less well-off: as the large number of people with incomes close to or lower than the mean income spend far more than the few rich, it is usual for the richest businessmen to strive to serve these ordinary customers. The surest route to wealth seems to be selling in quantity, and that means catering to a market far larger than a rich elite. In a society where these basic economic facts were understood there would be no resentment (which in itself would be a welfare improvement), and consequently the welfare-enhancing inequalities would not be destroyed.[212] So we can, again, reverse Hare's assertion that the preference utilitarian need not 'fear' that he will be accused of tolerating 'extreme inequalities'. Instead the preference utilitarian should *insist* that he tolerates them.[213]

Hare also attempts to show the correct preference-utilitarian rules for some typical problem cases. On the issues of consuming electricity contrary to the government's instructions and of not voting, Hare says that it cannot be correct to allow each individual to calculate that his behavior will make no difference to the others but benefit himself because 'it would be impolitic, in moral education, to bring up people to behave like this ... nearly everyone would consume electricity under those conditions, and hardly anybody would vote' (Hare 1982, 36–7).

He is supposing that the political facts are uncontentious and that only preference utilitarianism's correct applications require to be sorted out. But if electricity is in short supply thanks to a state-regulated monopoly, then there seems no reason that preference utilitarians who recognize the inefficiency of this need curtail their consumption. They might even care to opt for the supererogatory act of consuming extra electricity if that will hasten the collapse and deregulation of the monopoly. Similarly, if politics is an unnecessary evil, it might be better not to vote. Most people stand more chance of being run over by a bus on the way to the polling station than they have of influencing the outcome of election (and even if someone's vote were decisive he would only achieve a very crude and mixed package of promised policies). Statistically, it is not worth anyone's voting for the purpose of changing things (apparently, people vote partly because they don't grasp the statistics, partly because they value 'cheering for their team' or 'booing the opposition', and partly out of a sense of 'democratic duty'). And it can help to undermine the legitimacy of the political system if more people decline to vote (though not voting could lead to a worse regime if this were not done, and seen to be done, because a more libertarian system would be preferred). Hare's 'utilitarian rules' of 'law-abidingness' and 'public spirit' have no obvious welfare-merit, at least as he applies them here.

One final point. Hare objects to Bernard Williams's 'persuasive definition by which he labels the self-centred pursuit of one's own projects "integrity"' (29 n11). From the compatibility viewpoint, Hare is overlooking the powerful preference-utilitarian personal and 'invisible hand' reasons for *fully* respecting such 'integrity' (for not interfering with someone's voluntaristic plans and projects in any imposed way, whether in isolated cases or institutionally). It would be better to object to Williams's *inconsistency*: for Williams in practice advocates the (welfare destroying) disruption of innocent lives and voluntary associations to the extent that he advocates any state interference that does more than defend people from having others impose on them. Analogously with Rawls's criticism of utilitarianism for sacrificing other people's utility (4.4.b), Williams's criticism of utilitarianism for sacrificing 'integrity' is also quite ironic.

We now turn to another prominent preference utilitarian, John Harsanyi. His applications of preference utilitarianism are, if anything, even less consistent with the compatibility thesis.

b. Preference Autonomy and Free Personal Choice

Much of what John Harsanyi (1982) writes on morality and rational behavior is very abstract, and he says little about the practical implications by way of elucidation. He seems to confuse and conflate stipulative definitions, factual theses, and value judgements in an attempt to combine philosophy and mathematics 'rigorously'. At points he becomes less abstract, and his meaning becomes a little clearer. A few such points will be criticized.

Harsanyi claims to be a preference utilitarian. He sees it as fundamental that this version of utilitarianism is the only one 'consistent with the important philosophical principle of *preference autonomy*' whereby 'in deciding what is good and what is bad for a given individual, the ultimate criterion can only be his own wants and his own preferences'. The only sense in which someone can want something that is bad for him is if 'his own preferences at some deeper level are inconsistent with what he is now trying to achieve' (55). This might seem clear enough so far. We can imagine the simple case of someone who wants to drink some water, but fails to realize that it is poisoned. Harsanyi continues that 'social utility' must be measured in terms of people's 'true preferences' rather than their 'manifest preferences'. A person's 'true preferences' are defined as

> the preferences he *would* have if he had all the relevant factual information, always reasoned with the greatest possible care, and were in a state of mind most conducive to rational thought. (55)

Now the edifice begins to look a bit unstable. First, it looks like a persuasive definition to write of 'true preferences' here. Even if something is what someone would truly prefer in certain ideal circumstances the fact may be that he does not truly prefer it now. If we are using plain English then it is simply false to say that someone truly prefers what he does not prefer as a matter of fact. It would make more sense to refer to people's 'corrected preferences' or, more simply, 'general interests'. And is Harsanyi intending to go very far beyond such examples as that of the poisoned water? In the water example the person has only to be informed about the poison not to want to drink it, or even if we forcibly prevented him from drinking it at the time the poison can later be tested for and he will thank us (real examples of this type seem few and far between, and it would probably be rule utilitarian to have to pay libertarian restitution if we are mistaken). Does Harsanyi intend to include preventing people from smoking if they understand the likely damage and insist that they are willing to take the risk?[214] If so, then we do not seem to be dealing with the preferences of real people at all but rather the 'ideal' people that Harsanyi wishes existed instead.

There are several other problems with Harsanyi's position. There is a problem about 'all the relevant factual information'. As we cannot know everything, including what information might affect our preferences, any critic of an actual preference is only trying to come up with a better guess. He cannot be sure that he has 'all the relevant factual information' either. Further, even when reasoning 'with the greatest possible care' one often still makes mistakes. It is also often a mistake to invest 'the greatest possible care' in a decision when there are other things to be done in one's own life. Given that we have also to be in 'a state of mind most conducive to rational thought', are there many 'true preferences' left to real people on this view? Perhaps most preferences are 'false' most of the time. But then how is any real critic likely to be better placed to produce (enforceable) guesses, safely and reliably, than the individual whose life it is? (There is also a possible infinite regress of ever 'truer' preferences – some of which might be identical with our real preference anyway – if we only knew that little bit more.)

So if 'social utility' is defined in terms of Harsanyi's 'true preferences' it becomes a highly subjective and impractical goal. His so-called 'preference autonomy' would be quite contentious and of little use as a welfare criterion. In fact, it does not look as though autonomy has any real force in Harsanyi's system, despite his praise of the idea. For it now appears clear that what Harsanyi is really is advocating paternalism, and paternalism just means ignoring people's autonomy in order to rule them in their own, supposed, interests. The idea of 'true preferences' looks bound in practice to cause rule by a self-perceived, and self-serving, 'elite' that can only destroy general welfare and liberty.[215]

Harsanyi goes on to say that he wants to exclude some 'anti-social preferences' that even he concedes are 'true' by his definition. These include 'sadism, envy, hatred and malice'. He argues that these things are inconsistent with the 'general goodwill and human sympathy' which utilitarianism has as 'the fundamental basis of all our moral commitments' (56).

It seems quite anti-utilitarian to exclude these things. Preference utilitarians will surely not allow them to decide matters *except* where they give greater want-satisfaction than they cause dissatisfaction (and as utilitarianism involves long-term effects,

I see no realistic clash with liberty). There will be less utility if they are excluded. How can preference utilitarianism sanction a lower amount of utility promotion? Harsanyi has no proper pref-erence-utilitarian reason for asserting that these emotions should count for nothing. There are certainly many preference-utilitarian and libertarian ways of catering to 'sadism, envy, ha-tred and malice'. Boxing, gossip, prostitution, satirical maga-zines, and even career success can be – but need not be – tools for some of these. In any case, how are we to know whether someone's motives for involvement in one of these are 'antisocial' (and so count for nothing according to Harsanyi) or 'social' (and so add to welfare)? Harsanyi is really wanting to impose his own values on others in the name of preference utilitarianism.

Rawls was right, Harsanyi says, to point out that traditional utilitarianism is 'unreasonably strict' in requiring us 'to choose every individual action of ours so as to maximize social utility' because of the value that people put on having 'free personal choice' (60). But we can go *much* further than Harsanyi's modest admission and question how much welfare can really be in-creased by helping others altruistically. Aggressing against oth-ers in their persons and libertarian property – especially the ag-gression of state interference and taxation – is certainly a tre-mendous source of the loss of people's welfare. If this aggression stopped then the world would be a relative paradise. To offer positive altruistic help, however, will often be less useful than to be a peaceful profit-seeker who can only make money by serving the public. This is, of course, the fundamental insight of Bernard Mandeville, Adam Smith, and the early economists (for some more recent argument see Mises 1966).

Going beyond any spontaneous charity (what we happily give without suffering personal hardship) would probably not be preference utilitarian.[216] Give continuous sums of money to poorer people in one's own country and you can simply encour-age them not to work, as state money for unemployment does.[217] Send food regularly to people who are being starved by the poli-cies of their governments and it can undermine the indigenous farms, or feed the government troops, or reduce discontent at the policies of the government and thus enable them to carry on in power a little longer and do still more harm.[218] If the average person were to spend more than a small proportion (for I am not asserting that charity does no welfare good at all) of his income or time on general charities, then there would be a very real loss of welfare felt by him and his family and only a drop in the ocean towards some, possibly uncertain or even dubious, cause. Charity that is not based on personal acquaintance is much overrated. It certainly cannot provide significant welfare by comparison with the market. The creation of a freer market (by scrapping state immigration and import controls, employment and trade regulations, taxation, the state monopoly of the money supply, ...) would increase welfare more than a thousandfold increase in the income of charities (though the increased wealth of a freer market would also increase charity).

It might be thought that some greater 'general goodwill and human sympathy' is necessary merely to have less damaging aggression. There is some truth in this at the personal level, but most political aggression (and most aggression is political) is due to ignorance and confusion about economics. The welfare-diminishing political assaults on persons and their libertarian property occur chiefly not because politicians do not care but because they do not understand.

As with replies to other critics, this is hardly intended to be an exhaustive response. The detailed economic and social arguments and evidence have to be found in the relevant literature, only some of which can be indicated throughout this book. The focus here is on the philosophy and not the empirical evidence. The point is that it is at least a coherent and plausible position that preference-utilitarian welfare is best served by liberty and the market. And this is usually argued and referenced in this book in more detail than the opposite is argued, or merely supposed, by those to whom I am responding.

We have been looking at a few general and typical misinterpretations of maximizing 'utility' (or want-satisfaction) in practice. In the final section of this chapter, I now attempt to link utility more precisely to the observance of libertarian property.

4.6. Want-Satisfaction and Libertarian Property Rights

I always understand and intend *libertarian* property rights in what follows. I am defending the non-moral view that these property rights *considered merely as possible social rules* do not clash with maximizing want-satisfaction. This is done by responding to two writers who explicitly deny this possibility (though the previous writers examined were also at least implicitly against this). I focus on Peter Hammond's objection to 'the right to take risks as a kind of property right'. I criticize Alan Ryan's basic assumption that immediate equality, overriding any property rights, would at least maximize utility in the short term. Then I consider Ryan's arguments on various property cases that he asserts are more clearly defended by utilitarianism than by reference to anything like individual rights.

a. Private Risks versus Welfare?

Peter J. Hammond (1982) suggests, disapprovingly, that Milton Friedman 'views the right to take risks as a kind of property right which acts as a constraint on maximizing the expected value of the ex-post welfare function'. Hammond states that this entails, if one is to be consistent,

> that the failed capitalist has the duty to meet all the consequences of his failure, including discharging all his debts, if he can, and even selling himself and perhaps his heirs too into slavery if necessary.

He notes that, in fact, the right to go bankrupt exists in 'modern capitalist societies' and that this 'undermines the supposed property rights of other capitalists' (95).

Consider first, 'the right to take risks'. This is not so much 'a kind of property right' as part of any full property right: one owns a thing to the extent that one has the right to use it without external constraint. If people have the right to dictate the level of risks that we take with a thing, then thus far they are the owners of it. To dictate any rules of use about things in themselves (that is, when they are not being used to impose on the property of others) is to claim to have some ownership rights over the things in question. For instance, the people who think that you should be prevented from selling one of your kidneys must, logically, be asserting that you are infringing their property rights by so doing (or they would not have the right to stop you). They are effectively claiming a particular ownership right in your kidneys (they are not claiming a partial share in your kidneys, only a particular ownership right).

Now consider welfare. It must at least be logically possible that property rights, including any risk-taking aspects, do not act as constraints on welfare so much as promote welfare in the most efficient way known. Hammond's view sounds as peculiar to me as the following might sound to him: 'Hammond views the right to do welfare economics as a kind of property right which acts as a constraint on maximizing the expected value of the ex-post welfare function'. And though I do not think that Hammond needs to be censored – for free speech seems the best long-term strategy for welfare – I do think that welfare economists considered collectively, not in every case, have hitherto been a constraint on welfare. I cannot usefully do much more here than suggest that the author is mistaken in his background assumptions. But I can point out some of the more obvious flaws in those areas where these background assumptions are thrust forward, as in his 'failed capitalist' example.

Risks are, in any case, inevitable in this uncertain world. The difference with the 'capitalist' is, roughly, that he systematically risks resources to achieve a profit. That such risks be allowed is clearly preference utilitarian and libertarian, as long as they do not violate the property rights of anyone else. One can insure oneself against these risks, in a variety of ways, without such violations. Limited liability, for instance, could be a contractual and voluntary device. The state is currently involved, but only because of its imposed monopoly of the legal system. So logical consistency does not require, as Hammond states, that the right to benefit from risks implies that a 'failed capitalist has the duty to meet all the consequences of his failure' (in the sense Hammond implies). However, it is not a free-market phenomenon that businessmen can take risks at others' *non-contractual* expense. It is not only the 'other capitalists' (95) who bear the cost of bankruptcy: in the long term this has to be mostly passed on to the consumers, in higher prices or worse or fewer goods. Bankruptcy law was brought about by pressure on the state from powerful special interests: the rising business class. That UK travel agents can close down at any time without liability, appears to be another non-contractual example. Such things are, for the most part, due to state intervention in the market. If a enterpriser has not made it plain that he is trading on a limited liability basis (so that his clients have decided to accept that risk) or not insured himself by contractual and voluntary means, then it would be both a free-market outcome *and* prudent preference-utilitarian rule to make him liable for his enterprise's losses.

Selling oneself into slavery to meet these debts certainly sounds unlikely (if only because virtually no one would enter agreements which included this as a possibility). Being obliged to work off the debt as far as possible sounds both preference utilitarian and libertarian. This would probably involve the debtor working in a similar occupation to his normal one, if that would be libertarian and where his best earning potential is, and paying a significant percentage of his earnings to his creditors. The attachment of wages and property for debt is, of course, part of most Western legal systems. The idea that with sufficiently extreme losses strict private property rules might entail that one's heirs might become slaves is completely absurd: with strict private property the risk is the individual's alone; he does not own his children as chattel to forfeit them as part of his debts.

Hammond also worries about externalities. The example he uses is of everyone cutting down all their trees, which 'may create problems of soil erosion and landslides as well as having adverse effects on the local climate' (89). He sees only political solutions. It does not occur to Hammond that this problem could be the result of insufficient respect for private property: negative externalities conflict with full private property, and they could be better dealt with in a wholly private legal system (which would include the possibility of class actions where a negative externality is widespread). Instead he concludes that the

> significance of generalised [private] property rights has been greatly exaggerated ... with good governments ... insistence on [private property] 'rights' may often be little more than a selfish ploy to influence the political process unduly. (90)

'Good governments' and good fairies sound like wonderful things. If they exist then we should be grateful. But do they, or could they, exist just because welfare economists and storytellers talk about them? Like many welfare economists and utilitarians, Hammond starts with a theoretical defense of his basic stance – which is not disputed here – and then, before one can blink, concludes that some detailed aspect of state intervention is thereby obviously required. A welfarist who is more familiar with the economic literature which I accept, might again be inclined to invert Hammond's conclusion: 'The welfare efficiency of property rights has been greatly neglected; with any government the insistence on the "public good" may often be little more than a selfish ploy by special interests to interfere with property rights unduly'. This is an important insight of public choice economics (see, for instance, relevant writings of James Buchanan and Gordon Tullock).

One of the greatest threats to libertarian private-property rights is egalitarianism. It is time to ask how far egalitarianism even begins to be preference utilitarian.

b. The Immediate Effects of Equality

In the course of a discussion on 'Utility and Ownership', Alan Ryan (1985) holds it to be obvious that

> At any given moment, there would be an increase in welfare if we were to divide up everything equally; but to do it would set at risk the environment ... we rely on to create the wealth .... (183)

Ryan's egalitarian outlook is at least modified by some grasp of the wealth-creating aspects of the free market. But would equality even *immediately* ('At any given moment') be welfare-enhancing? I now criticize this specific assertion because it seems to be the thin end of the egalitarian wedge. As usual with matters which are more empirical, what follows is not intended to be a knock-down refutation so much as clearly more plausible than the mere assumption at which it is aimed.

Could the proportion of any national population (world redistribution seems even more problematic) with more than average wealth be forced to accept an egalitarian redistribution without bloodshed? Could the logistics of redistributing homes, consumer goods, factories, and so on, be solved in a way that did not lower welfare? Even assuming the answer is yes in both cases – two considerable assumptions – would the recipients be likely to gain as much welfare as the losers lose? Wealth transfers are not the same as welfare transfers. Property is usually carefully organized in ways that are of particular value to the owner. It seems probable that thieves, plus any eventual recipients of the stolen property, typically gain a value smaller than the value of the property to the original owner (if it were the other way round then theft might increase the 'national welfare'). So it is quite implausible that there would even be an immediate gain in welfare 'if we were to divide up everything equally'.

Ryan might suggest that such property redistribution is unnecessary because purchasing power could be given to people in proportion to their lack of wealth. Taxation of wealth via income redistribution would be impracticable as it could not be high enough to achieve the immediate equality Ryan has in mind (and announcing such a tax would cause many people to engage in tax avoidance and evasion). If equalization were attempted by printing and distributing money this would chiefly create a great price-inflation, with those with above-average, non-monetary wealth not selling enough of these assets. But let us suppose that we can take projected price-inflation into account when calculating such handouts (and still enforce 'legal tender' laws). What then? Many people would enjoy windfall gains. But what of the 'windfall losses' of everyone else – everyone above average wealth – who loses by this redistribution? Windfall gains are usually a relatively small source of welfare in anyone's normal life. An equal amount of monetary loss is usually a more than proportionate disaster. The things we normally budget for are threatened. We have to tighten our belts uncomfortably to cope with the loss. If there were not this difference then we would expect people regularly to gamble large amounts when the odds are even (for instance, two of us on equal incomes would think it a good bet to allow the toss of a coin to decide who gets both monthly salaries). If only because of the diminishing marginal utility of income, this is not normal behavior. It is far from clear that the utility from the windfall gains would be large enough to compensate for the disutility of the losses.

Consider a single, relatively extreme, example. Take a professional person undoubtedly above the average income for even the UK and imagine suddenly taking a mere month's salary from him and giving it to someone as poor as a homeless,[219] alcoholic beggar. All the wealthier person's normal financial arrangements will be in disarray. He will have to juggle drastically with his bills and go without many of the items or maybe one large item (his annual holiday?) he usually buys. Beggars often choose to live rough and even look down on those who work all day to pay for a house to sleep in. A beggar could usually get an immediate job day-laboring if he chose and maybe sleep in a Salvation Army hostel (where there are often empty beds,[220] as their regulations are not universally popular). He does not so choose and he is unlikely to change his ways because of this windfall. He will probably do with it what he normally does with any money he receives: he will spend it on drink and not bother to return to begging until it is spent. He might drink more than usual, possibly dying sooner as a result, and go longer without begging – that is all. Without this transfer, the beggar would have continued drinking on the income from his begging that people give *without* resentment or feeling a great loss. And what if we took half the wealthier man's entire property and gave it to the beggar? The beggar would stay drunk much longer. Meanwhile the poor man who has lost half of all he owned is having his normal life utterly disrupted. Can an impartial preference utilitarian see these as even an immediate increase in the overall welfare of the two? It is at least not obviously an increase.

The previous example was chosen because it seemed that if an immediate transfer of income or wealth were not preference utilitarian in a relatively extreme case, then the argument against milder cases should be stronger still. However, perhaps the example has peculiarities which invalidate that conclusion. Suppose, instead, that one took the wealth of an extremely rich man and divided it among fifty poor working people. Would there be an increase in immediate utility? Perhaps. On a society-wide scale though, which is what Ryan is supposing, it is more dubious that there are enough extremely rich men for every fifty poor working people (even ignoring anyone else's claims). We have to compare the extreme disutility of some rich people who are 'ruined' with the prospect of many poor people each receiving a modest cash payout. This would be a sort of reverse lottery: the exact opposite of how any lottery player chooses to gamble. Could that really cause a rise in overall utility?

It seems far more likely in reality that immediate equality would decrease welfare disastrously for various reasons. One large factor that would cause the decrease is simply people's expectations. This was seen by David Hume ([1739–40] 1968, 219). People are more upset by failing to receive what they are expecting, relying on, and think is properly theirs, than the reverse. Of course, if people did not have such expectations then total utility *might* go up *initially* (provided that the process of redistribution did not itself destroy too much wealth and welfare). In reality people do have such expectations, and Ryan is writing of reality. If equality were cautiously approached (to avoid any sudden disaster), then that might weaken the expectations argument against equality. But then there are the other long-term welfare arguments (not least, the destruction of investments in productive resources that would raise the standard of living), in this chapter and in the books cited, for not imposing equality. Here I only mean to criticize Ryan's fundamental axiom that immediate equality would raise welfare. Ryan is not being cautious enough when he suggests that it is 'wrong to attempt anything more than slowly operating methods of redistribution' (184). For if there is no sound reason to think that equality at 'any given moment' will raise welfare, then Ryan has not given us a sound reason that equality is even to be cautiously approached.

Ryan goes on to argue that utilitarianism can provide a much more plausible defense of property rights than can (libertarian) individual rights. He is, in effect, attempting to ally property with utility but divorce it from liberty (as libertarians use the term, at least). This is clearly at odds with the compatibility thesis and worthy of a reply.

c. Utility versus Individual Rights?

Ryan (1985) argues for the superiority of utilitarianism over individual rights in defending property rights (he argues thereby against non-libertarian rights also, but I can ignore that aspect). He considers four basic issues: self-ownership, original acquisition, taxation, and slavery. My general libertarian accounts of these were given in the previous chapter. Here I am concentrating on what seem to me to be the chief errors that cause Ryan to think that these are more of a problem for a, libertarian, rights theory than for utilitarianism. As ever, I avoid any intentional moral advocacy in my arguments.

On self-ownership, Ryan writes,

> It's hard to see what rights would be like at all if they did not
> include rights over one's body – but it is not hard to see how
> there could be such rights and no property rights. (193)

Property rights are, roughly, valid claims to use and control
things. To the extent that we have the legal or moral right – I do
not here assert any such rights – to use and control something,
we thus far have a (legal or moral) property right in that thing.
So to the extent that I have the right to use and control that
thing which is '*my* body' – the body that *is* me – it must also be
'*my* body' in a propertarian sense.[221] Contra Ryan, therefore, it is
impossible to see how there could be 'rights over one's body ...
and no property rights'. Of course, Ryan does not intend 'property rights' to include rights to control one's body. But his intention is irrelevant. Rights to control one's own body are *necessarily* property rights, and so are any rules limiting this control (as
we saw in reply to Hammond, above). In fact *any* putative right
is a claim to the use and control of something (though that can
be a type of thing rather than a specific item) and is therefore a
putative property right, whether or not the person asserting the
right realizes this.[222] How property in our own bodies follows *if*
the principle of liberty, as defined, is observed was explained in
the previous chapter (briefly, people impose a cost if they control
us without our consent, hence we control ourselves and thereby
own ourselves).

Ryan also asserts that

> The defense of leaving people to do as they choose is not
> based on the thought that they 'own' themselves ... There is
> no natural ownership, whether of ourselves or of others ... .
> (189)

Perhaps the only or best defense of 'leaving people to do as
they choose' is not that people are self-owners. But the idea that
people own themselves might well be 'the thought' that causes
many people to accept that we should leave people alone, and
Ryan seems to be denying this. A philosophy lecturer at the
London School of Economics once asserted that self-ownership is
a strange idea and that no one thinks that he owns himself. I

suggested that any of my fellow-students at the lecture who thought that he owned himself should raise his hand. Most, possibly all, raised their hands. I see no reason to think that this is a particularly unusual view. What people certainly do not usually do, in the case of normal adults at least, is a welfare calculation to defend 'leaving people to do as they choose'. Of course, I think that a welfare calculation would come to the same conclusion if done correctly. And perhaps the 'natural' presumption of self-ownership is the result of previous, socially absorbed and largely overlooked, preference-utilitarian effects. If we really would be better off as slaves then we might take that to be the most natural thing.

Having dismissed the idea of self-ownership, Ryan considers the thought experiment that compulsory transplant surgery could save lives. He does 'not think that utilitarianism can do very much to accommodate the idea that this is intolerable' though it can 'do a good deal to embrace the same conclusions as the theorist of the right to respect as a person would reach' (193). Here Ryan is somewhat at odds with his general theme that utilitarianism is clearer than individual rights in finding the 'right' answer on his basic issues. But the practical hazards of, and passionate objections to, making transplant surgery compulsory – which Ryan does see to a considerable extent – do indeed make it 'intolerable' from a *practical* welfare viewpoint. Ryan completely overlooks one crucial point that makes compulsion even less practical: the real problem of the shortage of human organs could be solved completely, relatively cheaply, safely, and almost overnight simply by allowing the incentives of the free market to operate. Large numbers of people die every year because this market is declared illegal by the state – thanks to the permeation of anti-market views propounded by such philosophers as Ryan. So Ryan sees much of the impracticality of compulsory transplants but is asserting merely that it is logically possible that utilitarianism could tolerate this. He offers no realistic difference in clarity or outcome between utility and (libertarian) individual rights.

Connected with self-ownership is Ryan's failure to see how original acquisition – though likely to be 'ceteris paribus' utilitarian – is entailed by (libertarian) individual rights. We are told that there is a temptation to think that a first user

has mixed what was his with what was nobody's and thereby
made it his too. It should not be a strong temptation, though,
since the sense in which our actions are *ours* is not much like
the sense in which a car is ours. (187)

By using unowned resources we invest our actions in them in
a fairly plain sense of investment: we make an effort with the
hope of reaping the rewards of that effort. The labor is obviously
'ours' in the attributive sense: *we* are laboring, not someone else.
Ryan sees this sense. The labor is *also* 'ours' in a propertarian
sense if we are self-owners – as follows from observing liberty –
and have not contracted to work for someone else (an employee's
actions are 'his' attributes though the investment made with
them is no longer 'his' property). This propertarian sense of what
is 'ours' is not understood by Ryan just because he mistakenly
rejects any plain sense in which people can be seen as owning
themselves. If we are self-owners then 'our' actions are also
'ours' in the sense that we have a property right to make them
and no one else has a property right to dictate them. With libertarian property rights, we *do* own the right to action as part of
owning ourselves in *just the same way* that we own the right to
do what we like with our cars as part of owning our cars: we can
do what we like with what is our property insofar as we do not
impose a cost on others (though if some imposition is unavoidable then the overall imposition has to be minimized). So if
someone were to take the 'new product' – in which we have invested our actions – without our consent, then he would usually
be imposing a cost on us. We, however, would not be imposing on
him merely by denying him this benefit (ignoring complicated
qualifications explained in the previous chapter). We therefore
control, or own, the new product, if liberty is to be observed.

Another idea that might mistakenly be thought to justify
original acquisition, according to Ryan, is seeing that people intend to become owners and respecting this intention. He thinks
this approach is more or less based on 'respect for persons' which
he thinks is 'altogether too like the doctrines of "abstract right"
that Mill deplored' (187). 'Respect for persons' is indeed vague.
The libertarian idea is the more precise 'respect for people's liberty'. This is not vague as defined and developed within this
book.

We are told that 'taxation is a forced contribution to social costs' and reassured that

> viewed in the utilitarian framework, ... there is no reason to
> think that we do have [a] sort of [private-property] right to
> our pretax incomes; rather, we are entitled to some share in
> the net proceeds of social collaboration .... (191)

It would be clearer to say that taxation is a forced contribution to the state. What the state spends the money on is immaterial to whether or not the forced contribution is taxation. The
expression 'social costs' in Ryan's usage seems a collectivist
euphemism that is intended to imply that taxation benefits society. There may be no logical inconsistency in being a preference
utilitarian and advocating taxation, but laissez-faire economists
provide plenty of practical reasons for thinking that taxation destroys welfare (for example, Rothbard 1977b, 83–167). Ryan also
fails to see that one's ownership of one's, libertarianly acquired,
income is an aspect of liberty. So within realistic preference-
utilitarian *and* libertarian frameworks we do indeed have reasons 'to think that we do have [a] sort of [private-property] right
to our pretax incomes'.

Also consider Ryan's description of the sum of individual incomes in a society as the 'proceeds of social collaboration'. In one
sense this is not nonsense: one can intelligibly call the aggregate
of individual incomes the 'proceeds of social collaboration' if one
wishes. But a society is not the single enterprise that Ryan
seems to be implying with this expression. There is not a single
goal but different goals for every single person in each of his interactions. If there are trades between Max and Stuart, Stuart
and Isobel, and Isobel and Max, they do not sum to a single arrangement. At any stage there is a gain from a mutually beneficial trade between particular consenting individuals. It is polycentric, and anarchic, rather than holistic. Ryan's implication is
that we have been short-changed in a single social process of
production if we do not receive some, unspecified, fair share.
This might look more obviously questionable given a non-
financial example. Suppose someone asserts that sexual relationships are part of the 'proceeds of social collaboration' and
that he is not getting 'his share'. It is true that no one would
have any sexual relationships without social interaction taking
place. This does not imply that voluntary sexual relationships

need be supplemented by compulsory redistribution of sexual partners. It is merely logically possible that preference utilitarianism might require this unlibertarian outcome. Thus it prejudices the issue to describe what are in reality discretely attained utility gains as the 'proceeds of social collaboration'.

More generally, behind Ryan's explicit statements on taxation is the implicit assumption – without addressing arguments to the contrary – that the preference-utilitarian share is other than that of, tax-free, laissez-faire production which tends towards individuals receiving their marginal revenue products.

Ryan thinks that if someone contracts into slavery

> we ought not to side with his 'owner' if he [the slave] changes his mind ... it is not that we stop people doing what they naturally can, but that we decline to provide institutional sanctions ... . (189)

Assuming such contracts, for the sake of argument, to disallow their enforcement would leave *all* parties worse off ex-ante in their own opinions (or they would not seek to make the contracts). I offer only this basic economic point because Ryan supplies *no* utilitarian argument for his view that 'we ought not to side with his "owner"'. Note also, that Ryan seems to be presupposing a monopolistic state legal system. Contra Ryan, left to themselves people *will* 'naturally' (that is, it is absurd to think they would usually behave in any other way) pay for the legal sanctions that are necessary to protect their property, including any slaves, on the free market. So what Ryan's state would do, and does do, is positively prohibit people from providing the private legal protection they would otherwise buy. The state does not merely 'decline to provide institutional sanctions'; it aggressively disrupts the spontaneous market-provision of sanctions.

I shall not attempt to make out detailed, practical, preference-utilitarian and libertarian cases for allowing people to contract into slavery. I would not expect even contractual slavery to exist in a libertarian society. Though there may be no 'natural right' to self-ownership in any factual sense, slavery is 'unnatural' in the senses that people usually see themselves and others as unquestionably self-owners, and it usually takes a state to enforce slavery. These days it is mainly state-prisoners who are often effectively slaves (though not strictly owned as chattel). As explained before (3.5.b), libertarian rectification would replace most incarceration of criminals with libertarian restitution. So we can expect vanishingly little slavery when law and order is depoliticized.

At one point in his criticism of (libertarian) rights, Ryan rejects the position of those who assert that 'people just *are* originators of value, creators of moral worth in the world, and begetters of their own projects – all of which requires expression in the appropriate ownership institutions', though he believes that 'this is what with luck and good social design they may become' (191–2). Ryan is apparently denying that people have any unimposed values, and morals, and know what they want to do; so social-engineering by the state ('good social design') should decide which values, morals, and projects to create in people (he does not say who should design the designers). But let us again take the most extreme example of someone in the power of another: a slave. A slave is not the psychological puppet of his master: he cannot genuinely value, or moralize about, or want to achieve something simply because his master tells him to (or it would not be necessary always to maintain slavery by coercion); he can only make his actions conform to his master's demands. It seems a fact of human nature that people have to value, moralise, and choose for themselves – even when their options are severely constrained by the lies, threats, and aggression of the state. Much of the history of the twentieth century can be seen as unintended welfare-destruction that is caused by attempts at the state-engineering of these things. Ryan is apparently sympathetic towards this state-engineering – albeit writ small thanks to some grasp of what is practical – just because of his blindness to the connections between (libertarian) liberty, the market, and utility.

It is a mistake to think that the principle of maximizing utility, compared with the principle of observing (libertarian) individual rights, is clearly the 'plainest and most compelling account' (193) of property rights. The arguments and literature discussed in this book show that both preference utilitarian and libertarian implications for property rights are complex and debatable, but that – for philosophical and economic reasons – private property and the free market is the general, practical conclusion in both cases.

Only anarchy now remains to be explained in relation to the

compatibility thesis. Since anarchy is here understood as nothing but interpersonal liberty and free markets at their most consistent, this final step will not require as much space as the previous aspects.

5. Anarchy

5.0. Chapter Thesis

Private-property anarchy is better than the state in the enhancement of liberty and welfare. Strictly speaking, market exchange is one aspect of private-property anarchy. But I here focus on market-anarchy as that is a main source of confusion and debate. Similarly, pluralism is another aspect of private-property anarchy. I focus on pluralism as an example of a currently popular topic where private-property anarchy is misunderstood. 'Pluralism' here means '(tolerating) different ways of life'. 'The market' means 'voluntary exchange'. 'Anarchy' means 'no rule'. Both interpersonal liberty and private property are inherently anarchic: no one is ruled to the extent that these exist. They are also naturally pluralist. The state, by contrast, coercively imposes ultimate control and is thus inherently illiberal and naturally Procrustean. Democratic prejudice obscures these facts.

This chapter is shorter because anarchy is simply interpersonal liberty and private property at their most consistent and because there is little serious philosophical criticism of anarchy to deal with. Basic conceptual confusion and mere prejudice are more the real problems. The social scientific literature is considerable, of course, but largely outside the scope of this book. First, I clarify various key matters about which there is popular misunderstanding. Then I consider some typical pro-state views of an influential 'modern liberal' philosopher, John Rawls. Consistent with the non-advocatory nature of the compatibility thesis, any mention of morals is intended merely to argue that anarchy is more compatible with some assumed example than is the state.

5.1. The State, Law, and Market-Anarchy[223]

I take 'pluralism' simply to be about different ways of life existing or being tolerated, rather than seeing plurality as an end in
itself – possibly to be promoted at the expense of liberty and welfare. To see how market-anarchy might be better than the state
in the enhancement of liberty, welfare, and pluralism, we need
to clarify in slightly more detail the natures of, and the links
among, a few other basic things about which there is considerable popular confusion: the state, law, anarchy, and the market.
My arguments are, as usual, primarily but not exclusively philosophical.

States clearly do not have the explicit consent of, or explicit
contracts with, their subjects. Locke's view is that we tacitly
consent to the state by not leaving its territory. He might as well
have said that we tacitly consent to accept gangsters, murderers,
or rapists by choosing to remain in a town they are known to occupy. As Hume argued in reply to Locke, there are ties of culture
and habit that make it undesirable to leave (not that there are
yet anarchic alternatives, anyway). Even on the assumption that
anarchy would be chaotic, and worse than the state, that still
cannot turn into tacit consent or contract merely remaining
within the territory of some state. There has to be agreement in
some form on both sides. This is clearly absent with the anarchist and at best hypothetical with the statist: if faced with a
genuine contract that included giving up their individual sovereignty, how many people would really sign? Only real consent or
contract are consistent with liberty, and that does not exist with
the state. The state is an organization that coercively imposes[224]
ultimate control over persons and property.[225]

It might in practise be unavoidable that the state's coercive
imposition requires the majority's opinion that this is necessary
(as famously argued by Hume [1741–42] and La Boétie [1577]);
but that is a contingent point, and it does not make the coercive
imposition somehow libertarian. The more powerful the state, in
terms of monopolizing superior arms and so on, the less popular
support it requires. We can conceive of a very powerful state
that simply does whatever it wishes and against which a popular

uprising would be a practical impossibility; we would still call it a 'state' (and some states must approach this extreme, perhaps in pre-industrial regions where the states buy foreign weaponry). The fact that the majority is often positively enthusiastic to have a state only disguises the illiberal coercion for people who think that democracy is somehow inherently liberal. I have said enough about democracy's inherently *illiberal* nature for my current purposes (3.6.d).

A state must *rule* (impose its control) to be a state, but it need provide no written law. Laws are enforced social rules. They can exist without the state's encoding them or doing the enforcing. In fact, there are powerful arguments that state legislation is, at least often, an anti-social interference with the spontaneously occurring systems of law that protect persons, property, and contracts.[226] Briefly, social interactions often have the game theoretical structure of iterated prisoner's dilemmas (Axelrod 1984). This means that people learn that it generally pays to respect persons, property, and contracts in order to continue successful interactions with others. Policing and adjudication of disputes also evolve without state interference. Private businesses compete to provide these valuable services. As Molinari [1849] observed, there is no reason to think that these services escape the general principles of economics. The market will provide such 'law and order' when that is what the overwhelming majority demand (that is, assuming a generally libertarian culture – or we should have something else, as we do now). By contrast, a state is bound to replace this competitive efficiency with illiberal pandering to special interests of one kind or another at the expense of general welfare (thanks to concentrated benefits to the special interests at the expense of widely dispersed imposed costs). But even without this incentive problem, the economic calculation argument (2.6) shows that it would be quite impossible for the state to determine what is efficient.

Even a so-called monopoly (really, dominantly successful) private protection agency – in the unlikely event that one should prove economic – would, ipso facto, be paid voluntarily and only to protect persons and (libertarian) property; hence it would not be coercively imposed, nor rule, nor be a state. Of course, libertarianism is logically compatible with very comprehensive control: complete contractual control of many persons and their

property, including vast areas of land.[227] However, a *fully* contractual organization would be quite libertarian and so not a
state at all (at least, not in the relevant sense that statists want
to defend and liberal anarchists to criticize). Apart from that,
though, no non-contractors – *including all future generations* –
would be bound by the controlling organization. So states (by
being coercively imposed) and private agencies (by being libertarian) seem to remain conceptually distinct even in the most
extreme conceivable cases.

To finance its rule, it is logically possible that a state need not
rely on taxation (resources extorted by the state) or on inflating
its, coercively imposed, currency: it could have sufficient voluntary donations. It is also logically possible that a state could tolerate a plurality of ways of life. Empirically, however, states are
both massive consumers of tax-money and always Procrustean
in their rule (relative to anarchy, at least).

'Anarchy' means 'no rule' (by etymology rather than pejorative connotation) in the sense of 'no imposed control of persons
or property by the state'. In a sense, there are 'anarchic holes'
wherever the state does not interfere with voluntary activity,
but only full anarchy *is* anarchy – though minarchy (minimal
statism) might come quite close. In a society where people interact without imposing costs on each other (that is, where liberty
exists), no one can be ruled. Anarchy is thus linked to interpersonal liberty in an analytic way: to the extent that we have liberty, we approach anarchy; to the extent that we lack liberty, we
approach totalitarianism. Anarchy is thus entirely compatible
with law, provided that the law does no more than protect individual liberty. Enforced rules (laws) do not 'rule' (impose control
on) individuals if the rules are libertarian: libertarian rules
merely stop people from imposing on each other. The conceptual
confusion of thinking that anarchy is incompatible with law as
such, rather than with state rule, often causes people to dismiss
anarchy without giving it proper consideration.[228] This crucial
error is not merely common, it is almost universal.

The market is inherently anarchic (Karl Marx criticized it for
being so): to the extent that a market is intentionally directed, it
ceases to be a market. Anarchy is possible without the market
(anarcho-communism), but only in very small, primitive societies
(as we saw in the economic calculation argument, 2.6). Market-

anarchy is naturally highly pluralist: with all the material advantages of the market and no illiberal restrictions, diverse ways of life flourish. 'The market' has become almost a term of abuse for some statists, but the expression is only another way of referring to voluntary exchange. The only liberal alternative to voluntary exchange is charity. The anti-marketeer is not usually advocating charity. The illiberal alternatives include, in the property sphere: fraud, theft, robbery, extortion, and vandalism; in the personal sphere: deceit, assault, rape, slavery, and murder. To the extent that one objects to the market, one must effectively be advocating one of these (or something similar) though probably under some statist euphemism: taxation, conscription, war, eminent domain, paternalism, egalitarianism, … .

The advocate of market-anarchy is not a Utopian in the sense that he believes it to be 'the perfect moral order'.[229] To be sure, the degree of market-created income certainly indicates the degree of public service as a good rule of thumb.[230] And all state-funded work that the market or charity would not support, if allowed, is thereby prima facie destructive of liberty and welfare. But libertarians certainly do not need to think that income is the only indicator of what is valuable. If everyone were guided by short-term profit-maximization then there would probably be entertainment, technology, and prudence but there would hardly be art, science, and philosophy; and the best of these latter may eventually give more service over the generations. The world would surely be a poorer place without these pursuits. However, the labor of individuals and the wealth they produce in the market are more efficiently used when voluntarily given to the promotion of these things as they are perceived by the givers to be valuable. Market-anarchy is the least bad framework in which to cultivate them.

I generally agree with Murray Rothbard's and David Friedman's *economic* arguments on the superiority and stability of anarchic 'law and order'.[231] I shall not rehearse the details of those economic arguments but merely urge people to read them.[232] Nor shall I tackle any rejections of full free-market anarchy – such as at the end of David Miller's book on anarchism (1984) – as I do not think that they seriously consider the explanations of 'public goods'[233] and of law and order to be found in the libertarian economic literature. I will, however, add a final brief word on nationalism. Miller argues that this is one of the

biggest obstacles to anarchy. I feel that many people will agree
partly due to presuppositional and conceptual errors which,
therefore, it is part of philosophy to tackle.

Nationalism, as Miller uses the word, is the ideology that a
society or culture needs its own state. Miller cites nationalism as
a powerful ideology of identity that is opposed to anarchy. In
this ideological sense, I am bound to agree with him. That does
not stop me from thinking such nationalism is a state-
propaganda tool that will eventually be replaced by two things: a
depoliticized affection for one's perceived geographical home and
culture (one can even now, after all, be a proud Yorkshireman,
Scotsman, and so forth, without wanting a separate state), and a
moral affirmation of liberty (which politics will correctly be seen
as destroying – along with destroying welfare, of course). As an
anarchist, I therefore have no ideological nationality. To think
that everyone must have some such nationality is rather like
thinking that everyone must have some religion – as would also
have been normal at one time. My situation can be contrasted
with the more familiar idea of some ideological nationalists
(Scottish and Welsh, for instance) who have not attained a separate state. When I call myself 'English', then, I mean only by ge-
ography and culture. On forms requesting my so-called nationality, I sometimes replace this state-propaganda term with 'state
subjection'; for I cannot deny that I am a de facto subject of the
declining, once relatively liberal, British state (and a de jure
subject of the infant, relatively authoritarian, European super-
state).

What I wish to focus on now are some real examples of the
mere unthinking dismissal of, or prejudice against, the market-
anarchist route to liberty, welfare, and pluralism. I tackle some
writings of only one erudite political philosopher, John Rawls. I
choose these for several reasons: the topics are precisely relevant; the presuppositions are fairly typical; the arguments often
fit anarchy better than 'liberal democracy' (rather like Popper's,
3.6.d); and Rawls's writings are highly influential.

5.2. The Prejudice against Anarchy

In some writings by John Rawls that are intended to clarify his
position in *A Theory of Justice* (1971), we can see his presupposi-

tions against anarchism brought out clearly. First, we look at 'Justice as Fairness: Political not Metaphysical' (1985).

In this article Rawls is looking for 'the public conception of justice' (a moral system of basic social rules) that supports constitutional democracy. To be more clear and robust, these rules are to be 'independent of controversial philosophical and religious doctrines' (223). Even if we grant that Rawls can achieve this goal, it is clear that he has side-stepped the clash with some political possibilities by simply refusing to consider anything outside some form of constitutional democracy. If there are no proper arguments against alternatives, and he is trying only to preach a clearer understanding of constitutional democracy to the converted (as he also did in his *A Theory of Justice*), then why should I criticize his writings? Because Rawls muddies the waters, albeit unintentionally, on the natures of such things as liberalism, liberty, democracy, society, and justice in ways that are quite typical and that help to sustain popular views against anarchy.

In a key example, Rawls writes of

> a conflict within the tradition of democratic thought itself, between the tradition associated with Locke, which gives greater weight to what Constant called the 'liberties of the moderns', freedom of thought and conscience, certain basic rights of the person and of property, and the rule of law, and the tradition associated with Rousseau which gives greater weight to what Constant called the 'liberties of the ancients', the equal political liberties and the values of public life ... . Justice as fairness tries to adjudicate between these traditions ... . (227)

The 'liberties of the moderns', as listed, do seem to refer to people being free from interference by others (with the possible exception of the rule of law, which is compatible with Draconian state interference provided that it is impartially applied). The 'liberties of the ancients', by contrast, seem to be not liberty at all but the right to have a hand in interfering with the liberty of others; for politics always entails ruling (imposing control on) people. As we saw in the reply to Popper (3.6.d), democracy is a political process that interferes with liberty. It is highly confusing to place liberty within a tradition with which it must be at odds. Rawls's 'justice as fairness' must be more about striking a balance *between* individual liberty and democracy rather than about adjudicating competing claims 'within' democracy, as he states.

Though perhaps intending only to distinguish one society from another, Rawls in fact drops into holistic views of society and justice without argument. He tells us that a society is 'a more or less complete and self-sufficient scheme of cooperation' and that a sense of justice is 'the capacity to understand, to apply, and to act from the public conception of justice which characterizes the fair terms of social cooperation' (233). Contra Rawls, a society is not a 'scheme' in the sense that it is an intentional arrangement or single plan. One of Adam Ferguson's most important ideas is that what might look like a designed order is often really a spontaneous order: a pattern that has arisen anarchically.[234] To the extent that we try to impose a plan on such things, the result is often chaos. A society is more like the *anarchic pattern* of cooperation in some geographical area. To view this anarchic pattern as a 'scheme' might tempt one, as Rawls is tempted, to feel that one can be justified in imposing a 'better' scheme – despite the real schemes, or plans, of the millions of individuals that this must override. The same holism is assumed in defining a sense of justice as something that must be derived from the public conception. There is no agent who is the public, nor are there sets of reasons which *everyone* accepts; there are only individuals with their own views on the matter. Perhaps Rawls is referring to the majority, but it is far from clear why the majority's view must be regarded as the correct view of justice. 'Fair terms of social cooperation' is also an expression that seems designed to lump together what are really quite distinct acts of cooperation, in a similar way to Ryan's expression 'proceeds of social collaboration' (4.6.c).

We are told that one of the clearest differences among political conceptions of justice is between those that 'allow for a plurality of opposing and even incommensurable conceptions of the good and those that hold that there is but one conception of the good' (248). Plato, Aristotle, Augustine, Aquinas, and classical utilitarianism are said to be in the singular category. Liberalism is in the plural category. This is supposed to be because in liberalism the conception of justice is 'independent from and prior to the conception of goodness in the sense that its principles limit the conceptions of the good which are permissible' (249). Can a theory of 'justice' (by which Rawls means a moral system of basic social rules) ever be entirely independent of a theory of the good? No: these basic rules must themselves be thought good, or they would not be advocated. The real difference here is that they can be limited, if deontological, while (teleological) classical utilitarianism, and so on, are fairly comprehensive. *All* systems of such justice set 'good' limits on the conceptions of the 'good' but also allow *some* leeway for individual choice. With liberalism you must observe liberty because it is good, and otherwise you can pursue whatever you personally regard as good. Now, constitutional democracy might allow for more diversity (but only if the constitution sufficiently limits the democracy) than, say, most religions – but this is a contingent difference and a matter of degree: within most religions many kinds of lifestyle are possible as long as they do not flout the religion; within a constitutional democracy many kinds of lifestyle are possible as long as they do not flout constitutional democracy. Flouting democracy, however, is just what anarcho-libertarians want to do – because they believe that private-property anarchy would be more liberal and pluralist.

Rawls seems to presuppose that it is self-evident that there would be maximal toleration of different lifestyles under some form of constitutional democracy. He is overlooking the anarchist argument that the state is a cause of strife because it creates the conditions for predation by a host of special interests; that constitutional democracy is a way of setting people against one another in a negative-sum game. Intolerance of liberty and diversity, and the destruction of welfare, are the effects of this system. Pluralism could better be achieved by simply allowing everyone to do what he wishes as long as he does not impose on the persons or property of others. This anarchist possibility is not merely left entirely unconsidered but is positively obscured by Rawls's accounts of the relevant concepts.

In his article 'The Idea of an Overlapping Consensus' (1987), Rawls combines a tacit dismissal of anarchy – among other possibilities – with claiming for democracy several of the moral and social ideas that are more compatible with defending anarchy.

Rawls thinks that within a constitutional democracy a 'political conception of justice' that rests on self-interest or group-interest would be a mere modus vivendi and hence unstable.

Stability comes with a democratic system where there is 'the support of an overlapping consensus' (1987, 1). A liberal anarchist can happily agree that a conception of basic social rules will not be as stable if it is based on pure self- or group-interest. There is nothing about this idea that is peculiar to democracy rather than to any other basic rules of social interaction, whether another kind of archy or even anarchy. Both extreme authoritarian regimes and extreme voluntaristic societies will tend to persist only in so far as the general populace feels approval of them and loyalty towards them (that is, there is an 'overlapping consensus'). While authoritarianism obviously limits the pluralism that Rawls feels is desirable, it is still not clear how constitutional democracy could defend this pluralism better than anarchy. Rawls writes of having clear aims and limits to a constitution, as though this is some guarantee of their being respected. But the very constitutional mechanism can give interest groups a powerful way to infiltrate and lobby to subvert liberties that would have been more stable left to unregulated, anarchic support.

The liberalisms of Kant and Mill, and 'many liberalisms' besides, are rejected because their doctrines are 'not generally, or perhaps even widely, shared in a democratic society' (6). They are held to be too comprehensive to be practical for Rawls's purpose. What is needed is 'implicitly shared fundamental ideas and principles' (6). He recognizes that it might not be possible to avoid comprehensive doctrines entirely but sees the crucial question as 'what is the least that must be asserted; and if it must be asserted what is its least controversial form?' (8). The 'fact of pluralism', we are told, makes an answer necessary if we are to reach a consensus. Here Rawls is not merely rejecting 'many liberalisms' that do not fit his purposes, he is rejecting *full* liberalism because he sees it as conflicting with his other ideals – including that of democracy. From the anarchist point of view, Rawls is really wanting to limit pluralism with his own relatively comprehensive view of how society should be organized. Pluralism does indeed make it desirable that we reach a consensus on liberal social rules, but the anarchist answer to Rawls's question about the least that must be asserted – and in its least controversial form – must be 'Live and let live', that is, 'You let me live without interference and I shall not interfere with you'. This would seem to be far more pluralist than Rawls's implicit answer, which to the anarchist looks rather like 'Rule and let rule', that is, 'Let us share in the rule of everyone' – a Rousseauian travesty of interpersonal liberty. Of course, most people do currently see democracy as desirable and so, strictly speaking, 'Live and let live' is controversial; but this is because people do not see that democracy is the enemy of liberty and welfare. Were Rawls to see this, he would surely agree that we should not pander to the prevailing conception of justice but, instead, argue for the anarchic liberalism that is a better option.

Rawls deals with the criticism that an overlapping consensus is itself a mere modus vivendi. He thinks that with an overlapping consensus 'the political conception of justice, is itself a moral conception' (11). Only where people are prepared to support the system despite changes in the balance of power is stability caused by an overlapping consensus rather than a mere modus vivendi. However, this would apply equally – mutatis mutandis – to an anarchic society: only where people are prepared to continue to give support to private-property anarchy despite changes in their fortunes is stability caused by an overlapping consensus rather than a mere modus vivendi. Surely it is possible for people morally to affirm voluntary association at least as sincerely as state aggression. What is more, the very existence of a democratic system constantly tempts and makes possible political actions at the imposed expense of others, which must itself partly undermine any consensus.

The 'method of avoidance' (12) is Rawls's expression for attempting to come up with a view that is maximally acceptable to all citizens from 'religious, philosophical or moral' points of view. He thinks of 'basic rights and liberties as taking certain questions off the political agenda' (14) because, 'faced with the fact of pluralism, a liberal view removes from the political agenda the most divisive issues' (17). Rawls is analytically bound to be doing the exact opposite of what he asserts here. Politics is about what states do. To use the state to enforce certain so-called 'basic rights and liberties', come what may, is not to take them 'off the political agenda', but precisely to politicize them permanently. Rawls is really trying to rule other social systems out of (the state) court. One of the systems is anarchy with its greater toleration of pluralism, the very thing he maintains that he wants to preserve.

We are told that eventually citizens may not be able fully to explain their agreement with each other because 'they view the political conception as itself normally sufficient and may not expect, or think they need, greater political understanding than that' (16). Again, this is just what an anarchist would expect to happen. Initially, people would need to be persuaded by relatively complicated arguments to see that anarchy gives them more liberty and welfare while also – which is an additional matter – being more moral. Eventually, people would be likely to become more tolerant of all voluntary activities (in both the personal and the property spheres) and simply feel that it is 'obvious' that it is a bad idea to interfere with them. Such habitual toleration is a vain hope in any political system: politics necessarily entails the initiation of impositions by a coercively imposed ultimate power, and this naturally provokes privilege, parasitism, persecution, and Procrusteanism – instead of the mutually beneficial co-operation that private-property anarchy ensures.

Rawls is altogether representative of so-called liberals (in the modern sense). None of them takes liberty (in the sense of not being imposed on by others) seriously and so cannot see its compatibility with welfare and anarchy. They are more interested in defending inherently political 'liberties' or 'rights'. But 'liberties' and 'rights' that are inconsistent with liberty have pernicious unintended consequences. They set up perverse incentives and moral hazards to such a degree that they undermine the very things they are supposed to be defending or promoting. To the extent that the state guarantees or regulates things, those things tend to be damaged or destroyed (at least, relative to what anything nearer anarchy would produce). This applies to pluralism, law, money, healthcare, housing, pensions, education, roads, the arts, the environment, ... you name it.[235]

Thanks to the intellectual resurgence of private-property ideas in recent years, state growth has been generally slowing (and has even shrunk in some areas). We may yet see genuine movement towards private-property anarchy, with the greater liberty and welfare it allows. In terms of the public debate, I see general progress worldwide. The role of the libertarian philosopher in all this must be to correct the erroneous conceptions, arguments, and presuppositions that impede this progress. I hope that this book has made some contribution to that end.

Notes

1 Introduction

1 I generally use 'liberal' in the broadest classical sense throughout (which includes modern libertarians but excludes statist, so-called, liberals), unless the context clearly indicates otherwise.

2 In a sense that includes, without going into more precise categories, such writers as Hugo Grotius, Samuel Pufendorf, John Overton, John Locke, David Hume, Adam Smith, Adam Ferguson, Baron de Montesquieu, Marquis de Condorcet, James Mill, John Stuart Mill, Richard Cobden, John Bright, Herbert Spencer, Benjamin Constant, Alexis de Tocqueville, Wilhelm von Humbolt, Ludwig von Mises, and F. A. Hayek (this list could be much longer, and it omits many with at least as good classical liberal credentials).

3 Robert Nozick (at least as found in his 1974) is the most widely known libertarian. The free-market anarchist writings of Murray Rothbard and David Friedman are becoming better known. See also the libertarian philosophical writings of John Hospers, Tibor Machan, Jan Narveson, and Hillel Steiner.

4 For instance, many in what are sometimes known as the Chicago School (such as Milton Friedman, George Stigler, Ronald Coase, and Gary Becker), the Virginia School (such as James Buchanan and Gordon Tullock), and the Austrian School (such as F. A. Hayek, Ludwig von Mises, and Israel Kirzner). Hayek, Buchanan, and all those listed as Chicago School economists, have won Nobel Prizes for Economic Science.

5 I shall not discuss how far this is true in individual cases. For expositions and discussions that include this issue, see Barry, N. 1986.

6 I use 'non-moral' because of the somewhat pejorative connotations of 'amoral'.

7 Many of Karl Popper's epistemological writings argue for the importance of problem specialization instead.

8 As John Zvesper observes, 'This division between utilitarians and deontologists makes contemporary liberal theory less able to rise to the radical challenge than was the older, Lockeian liberalism, which at least provided a united front by combining utilitarian and rights-based arguments' ('Liberalism' in Miller 1987, 289). We focus here on the objective compatibility of utility and liberty rather than their moral aspects.

9 Popper does allow that it can be proper to clarify one's concepts: 'Two fundamental concepts that I have used here require a brief elucidation: the concept of truth and the concept of explanation' (1992, 76).

10 Most people certainly want to limit liberty in the sense used here, but such is the positive connotation of 'liberty' that people will often not admit to wanting to limit it; instead they define it to include their welfare goal.

11 I adapt this example from W. V. O. Quine's essay 'Two Dogmas of Empiricism' (1980, 21).

12 This is analogous with mere thought-experiment attacks on the compatibility of liberty and welfare.

13 Strictly speaking, I follow Bartley 1984 in accepting *pan*critical rationalism, which denies the need for a dogmatic attachment, or commitment, even to criticism. To avoid making the expression even longer and getting into a separate debate, and as Popper eventually came round to accepting Bartley's position without changing his terms (Bartley 1984, 105), I shall stick with 'critical rationalist'.

14 I have always thought that truth-content makes good intuitive sense (that two theories can be false but one be nearer the truth; that is, a more accurate description) even though it is not possible to characterize this formally (see Popper 1979, Appendix 2).

15 As Bartley replied to John Post, 'To demand for every putatively criticizable statement a specification or presentation of a potential criticizer is in effect *to demand a justification of the claim that the statement is criticizable and so to refuse to hold that claim hypothetically* (which is to say critically)' (1984, 235).

16 Things might seem this way in the development of the implications of observing liberty in the 'state of nature', but drawing out the implications of an idea is more like an attempt to test it than to justify it.

17 'Thus the dialectic of criticism, unlike the monologue of justification, is not committed to the endless iteration of the same point.' (Miller 1994, 69.)

18 No doubt I have done so, if only by the tone of some arguments, but I hope that such slips do not undermine the overall approach.

19 See Popper's Addendum I 'Facts, Standards, and Truth: a Further Criticism of Relativism' (1977, 2: 369–96).

20 Liberty cannot be an ultimate value, because not all things have to aim at it even indirectly. Within this social rule I am a value pluralist.

2. Rationality

21 The a priori/a posteriori distinction (that we know some things *independently of/not independently of* experience) is a matter of philosophical controversy. It has been challenged, for instance, by Lakatos (1976) and Quine (1980, 21ff). Bartley (1990, 240) completely agrees with Lakatos in rejecting the distinction. However, I see no convincing reason for not entertaining the distinction conjecturally and critically, as Bartley himself does with 'necessary truths' (239): we are entitled to conjecture that we know a priori that agents

are rational, in the sense to be defined, given that we cannot think of any logical argument or empirical evidence that would refute the thesis but concede that this could just be our failure of imagination (arguments and evidence will be examined). In any case, it seems wise to stick to this distinction as used by Mises, Kirzner, and Rothbard until there are better arguments that it must be abandoned.

There are complicated arguments on the relationships among the three pairs of concepts: a priori/a posteriori, necessary/contingent, and analytic/synthetic. I have ignored these as being distractions and used the terms in philosophically standard ways.

22 For brief but sophisticated accounts of Austrian apriorism generally, see Smith, B. 1986 and 1990.

23 In McKenzie and Tullock 1978, the authors quote Mises in the introduction to the second chapter, but their conception of rationality is not fully comprehensive and a priori, as they explicitly concede (30).

24 For a general criticism and defense of Austrianism see, respectively, Nozick 1977 and Block 1980.

25 There will be no discussion here of what is called 'Rational choice theory' . That is to do with what supposedly objectively maximises utility, in some sense, and so is not directly inconsistent with the subjective theory that follows (though I disagree with much that appears under the name of that theory).

26 In a broader sense of 'interest', something can be in one's interests without one's desiring it. We are ignoring that welfare possibility in this chapter. In the chapter on welfare it is argued that such interests must relate to a real felt interest at some point, and that it is more welfare-efficient in practice to allow people to make errors than impose one's perceptions of their interests.

27 Preference *autonomy* is a separate issue that is raised in 4.5.b.

28 If it is not true that firms tend to maximize their profits ultimately because in some way that tends to maximize the want-satisfaction of the stockholders involved, then the assumption that firms do throws doubt on any economic conclusions that are supposed to follow (though firms might need to approximate a profit-maximizing strategy if they are to survive at all).

29 For a useful account of the debate between Kirzner and Becker on this issue, and what is at stake, see Lagueux 1991.

30 Economic analysis has been very usefully extended to study the efficient allocation of scarce resources in other animals and even plants (see McKenzie and Tullock 1981 and more recent developments of these ideas).

31 I write 'despite' because once the physical world is held to be as certain, or uncertain, as consciousness then the idea of a distinct mental substance losses much plausibility.

32 For a philosophical defense of this see Flew 1987, ch.s 7–8.

33 No important distinction need be made between these, as what we value we desire, and vice versa, in some sense (this will be argued in more detail later); and the common contrast between interests and desires can be seen as

really between the long term and short term or between being informed and uninformed (more on this in the welfare chapter).

34   Though I also write of 'addicts' and 'addiction' at several places in this book, I do not intend to imply anything pejorative by this. It is not absurd to assert that a good life often contains a multitude of enjoyable 'addictions' (physiological and psychological, innate and acquired).

35   I think that acting while 'not being forced by another' is the ordinary sense of free will and that it is unconvincing to deviate from the ordinary, without adequate explanation, to create paradoxes. I have in mind such common usages (which should be unambiguous even if used in a court of law) as, 'no one forced you to do it; you did it of your own free will.'

36   However, even a person who has an effective desire electrically stimulated in him by another must, strictly speaking, still be an *agent* when acting on the implanted desire, because his will (albeit externally stimulated) is what brings about his behavior. To the extent that another agent can interfere with his will in this way, this only stops him from being a free or *autonomous* agent (in the sense that the effective desire is not physically generated within one self).

37   This 'compatibilist' thesis is quite different from – and not presupposed by – the compatibility thesis that this book defends. But it is worth mentioning if only for those people who do think that determinism is true and that it rules out free will in a way that makes rational state-controls prima facie more likely to improve on merely arbitrary natural influences (some cases arise later in this chapter and in the welfare chapter).

38   I do not accuse Frankfurt of this; I agree that his 'conception of the freedom of the will appears to be neutral with regard to the problem of determinism.' ([1971] 1982, 95)

39   This is not an unusual position. Antony Flew, for example, has a similar view of free will in his 1978 and 1993a.

40   What if Frankfurt's position is modified so that one is only unfree if one cannot change desires one actually wants to change? Such unfreedom would be undesirable, but I would see this as a limitation on one's tastes rather than one's will.

41   For the more general purpose in this book of reconciling liberty and welfare, it should to be noted that the strength of drug addiction that is here being supposed by Frankfurt is apparently imaginary. Even if we take a drug as addictive as heroin and look at the severest case we find the following admission in a Department of Social Security information booklet: 'After several weeks on high doses sudden withdrawal results in a variable degree of discomfort generally comparable to a bout of influenza' (DSS 1985). Giving up narcotics seems to be made difficult more by the user's circle of friends and daily habits than by the physically addictive quality of the drugs themselves.

42   For a discussion of the extent to which such changes are really desirable, even if possible, see Luper 1996.

43 By 'unitary conscious self' I mean a self that is aware of conflicting desires, of whatever origin. I am merely ruling out such examples of split-consciousness as can occur when the mid-brain is cut or 'subconscious' desires exist, if they really can. Those who accept weakness of will do not usually use these as explanations.

44 As with Frankfurt, 'will' is defined as 'effective desire'.

45 The literature is vast. A good place to start looking might be at a libertarian website (see the Afterword).

46 Perhaps both Watson and Frankfurt need an account of *objective* values, but neither provides one and so I cannot criticize them.

47 For example, Hayek [1979] 1982, 3:166.

48 This is well known as a standard theme of Karl Popper's epistemology, for instance in his [1963] and [1972]. Though as David McDonagh has observed 'ideas do not die ... constructive criticism is a pleonasm' (personal communication).

49 For instance, Hayek 1948, 26.

50 See the writings of the psychiatrist Thomas Szasz for some of the most informative and damning criticisms of the psychiatric profession.

51 Though some of the best economists of their time did not make this assumption: Hume, Smith, Marshall, and Wicksteed.

52 As a consequence of such economic work, this professor of economics at Chicago has also been made a professor of sociology.

53 Becker goes on to give an economic analysis of altruism. He argues that it increases genetic reproduction in various ways, and hence it is really a sort of genetic egoism.

54 Alasdair MacIntyre expresses these two views thus: 'philosophers have oscillated between these two positions: the Hobbesian doctrine of altruism as either a disguise or a substitute for self-seeking and the assertion of an original spring of altruistic benevolence as an ultimate and unexplained property of human nature.' (MacIntyre 1967)

55 Hare cites Kant in his support, and I think that he therefore fails to see that Kant's moral system lacks a clear emotional motive. Like Kant, he thinks morals are decided rather than felt (for example, Hare ([1952] 1986), 44 and 54).

56 In Butlerian *terminology*, however, only actions done out of self-love, the desire for one's own happiness, are sensibly called 'interested'; actions done for any other motives are 'disinterested'.

57 For example, Singer 1983, especially chapter six.

58 This is contra the many moral philosophers who hold this view (such as J. L. Mackie (1979) and Hare [1952]), which seems to be imposing unnecessary content on the form of moralizing.

59 It might even be only himself that is valued morally, perhaps because he feels that all people should neglect others (moral egoism), or because he feels that he has qualities that simply happen to put him above others, but he

would respect anyone who came to have these qualities. Both of these are still being formally impartial.

60 One can also have *objective* commitments, such as contractual obligations, but Sen does not mean these. One need not be subjectively committed to one's objective commitments.

61 As Ray Percival observed on reading this, the melting and freezing examples are in a sense explained by the same factor, temperature, but going in different directions.

62 It seems that there have been natural science measurements which were only ordinal, such as the hardness of substances (now used only in geology, I am told). But there must always have been degrees of hardness (an ontological issue), whether or not we could accurately or usefully measure them in units (an empirical issue).

63 The idea in Simon, H. 1955 that we can settle for what is good enough ('satisficing' instead of maximizing), seems to overlook search costs: at some point we guess that the disutility of these is likely to outweigh any other utility that we will achieve. That is still maximizing as best we can.

64 For example, Hare ([1963] 1972). Hare denies that we *always* do what we think is moral: we sometimes suffer 'moral weakness'. He claims consistency on the basis that the moral view is genuinely held but we are 'psychologically' weak. He says very little to explain what this means except that 'this is clearest in the case of compulsive neuroses in which "psychological" impossibility comes close to "physical" ... ' (82).

65 In the welfare chapter, preference utilitarianism is defended (hypothetically: to argue that it entails libertarianism in practice) only as a welfare theory and not as a moral theory.

66 Steele 1992 is an excellent place to start: this must be the definitive account of the nature and significance of the economic calculation argument and the numerous failed attempts to answer it.

67 One such example is David Ramsay Steele (see previous note).

3. Liberty

68 '*Contingently* deontological' here means not allowing that X be done in an *attempt* to prevent more examples of X's being done – because the attempt will usually fail. In this book consequentialism is accepted in principle, at least for the sake of argument. So this is a form of rule consequentialism. This view thus differs from Nozick's conception of a 'side-constraint', which is inherently anti-consequentialist (Nozick 1974, 30); see 3.5.c.

69 A version of 3.1, 3.2, and 3.4.a first appeared as Lester 1997a.

70 Obviously, such prevention and redress do not themselves *initiate* constraining, interfering, or imposing.

71 As found, for instance, in the works cited in the bibliography by David Friedman, John Hospers, Tibor Machan, Jan Narveson, Robert Nozick, and Murray Rothbard.

72 Since coming up with this simple but comprehensive formulation of interpersonal liberty in 1989, I found that David Gauthier (1986) uses the idea of not imposing costs, though less consistently, in an attempt to derive morality contractually. He would also, unwittingly, be deriving the objective libertarian solutions to problems – which he thinks will clash with welfare-maximization (104–5) – but for certain key differences. It seems relevant to mention a few of these differences and then briefly comment (in brackets), though his *general* contractual-morals thesis is not strictly inconsistent with my non-contractual, non-moral use of 'not imposing costs' (which can only be elaborated during the chapter).

In a state of nature, Gauthier supposes, imposed costs do not require rectification unless social interaction takes place (207–12) (rectification follows from merely observing 'liberty', as used here). He takes perfect competition (for example, 97) to be a realistic criterion of market efficiency (contra many pro-market economists, but especially Austrians) that the state can correct for without imposing costs (as though taxation need not impose on people). He uses fantasy-world possibilities (for example, 263) – what things *might* have been like in a so-called 'fair' social situation – to decide what *actually* counts as imposing costs in this world (as though one can positively impose on others merely by enjoying one's good fortune). Not least, Gauthier elaborates a complicated theory of constrained maximization (but, as Axelrod 1984 shows, iterated Prisoner's dilemmas mean that this is quite unnecessary: such 'morals' are not needed for co-operation when we know that there will be repeated interactions with identifiable others).

73 The formula is certainly not intended or obliged to be a defense of libertarianism as an ideology, as Will Kymlicka suggests (personal communication), though I can see how one could also use the formula in that way.

74 For problems with equal liberty in Spencer, Steiner, and Hart see Gray, T. 1993.

75 'License' is here understood as roughly the opposite of 'liberty': imposing a cost on another. I do not see that the liberty/license distinction is inherently moralised. For instance, Roger Scruton's example looks objective enough to me: 'Intuitively the distinction is easy to grasp: it is an infringement of my liberty to prevent me from walking out of my house, but only the removal of licence to prevent me from then abusing, assaulting or murdering my neighbour.' (Scruton 1983, 'Liberty', (ii) Liberty and licence). Modern 'liberalism' would be more accurately called 'licensism' (and 'liberals', 'licensists'): it is not about tolerating liberty but, rather, acts which impose on others.

In any case, given the definition of libertarian liberty that I come up with, any action that does not fit that definition will be, by that definition, a license from a libertarian point of view. This is only like saying that granted the truth of the bible, for the sake of argument, certain things will be 'sins'. That is not to say that there really are sins or that these are what they are.

76 The search for this distinction, with respect to the morality of abortion, put
    me on the path to libertarianism in 1979.

77 An ethical aside: for some of the moral differences between imposing a cost
    and withholding a benefit, see Nesbitt 1995.

78 Readers might notice that this criticism is similar to a well known one used
    against a strict interpretation of Popper's 'negative utilitarianism', which is
    another 'bad'-minimizing theory. See Smart, R. 1958, and Popper ([1945]
    1997) 1, ch 5 n6 (2), 235, and ch 9 n2, 284–5.

79 Voluntary birth control is different because that is merely withholding the
    benefit of life that is within one's own gift.

80 It might more straightforwardly be suggested that all lives are full of im-
    posed costs that outweigh the imposed cost of early murder. But that seems
    more straightforwardly implausible given that people do not usually regret
    having been born even when they have extreme disabilities or live in terrible
    circumstances. To conceive and raise a person who does not regret his birth
    cannot itself be to impose a cost even though he will suffer many imposed
    costs throughout his life. Though if there are cases where great suffering is
    bound to make not being born, on balance, preferable to life, then it seems
    that we do impose a cost on the suffering person by causing his existence. I
    guess that this is very rare.

81 Statists usually hold something like this definition (explicitly or implicitly).
    As they all think they are only in favor of moral constraints, they 'know' a
    priori that they are all in favor of liberty and can ignore libertarian concep-
    tual arguments to the contrary.

82 In reality it might be easy to avoid communicating the disease. In the notori-
    ous case of Typhoid Mary, she was a cook who passed it on (apparently unin-
    tentionally but knowingly) mainly when she prepared cold dishes.

83 Supposing his existence, what about the imposed cost to God? If he is small-
    minded enough to worry and, contra Locke, thinks that genuine piety can be
    coerced, then he is probably big enough to look after himself.

84 On this area more generally, all honest defamation must be liberal, as liber-
    tarians standardly argue. However, dishonest defamation is fraudulent, but
    the fraud is against the people misled and not against the defamed person.
    He merely ceases to receive any benefits that would have come his way be-
    cause of their good opinions. Perhaps the defamed person can take out a lib-
    ertarian class action on others' behalves for the cost to them of the fraud. It
    might be hard to prove dishonesty though.

85 If a speaker intends or should reasonably be able to foresee that his oratory
    is quite likely to cause others to commit crimes, of any unlibertarian kind,
    then that looks like incitement to commit a crime. I guess that does impose
    to a greater or lesser degree, depending on the case. It is one thing to advo-
    cate that someone be sacked (itself quite legitimate); another seriously to ad-
    vocate that he should be shot (if said on television there is always a good
    chance that someone might take this as an 'order' from the person whose
    follower he considers himself to be). Or suppose that I publish the home ad-
    dresses of abortion doctors in the USA without advocating their murder, but

knowing that others might use the information to find and murder them. In the context, this looks like a tacit incitement to murder. Obviously, a great deal more can be said on all this – but no more here.

86 Suppose that at some future time it were to be demonstrated that there is an identifiable group of people who systematically and incorrigibly approach being 'utility monsters' to even a very minor degree. Then we might well wish to opt for different conceptions of liberty and welfare than are defended in this book. But that logical possibility is not a problem for the *practical* compatibility thesis now.

87 For instance Pattanaik 1988 broadens the idea in an explicit attack on libertarian values.

88 Pressler (1987) and Barry, B (1991, chapter four), among others, have fundamentally similar arguments to what follows but more technically expressed and, more to the point, in terms of rights instead of liberty (and Barry also defends various other views inconsistent with the compatibility thesis).

89 There are other philosophical problems with the Pareto criterion (see, for example, Rowley and Peacock 1975) which I will avoid here as the issue turns out really to be about the nature of interpersonal liberty.·

90 Nozick analyses 'coercion' in his paper of that name (1969). There is this loose usage on the first page, where he writes that you 'threaten to get me fired from my job if I do A, and I refrain from doing A because of this threat and am coerced into not doing A'. There is no mention of force here. Other philosophers use coercion to include even such things as moral censure. These are probably better described, following Kant, as 'influence'.

91 Though conventions can arise liberally (such as eating a restaurant meal without explicitly contracting to pay) and it can then become illiberal to flout them (by eating and then not paying).

92 As J. L. Mackie puts it, after some moral argument of his own: 'Of course, to say this is to deal hastily with considerations of kinds that lawyers weigh carefully in concrete particular cases; here and elsewhere moral philosophy appears as a poor relation of law.' (1977, 164). The philosophical application of non-moral formulae in similar areas is hardly different.

93 Even if we assume that persons are Cartesian minds who are contingently attached to particular bodies, it must minimize imposed costs to allow people to control the bodies to which they find themselves attached.

94 This is Locke's proviso (Locke [1690] 1966, 130) of leaving 'enough, and as good' – to which we shall briefly return.

95 In one sense Robert Frank (1985) is right to assert that merely knowing that those around us have greater benefits is usually a cost to us (for example, 113); but in a *voluntary* society this is no more an *imposed* cost than is losing at a game we freely choose to play. Frank fails to make this crucial liberal distinction.

96 There will, no doubt, be some people who are more sympathetic to envy than I am. For them it will take far more than this outline of my view of envy to

convince them otherwise. But as pure envy is rarely explicitly held to be a serious and major libertarian, or even utilitarian, reason for redistribution, I will not go into this subject further here (see 4.5.a).

97 What of less extreme and clear-cut cases? Suppose I just happen to find the best, but not only, spring for miles around. If it really is so superior and others would have found it soon enough anyway, then my *direct* libertarian claim is thus less secure. But we would probably still allow it on the practical libertarian effects of having a prima facie 'finders keepers' rule: of there being some private owner to husband the resource and of avoiding conflict and expense over disputing the possession. Thus we are not obliged to jump out of the frying pan of absolute property rights into the fire of radically indeterminate property rights.

98 This sentence might appear circular, but I have already explained the ideas of 'imposing a cost' and 'acquisition without imposing a cost'. This sentence explains the general sense in which 'seizing acquisitions' can impose a cost. Analogously, to explain a 'prime number' as 'a number divisible by only itself and the number one' is innocuously to presuppose the understanding of 'number' and 'divisibility'.

99 Strictly speaking, insofar as you would have used the same particular raw materials in any way, my use of them would impose on you a very slightly higher search cost for similar raw materials. But, to look ahead, it would clearly impose an immensely greater cost on all to disallow such use and security of possession. The fruits of everyone's labors would be liable to seizure. Efficient economy would not be possible. It clearly minimises imposed costs to avoid this.

100 Once libertarian private property is established, it will be a good rule of thumb that it will be unlibertarian to interfere with it. However, all property rules will impose to some extent and the only thorough test of their overall libertarianism will be what minimises imposed costs. In a somewhat similar way, Newton's view of absolute and Euclidean space will do for many purposes but Einstein's relative and curved space is sometimes needed to be more precise.

101 Economic efficiency is usually contrasted with technical efficiency, understood as goal maximizing irrespective of the relative scarcity of resources.

102 However, one does not impose a cost to the extent that one finds a way of merely preventing others from, or charging others for, enjoying some benefit one causes. And people do impose a cost to the extent that they take some benefit against its producer's wishes. Thus I do not need to mention benefits as well as costs in the libertarian formulae.

103 It might appear that there are similarities here with the Coase theorem (Coase 1960). Roughly, the Coase theorem is that, whatever the initial allocation of resources, free exchange will ensure that they will be employed in their most highly valued uses (as defined by willingness to pay) given zero transaction costs. But I am only allowing the *initial* allocation of resources that minimizes imposed costs. This will not even be *finally* achieved given Coase's assumptions, except by unlikely coincidence.

104 See the section on critical rationalism (1.3) in the introductory chapter.

105 On libertarian restitution and retribution see 3.5.b.

106 This is argument is therefore at odds with Rothbard's libertarian account of promises (1982, 134 ff.) where people rely on promises entirely at their own risk.

107 I have profited here from reading Rothbard 1982 chapter 19, which I recommend despite its rights approach and the criticisms in what follows.

108 To understand Locke's proviso one must see Locke's intention behind the proviso; his 'problem situation' as Popper calls such things. This was that Locke wanted to avoid having any man exercising natural (or automatic) authority or privilege over any other; by which he clearly meant to advocate non-interference or liberty in more or less the libertarian sense. Once one understands Locke's problem situation, one sees that his proviso is only one, somewhat ambiguous, interpretation of one aspect of this. I think that 'avoiding, or at least minimizing, imposed costs' is a way of formulating the same general problem situation as Locke's but expressed more generally and exactly so that it gives more and clearer answers.

109 By contrast, the finders-keepers rule, as defended in Kirzner 1989, is a good libertarian rule of thumb: it will almost always approximate to what minimises imposed costs (but it will have to be overturned in cases where it clearly clashes with this). Minimizing imposed costs is much more clearly related to interpersonal liberty than a finders-keepers rule.

I must also dispute Kirzner's defense of the idea that pure entrepreneurial discovery does not contribute to production (for example, 110). It fits the general picture of production better to interpret entrepreneurial discovery as the *intellectual production* of new economic opportunities. Following Popperian epistemology, these opportunities will be produced by trial and error rather than merely being noticed whenever they occur. Having intellectually produced the opportunity surely provides a better property claim, which is what Kirzner seeks, than supposedly 'costless' (29) discovery – which could be used to argue for redistribution. Even if Kirzner would hold this to be a terminological disagreement, I would say that a bad choice of words can be misleading.

110 If I were to pay ten ducats then I would suffer the whole imposed cost for which we are, ex hypothesi, equally responsible.

111 Nozick (1974, chapter 4) has a roughly similar though much more detailed account but, as always, it is based on moral rights rather than an explicit theory of liberty. One disagreement with his conclusions was mentioned in a part of the 'mob rule' criticism, 3.2.c.i. I only further suggest here (we return to this topic later) that Nozick needs the liberty formula for clarity of libertarian solution and sometimes errs because of the lack of it, as in his calculation of compensation based, instead, on 'the normal situation' (82).

112 There might be the insignificant, and reciprocal, cost that someone else cannot now use just those resources.

113 For completeness, it should be added that abortion must be libertarian even if the foetus were a person, in the intellectual sense, which it is not. Remov-

ing the foetus is really ceasing to continue the uncontracted-for benefit of sustenance rather than imposing the cost of death. Also, as a practical policy, coercively preventing women from having abortions cannot plausibly increase overall welfare. Women will have wanted children instead, or be paid to be surrogate mothers. (The position on abortion and children here is roughly the same as Rothbard 1982, chapter 14, but the argument uses the definition of liberty rather than rights.)

114 People sometimes say that intellectual property is about ownership *in the expression* of ideas rather than the ownership of ideas. As ownership means rights of use and to express an idea is just to use it, I do not see a difference.

115 Dawkins 1976.

116 Such things as maps, mathematical tables, and telephone directories, are more like patents just because very similar things are independently producible.

117 It could even be that acts of donation to the public domain are a nuisance and found to be invalid on libertarian grounds (or at least open to the first person to acquire by use). One cannot donate one's land to the public domain in perpetuity without thereby creating a tragedy of the commons, and the same might be true of *some* intellectual property.

118 However, if others would likely have re-discovered it in time, then we have a patent-like situation and patent rules might then apply.

119 Nozick, for one, outlines a broadly similar account of patents but, as usual, in terms of rights instead of liberty and not explicitly linked with welfare (1974, 182).

120 Or they might not. The wheel was not invented in every civilization.

121 I assume that, with modern world communications, genuinely independent later invention becomes less and less likely.

122 Though if one party wished to sell the use of the invention at a low price, or even donate the invention to the public domain, the other could have no libertarian claim to prevent this.

123 If such agents are plausibly identifiable, then they ought to receive a share of the patent from the supposed time that they would have come up with the idea.

124 Though perhaps the consumers merely miss benefits they could not own rather than have a cost imposed on them.

125 That inventions would eventually enter the public domain does not seem to create the same promotion and revival problem as with copyright. Perhaps this is because of the wider usefulness of general inventions, often followed by eventual complete obsolescence due to further inventions.

126 Rothbard 1962, 652–60; 1977b, 71–5; and 1982, 123–4.

127 This is Hume's example of the problem when he criticises Locke (Hume [1739–40] 1968, 234).

128 Though if we impose a greater cost on them for some reason, they will obviously have the better libertarian claim.

129 By 'public places' I mean private land which the owner voluntarily opens, pro tem, to the general public, perhaps for shopping or recreation. I do not mean state-owned land.

130 Sometimes this will be determined case by case and sometimes by general rules. The problem of interpersonal comparisons has been mentioned (3.2.b) and arises again in the next chapter (4.2). The epistemological problem always exists; it should not be muddled with the fact that we have a clear theoretical answer.

131 What if someone, for whatever fantastic reason, makes an explicit and witting contract with me to be thus imprisoned? This someone would then have bound himself voluntarily and could not be freed against my wishes without lessening interpersonal liberty. Observing interpersonal liberty must usually include the keeping of a contract be it never so onerous (unless other debts, and so on, offset it). Enforcing a contract is always prima facie liberty-maximizing because you impose a cost on me if you try to deny me what you have *already* ceded ownership of, but I impose no cost on you by merely keeping what you freely contractually gave me.

132 A version of this section first appeared as Lester 1999a.

133 Chapter twelve of Rothbard 1973 remains one of the best introductions to this line of argument.

134 I mean 'restitution' in the broad sense that includes compensation, not necessarily putting things back as they were (which might not be possible).

135 I use 'rectification' in only this hypothetical sense (of 'libertarian correction of an infraction of liberty') and not any moral sense.

136 Benson 1996, 77.

137 As Roger Pilon notes (1978, 355 n13).

138 However, detecting the risk and finding the risk-victim might often be too difficult to determine in practice.

139 The view on crime given here differs to varying extents from the accounts that have chiefly inspired it, and perhaps from all of them in that no moral views are used to draw the conclusion. See, for instance, Epstein 1977, Ferrara 1982, Hospers 1977, and Pilon 1978.

140 Let me put it another way: on what libertarian basis could he complain, if we take a similar action against someone to that which he initially imposed on us?

141 Contra Barnett (1980, 150), Hajdin (1987, 85), Kleinberg (1980, 277 n9, and 278), and Miller (1978, 359–60).

142 In the case of torts, by contrast, it is hard to see how one could create the claim that someone could *accidentally* impose on one, as Pilon observes (1978, 354).

143 However, where the attempt stood no reasonable chance of success things are quite different. Attempting to kill someone by sticking pins in his effigy cannot be any serious imposition, except for the highly superstitious. I would not pay a penny to stop such 'attempts' on my life. In such cases we have

really no more than the daydream of the murder of another. Though we might allow proportional 'effigy retribution' (sticking pins into the daydream murderer's effigy or requiring money not to do so) for those who insist on taking such things seriously.

144 Lex talionis is not introduced to avoid the moral hazard of 'buying crime'. There just seems no libertarian reason that a victim of a crime should not have an equivalent claim against the perpetrator.

145 Some might suggest that even calculating such a balance makes this somewhat like a trade, which therefore undermines the proper notion of punishment. But there is no similar balance in trade, where both sides usually gain different amounts. *Because* lex talionis is obviously a form of balance it is unlike a trade. The crime is never made libertarian after all, but some balance with retribution is possible. In any case, even under an illiberally harsh punishment system the criminal can regard the risk and type of punishment as a 'price' in some sense, and respond economically to different such 'prices'. For those set on some crime, even the certainty of such punishment can still be a 'price' they feel worth 'paying'.

146 On a related point, what of the degree of resistance that can libertarianly be offered during the course of a crime? This must not be out of proportion to the apparent imposition. To shoot a shoplifter is clearly to go so far beyond his imposition as to become yourself the criminal. We must give the victim some extra leeway though, for the criminal might otherwise escape too easily and one cannot know how far a criminal might be prepared to go with his impositions. It is his choice that he has put others in that situation. It is therefore libertarian to assume, for instance, that an armed robber might shoot to kill and so to shoot him dead before he tries this (or even to assume the worst with any physical attacker). Not to allow the victim this leeway is to give the criminal an illiberal advantage in all situations, which can only promote crime and thereby be unlibertarian.

147 Pilon has this correct (1978, 356–7) though based on morals rather than a theory of liberty, and without a theory of proportionate libertarian punishment.

148 I write of 'financial restitution' and 'physical retribution' rather than simply 'restitution' and 'retribution' because perhaps libertarian retribution is not fully separable conceptually from restitution but is a part or form of it. For it is surely a form of restitution (though usually imperfect in that the status quo ante was preferable) that the victim comes to own an equally-valued claim to the criminal's person or goods. For the victim who wants this to be given anything less than this claim, is for him to be less adequately compensated for no libertarian reason.

149 This might sound mistaken. Of course the innocent person will *suffer* a great personal cost if he, for instance, receives the death penalty. This would be like flying with an airline when the plane crashes. In both cases someone is dead as a result of a fault in the system he contracted into. The airline does not *impose* a cost, though he *suffers* a cost, by mistakenly killing him (unless it was negligent). Neither does a contractual judicial system *impose* a cost, though he *suffers* a cost, by mistakenly killing him (unless it was negligent).

This might *seem* more like an 'imposed' cost only because in one sense they 'deliberately' kill him, but that description is incompatible with the definition of liberty and the analysis of contracts.

150 If so, this is because of increasing marginal disutility.

151 For example, Kleinberg 1980, 275 and 278–80.

152 See Benson 1990.

153 For the much misunderstood theory and history of more honest and efficient 'free banking' (that is, with private note issue and no state regulation), see the relevant writings of Kevin Dowd, George Selgin, and Larry White.

154 Private prison factories are one way to pay for this (eating being contingent upon working).

155 What if a shop carried a sign outside saying, 'Those who enter contract to be shot if caught shoplifting.'? Entry to the shop would probably not create a contract. A contract has to be at least implicitly agreed to by all concerned parties, and it is not reasonable to suppose that any shoplifter would agree. Neither would it create a contract if someone were allowed to enter a shop with a t-shirt saying, 'Shops which allow me in contract to allow my shoplifting.' However, there is an important asymmetry in that it is the would-be shoplifter who is taking the *action* of entering the shop, and thereby at least prima facie accepting the shop's contract.

156 Rothbard 1977, 263.

157 So-called chaos theory implies that the universe is infinitely complex ('infinite complexity' theory is a more accurate name for it) but determinate. It is of no metaphysical significance that the epistemological problem is thereby greater than hitherto thought.

158 As Hajdin suggests (1987, 81).

159 This could bring down the price of crime insurance considerably; it might even approach being free of charge if the insurance company gets enough whenever a criminal is convicted.

160 What of the moral hazard posed by the possibility of frauds claiming enormous 'restitution'? (Pilon 1978, 351 n4) Here it must be realized that a false accuser will be liable to pay an even greater amount (roughly, the sum fraudulently claimed multiplied by, for instance, ten if there is a ten per cent chance of detection). This makes such fraud a very bad gamble for most people.

161 As held by, for instance, Dagger (1980 and 1993), Kleinberg (1980, 277), and Miller (1978).

162 I initially dismissed the option of passing on all and any policing and security expenses no matter how high they might be. Even though we now have the risk multiplier as a libertarian principle, it might still be thought that we have the problem of how much of the general policing and security costs can be passed on in addition. However, apart from any unforeseen additional expenses which the criminal causes (by violently resisting arrest, say), I suppose that this would be double counting. The ex-ante price that someone

would reasonably be prepared to accept to suffer the risk of some crime will include any policing and security expenses that he actually does pay.

163 What if someone steals only one ducat with a million-to-one chance of capture, but he is then caught? Can it really be libertarian and preference utilitarian to make him pay one million ducats restitution? In a world where such thefts regularly occurred, only such a ratio could be adequate to internalize illiberal externalities. This might not fit our current intuitions as to what is libertarian and preference utilitarian just because such low capture rates are a fantasy. The victim is always at liberty to exercise mercy if he wishes and waive his claim. Other people are also at liberty financially to assist any criminal for whom they feel sympathy. However, they will run a real risk of encouraging crime if they are too soft-hearted.

164 My own use of fantasy examples was only to test whether the libertarian formula is clear, consistent, and comprehensive.

165 Nozick does not seem to extricate himself from the inconsistency charge against absolute libertarian 'side-constraints' (deontological libertarianism). He asserts that absolute 'side constraints upon action reflect the underlying Kantian principle that individuals are ends and not merely means' (Nozick 1974, 30–1). But if we want to respect people as ends *as far as possible* then surely it is logically required that *fewer* are used as means (or, perhaps more precisely, that people are used to a lesser degree overall). This Kantian approach still does not seem to rule out libertarian consequentialism *in principle*.

166 What if someone had from birth been merely socialised (without any use of force or fraud) into contented slavery? I do not see that there ever have been such merely socialised – or even originally coerced – fully contented slaves that needed no threats or lies to stop them taking paid employment at market rates and generally living as they chose. This is a mere fantasy possibility, and so it cannot undermine the practical adequacy of the conception of liberty under discussion.

The general account in the paragraph (to which this is a note) should, mutatis mutandis, be relevant to analogous utilitarian views concerning adapting and manipulating desires (such as Elster 1982).

167 Though any species will need a sufficient intellect to be capable of intellectual autonomy, and maybe there are no others on this planet.

168 Gauthier deals with a similar case (1988, 211 ff.). He accepts that polluters impose a cost on the fisher folk, but thinks that this only violates the Lockean proviso (and so they would have to pay compensation) if they also engage in voluntary interaction with them. Without such interaction he denies that the polluters gain by worsening the condition of the fisher folk, because the imposed cost is incidental. This seems a version of the, dubious, doctrine of double effect: that the foreseeable consequences of some intended action are not themselves culpable if not also somehow intended. I fail to see how not interacting with people can negate their libertarian claim to compensation for any cost one imposes on them.

169 If the fisher folk were new and the industrial activity were traditional then the situation would be more or less reversed. The new fisher folk would have to put up with the smaller catch or, if economic, pay the industry to stop its activity.

170 A fortiori, for a small population of aboriginals to hold a vast area to be a 'sacred wilderness' imposes even more on innumerable would-be migrants who would otherwise develop it and live in it. They could also assert a countervailing 'rational duty' (which it would impose a cost not to respect) to exploit and civilize wildernesses. I guess that the price of 'sacred wilderness' is not so much when the usefulness of money becomes understood by the aboriginals.

171 A version of this section first appeared as Lester 1995.

172 See, for instance, Popper [1963] and [1972].

173 It is this last point about bold conjecture that has been mistaken as a sanction for revolutionary state experimentation. But, as dry logic and bloody history shows, such state experimentation really replaces millions of individual experiments with one Procrustean one.

174 A free science and a free society are different things, of course. I am sure it is possible to come up with some relevant disanalogies as well. I will not attempt to list all these and reply to them. This is partly because one has to stop somewhere, but more important is that I cannot think of any that seriously threaten the general thesis being defended here: full anarchic libertarianism fits Popper's epistemology and scientific method *much better* than liberal democracy does. I do not assert that the fit is perfect in every way.

175 To name but three who have made out general cases that private provision of law and order is not only possible but far superior: Molinari 1977 (a translation of his 1849 essay); Rothbard [1970], [1973]; David Friedman [1973].

176 The publications of the Institute of Economic Affairs (UK) are a good place to start on protectionism.

177 On this point see Robinson 1993, 11 ff. This work is a case study on state energy policy that touches on many of the points in this section. The conclusion is a succinct introduction to the economics of government failure.

178 So-called piecemeal engineering (Popper's expression and suggestion) by the state is simply authoritarian rather than totalitarian. 'Social planning' that is imposed by force has the objectionable character of a revolution even if it is writ small. Only genuinely peaceful persuasion along libertarian lines completely avoids the problems of state planning.

179 Microeconomics is really just economics. Macroeconomics is mainly about unsound arguments for political intervention. One brief discussion of this is area is Simpson 1994.

180 For instance, rent control and minimum wage legislation are policies that are bound to decrease welfare in the long term (though economic controversy on minimum wages has revived; see Lal 1995). Again, Popper often sees such things but fails to see that this is a practical inevitability in a vote-buying liberal democracy.

181 This is despite the fact that Hayek's pro-market views must have had some influence on him. *Conjectures and Refutations* is even dedicated to Hayek.

182 Can the market itself be seen as a sophisticated and fair form of democracy (with money as a store of voting power, which is voted to one by others)? That cannot literally be true as there is no rule in the market, only voluntary co-operation. The consumer is sovereign over only himself and his purchases.

183 For more on politics and pluralism see the final chapter.

184 The absence of a clearly identifiable opposing state seems at least partly why the English state took so long to dominate Ireland and why the USSR ultimately failed in Afghanistan.

185 Popper points out the mistakes of conflating individualism with egoism and collectivism with altruism ([1945] 1977 , 100–6).

186 It seems inappropriate to call it the 'welfare state' when it does little but undermine people's welfare and make them dependent.

187 See especially Patricia Morgan's 1995 and her other contributions to the Health and Welfare Unit of the Institute of Economic Affairs.

188 Though the rising incomes of a market are eventually correlated with having fewer children.

4. Welfare

189 See the first note of the previous chapter.

190 I mean people not receiving what is advertised. I do not mean the anti-market idea that honest advertising creates 'false demand'. For a brief reply to that view see Steele 1992, 303–8.

191 Parfit's preferred Objective List Theory (1984, 499) is really the goals that he subjectively prefers that others have, unless he can show that values can literally be true.

192 For a refutation of the popular error that the market can and ought to be made to approximate to the impossible abstraction of 'perfect competition' see, for instance, Hayek [1979] 1982, vol. 3, ch. 15.

193 For arguments on the importance of status and the role of the market in accommodating status goals, see the first five chapters of Frank 1985. However, I should mention that the subsequent chapters in that work consistently underrate the following, overlapping, areas: 1) the possibilities of real, not hypothetical, contractual constraints on competitive consumption; 2) the real value of the goods to those who would not so contract; 3) how full private property internalizes illiberal externalities, as it would with Frank's problems with free speech (214–15), nudism (218), and pollution (120, 229); 4) the fact that theoretical market-failure is often unintentionally caused or exacerbated by state-failure, for example various 'public good' problems, such as state-benefit levels (244), 'national defense' (245), and state education (192).

Points (3) and (4) are obviously the subjects of a vast empirical literature. Any introduction to the economics of libertarianism should deal with them.

194 Though we need not desire our desires, as with the phenomenon of 'weakness of will', 2.2.c.

195 What are we to say about a person who would suffer a broken leg himself in order to save someone from a scratch (or to inflict a small scratch on him)? He is probably (it depends on whether he cares about how the other person *feels* about the scratch) still making an IUC. He simply gets more utility by changing the other's degree of utility than he does by purely self-referential acts (that is, acts not involving this other). Such things are not unusual with great lovers (or with great haters). Assuming normal supply and demand curves, we would expect the lover, for instance, to 'buy' less utility for his beloved if the price went up to, say, two broken legs to prevent a scratch (and the same, mutatis mutandis, for the hater). Thus the two utilities (though guessed in the case of the other party's) are still compared by the agent.

196 There is an interesting account and defense of analogous 'Rights of the Dead' in Lomasky 1987 (212–21), though 'rights' as such are not relevant here.

197 Past or future generations – even if we allow them to count and assume we could know their views – could not have a general preference utilitarian say in deciding matters today, for people are considerably less concerned about times before and after their own.

198 By 'brainwashing' I mean somehow forcing, not merely suggesting, ideas or desires directly into the brain of another. I am sceptical about the possibility in reality.

199 If it really could be preference utilitarian to persecute minorities, then I would have to abandon preference utilitarianism as a plausible and practical criterion of welfare.

200 Rothbard 1978 is a good place to start reading the social scientific arguments.

201 To the extent that a society is deliberately ordered it ceases to be a society and becomes an organization.

202 'Anarchic' and 'spontaneous' mean roughly the same thing here. Hayek prefers the term 'spontaneous order'.

203 They are also known, less politely, as tax-parasites. Some tax-parasites could, of course, make a living doing very similar things in the market. Their jobs are thus far less antisocial than those who could not. But they are still antisocial because even these are likely to be displacing cheaper, better, and voluntarily-funded alternatives.

204 I avoid a discussion of the income-versus-substitution effect here, but it is necessary for a rigorous argument. The substitution effect is likely to dominate in the long run.

205 In fact all taxes on market income – indeed, all taxes on market transactions, including value-added and sales taxes – will be likely to make work less attractive.

206 But it need not be the case that the drop in production and hence welfare will be *larger* because higher-paid people are affected; it is enough to defend their higher incomes utilitarianly that any money coercively denied them, or transferred from them, has no more-productive use.

207 See Frank 1985, first five chapters. Frank thinks that in society as a whole those who have high incomes are getting a free ride as regards status and so can fairly be taxed for this (115–17). But surely the attraction of high status due to income is included in people's calculations as regards the value of the different occupations. This means that the market will tend competitively to reduce salaries with high status to normal rates of (pecuniary plus non-pecuniary) return for the (human capital) investment. Status differences are a normal part of the incentives that make the market so productive. Frank is guilty of a sort of double counting.

208 Both of these points are corroborated prima facie by the annual *Sunday Times* list of Britain's wealthiest people.

209 On the trade-off between total welfare and equality of welfare see Okun 1975.

210 Even 'equality of opportunity' is welfare-destroying in its undermining of market competition, as well as being ultimately impossible (we are bound to have an indefinitely large number of diverse and ever-changing opportunities throughout our lives, which cannot be known about by others or equally distributed even if they were).

211 For informative histories of the state's destructive role in education, see West 1975 and 1994.

212 For an impressive study of the social effects of envy see Schoeck 1969. A more polemical and popular book on the subject is Sheaffer 1988.

213 Strictly speaking, the welfare-enhancing free market is only incompatible with equality in the same sense that it is incompatible with an infinity of in-equalitarian outcomes: imposing a particular income distribution of any kind is inimical to the free market.

214 For more on the rationality and utility of smoking see 2.2.c.

215 Economists are putting themselves in this role when they write of merit goods (which are supposedly undervalued by consumers) and demerit goods (which are supposedly overvalued).

216 I include charitable organizations, of course, especially where they would re-place state intervention. For some recent work on charity, welfare, and mar-kets (though all are far from being consistently anarcho-liberal), see Dennis 1997, Green 1993 and 1996, Himmelfarb 1995, Seldon 1996, and Whelan 1996. To see how things have not changed much, see also Tocqueville ([translation of 1835] 1997).

217 In a totally free market, there is no involuntary unemployment: the labor market will always clear if the wage rate is allowed to fall to the market-clearing level (though this will be rising as the marginal revenue productiv-ity of labor increases because the rate of capital accumulation and innovation typically outstrips population growth). Even 'frictional unemployment' is

voluntary insofar as people search for a 'good enough' job instead of taking the first available job. There is no reason that market clearing need take long when people realise that tax-funded idleness is not an option. With a state, unemployment is mainly caused by the destruction of prosperity due to state taxation, inflation, and regulation being combined with state welfare payments to bribe the disaffected workforce (unless there is a minimum wage above market-clearing to cause involuntary unemployment).

218 Bauer 1971 shows this with state 'aid', but it applies to charitable aid too. In fact, much charitable activity now includes lobbying the state for one reason or another.

219 The practical problem of homelessness is not due to 'inequality' in any important sense. Rather, it is due to state legislation and taxation. State accommodation standards mean that some people receive nothing instead of something affordable but below that standard. Similarly, state rent-control means that much potential accommodation is kept off, or taken off, the market, or simply not built in the first place. Moreover, property (and other) taxes drive some marginally-coping people from their homes. In these ways the state raises the price of accommodation to the majority while consigning a very small minority to homelessness.

220 There is an interesting logical point here. The number of beds need not be as many as the number of people for those sleeping rough to be doing so voluntarily. If there is only one empty bed available and all those who are sleeping rough decline to accept it (as it appears they do) then, under the circumstances (see previous note), they *all* sleep rough through choice.

221 It was argued earlier that we can also make sense of 'property' where someone has the effective use and control of something whether or not he has a legal or moral right to that use and control (3.4.a).

222 The right to something abstract, such as happiness, is a claim to whatever property rights are needed to achieve that abstract end.

5. Anarchy

223 A version of this chapter first appeared as Lester 1996a.

224 As ever, I mean 'impose' to refer to '*initiated* impositions' and not anything that merely *defends* people from such initiated impositions.

225 It is sometimes suggested, by libertarians and others, that the state is a monopoly. As the state is not necessarily a single seller of any kind, I do not see that this is strictly accurate. It is correct, however, in the looser sense of 'exclusive possession' (of which 'ultimate control' is, ipso facto, a form). I have no objection to this looser sense, and otherwise use it myself throughout this book.

226 See Benson 1990, Fuller 1969, Hayek [1973] 1982, and Leoni 1991.

227 I would guess that such contractual control would be highly unlikely except for a very few, small, and eccentric communities.

228 For instance, James Buchanan has this assumption throughout his *The Limits of Liberty: Between Anarchy and Leviathan* (1975) and 'A Contractarian Perspective On Anarchy' (1978), despite having relevant works by Murray Rothbard and David Friedman in his bibliography and notes. Lomasky also has this error (1987, 109–10).

229 As absurdly supposed in Haworth 1994, 3.

230 Generally, the products of individuals with higher market-incomes are more want-satisfying than those with lower market-incomes (though they might well be less want-satisfying considered as a *type* of producer).

231 For instance, I endorse Rothbard's (1977) and Roy Childs's (1977) criticisms of Nozick's argument (1974) for the minimal state, and David Friedman's (1994) reply to Tyler Cowen (1992). I should say that even in his 1994 rejoinder, Cowen seriously underrates the role of libertarian ideology and market operation: in a genuinely libertarian society, so-called protection agencies (why not independent police, courts, and lawyers as we have now?) would be far more likely to be checked by public scrutiny and (potential) competition.

232 As I stated in the introduction, this book is chiefly intended to be a philosophical complement to libertarian social science and not a primer in it.

233 Some examples include Coase 1974, Cowen [1988] 1992, Goldin 1977, Hoppe 1989, Hummel 1990, and Zandi 1993.

234 Ferguson ([1767] 1995, 119) famously writes of 'establishments, which are indeed the result of human action, but not the execution of any human design.'

235 For information on where to obtain much of the literature relating to these and other topics see the Afterword.

Afterword

Two useful addresses for obtaining relevant literature (though very little of it will be consistently anarcho-libertarian):

Free-Market.Net: The Freedom Network
http://www.free-market.net/
(This has very comprehensive connections to every kind of libertarian organization.)

Institute of Economic Affairs
2 Lord North Street
Westminster
LONDON SW1P 3LB
UK
http://www.iea.org.uk/

Bibliography

Acton, John Emerich Edward Dalberg. [1887] 1993. *The History of Freedom.* Grand Rapids, MI: The Acton Institute.

Arthur, Terry C. 1975. *Ninety-Five Per Cent Is Crap: A Plain Man's Guide to British Politics.* Cranfield, Bedfordshire: Libertarian Books.

Axelrod, Robert M. 1984. *The Evolution of Cooperation.* New York: Basic Books.

Barnet, Randy E. 1977. 'Whither Anarchy? Has Robert Nozick Justified the Minimal State?' *Journal of Libertarian Studies* 1, no. 1.

—— 1977. 'Restitution: A New Paradigm of Criminal Justice.' *Ethics* 87, no. 4:279–301.

—— 1980. 'The Justice of Restitution.' In *Moral Issues*, ed. J. Narveson. Toronto and New York: Oxford University Press, 1980.

Barnett, Randy E., and John Hagel III, eds. 1977. *Assessing the Criminal: Restitution, Retribution, and the Legal Process*, Cambridge, Mass.: Ballinger Publishing Co.

Barnett, Randy E., and John Hagel III. 1977. 'Assessing the Criminal: Restitution, Retribution, and the Legal Process.' In Barnett and Hagel, 1977.

Barry, Brian M. *Political Argument.* [1965] 1990. Hemel Hempstead: Harvester Wheatsheaf.

—— 1991. *Liberty and Justice.* Volume 2 of *Essays in Political Theory.* Oxford: Clarendon Press.

Barry, Norman P. 1979. *Hayek's Social and Economic Philosophy.* London: Macmillan.

—— 1981. *An Introduction to Modern Political Theory.* London: Macmillan.

—— 1989. *On Classical Liberalism and Libertarianism.* London: Macmillan.

—— 1990. 'Libertarianism: Some Conceptual Problems.' *Philosophy*, Supplement:109–127.

—— 1990. *Welfare.* Milton Keynes: Open University Press.

Bartley, W. W., III. 1990. *The Retreat to Commitment.* 2nd ed. La Salle, Ill.: Open Court.

—— 1990. *Unfathomed Knowledge, Unmeasured Wealth: On Universities and the Wealth of Nations.* La Salle, Ill.: Open Court.

Bauer, P. T. 1971. *Dissent on Development.* London: Weidenfeld and Nicolson.

Becker, Gary S. 1962. 'Irrational Behaviour and Economic Theory.' *Journal of Political Economy* 70:1–13.

—— 1971. 'Altruism, Egoism, and Genetic Fitness.' *Journal of Economic Literature* 14.

—— 1976. *The Economic Approach to Human Behaviour.* Chicago: University of Chicago Press.

Benson, Bruce Lowell. 1990. *The Enterprise of Law*. San Francisco: Pacific Research Institute for Public Policy.

—— 1996. 'Restitution in Theory and Practice.' *Journal of Libertarian Studies* 12, no. 1:75–97.

Bergland, David. 1990. *Libertarianism in One Lesson*. 5th ed. Costa Mesa, CALIF.: Orpheus Publications.

Berlin, Isaiah. 1969. *Four Essays on Liberty*. Oxford: Oxford University Press.

Block, Walter. 1976. *Defending the Undefendable*. New York: Fleet Press.

—— 1980. 'On Robert Nozick's "On Austrian Methodology".' *Inquiry* 23:397–444.

Boaz, David, ed. 1986. *Left, Right, and Babyboom: America's New Politics*. Washington: Cato Institute.

—— 1997. *Libertarianism: a Primer*. New York: The Free Press.

Brittan, Samuel. 1968. *Left or Right: the Bogus Dilemma*. London: Secker and Warburg.

—— 1973. *Capitalism and the Permissive Society*. London: Macmillan.

Broad, Charlie Dunbar. [1950] 1971. 'Egoism as a Theory of Human Motives.' In *Broad's Critical Essays in Moral Philosophy*, ed. David R. Cheney. London: Allen & Unwin.

Buchanan, James M. 1975. *The Limits of Liberty: Between Anarchy and Leviathan*. Chicago: University of Chicago Press.

—— 1978. 'A Contractarian Perspective on Anarchy.' In Pennock and Chapman, 1978.

Buchanan, James M., and N. E. Devletoglou. 1970. *Academia in Anarchy*. Guildford: Tom Stacey.

Butler, Joseph. [1726] 1967. *Fifteen Sermons Preached at the Rolls Chapel*. London: Bell.

Carter, Ian. 1992. 'The Measurement of Pure Negative Freedom.' *Political Studies* 40, no. 1:38–50.

—— 1995a. 'The Independent Value of Freedom.' *Ethics* 105, no. 4:819–845.

—— 1995b. 'Interpersonal Comparisons of Freedom.' *Economics and Philosophy* 11:1–23.

Charlton, William. 1988. *Weakness of the Will*. Oxford: Basil Blackwell.

Charvet, John. 1981. *A Critique of Freedom and Equality*. Cambridge: Cambridge University Press.

Childs, Roy A., Jr. 1977. 'The Invisible Hand Strikes Back.' *Journal of Libertarian Studies* 1, no. 1.

Coase, Ronald H. 1974. 'The Lighthouse in economics.' *Journal of Law and Economics* 17, no. 2 (Oct).

—— 1960. 'The Problem of Social Cost' *Journal of Law and Economics* 3 (October):1-44.

Cohen, G. A. 1979. 'Capitalism, Freedom and the Proletariat.' In Ryan 1979.

—— 1986a. 'Self-Ownership, World-Ownership, and Equality.' In *Justice and Equality, Here and Now*, ed. F. Lucash. Ithaca: Cornell University Press, 1986.

—— 1986b. 'Self-Ownership, World-Ownership, and Equality, Part II.' *Social Philosophy and Policy* 3, no. 2.

Cowen, Tyler. 1992. 'Law as a Public Good: The Economics of Anarchy.' *Economics and Philosophy* 8:249–269.

—— 1994. 'Rejoinder to David Friedman on the Economics of Anarchy.'

Economics and Philosophy 10, no. 2:329–332.

—— ed. [1988] 1992. Public Goods and Market Failures: A Critical Examination. New Brunswick, N.J.: Transaction.

Dagger, Richard. 1980. 'Restitution, Punishment, and Debts to Society'. In *Victims, Offenders, and Alternative Sanctions*, ed. Joe Hudson and Burt Galaway. Lexington, Mass.: Lexington Books, 1980.

—— 1993. 'Playing Fair with Punishment.' *Ethics* 103:473–488.

Danto, Arthur C. 'Constructing an Epistemology of Human Rights: A Pseudo Problem?' In Paul and Miller 1984.

Dawkins, Richard. 1976. *The Selfish Gene*. Oxford: Oxford University Press.

Day, J. P. 1983. 'Individual Liberty.' In Griffiths 1983.

Demsetz, Harold. [1967] 1974. 'Toward a Theory of Property Rights.' [1967.] In *The Economics of Property Rights*, ed. Furubotn Pejovich. Cambridge, Mass.: Ballinger, 1974.

Dennis, Norman. 1997. *The Invention of Permanent Poverty*. London: IEA Health and Welfare Unit.

Department of Health and Social Security. 1985. *Drug Misuse*. London: ISDD.

Edgeworth, Francis Ysidro. [1881] 1932. *Mathematical Psychics*. London: C. Kegan Paul.

Edwards, P., ed. 1967. *The Encyclopaedia of Philosophy*. London: Macmillan.

Elster, Jon. 1982. 'Sour Grapes – Utilitarianism and the Genesis of Wants.' In Sen and Williams 1982.

Epstein, Richard A. 1977. 'Crime and Tort: Old Wine in Old Bottles.' In Barnett and Hagel 1977.

Eysenck, H. J. 1954. *The Psychology of Politics*. London: Routledge & Kegan Paul.

Ferguson, Adam. [1767] 1995. *An Essay on the History of Civil Society* Edinburgh. Reprint, Faina Oz-Salzberger (ed). Cambridge and New York: Cambridge University Press.

Ferrara, Peter, J. 1982. 'Retribution and Restitution: A Synthesis.' *Journal of Libertarian Studies* 6, no. 2:105–136.

Fishkin, James. 1984. 'Utilitarianism versus Human Rights.' In Paul and Miller 1984.

Flathman, Richard E. 1984. 'Moderating Rights.' In Paul and Miller 1984.

Flew, Antony. 1978. *A Rational Animal.* Oxford: Clarendon Press.

—— 1979. *A Dictionary of Philosophy*. London: Pan Books.

—— 1981. *The Politics of Procrustes: Contradictions of Enforced Equality*. London: Temple Smith.

—— 1983. '"Freedom is Slavery": a Slogan for Our New Philosopher Kings.' In Griffiths 1983.

—— 1987. *The Logic of Mortality*. Oxford: Basil Blackwell.

—— [1985] 1991. *Thinking About Social Thinking*. London: Fontana Press.

—— 1993a. *Atheistic Humanism*. Buffalo, N.Y.: Prometheus Books.

—— 1993b. 'People Themselves, and/or Their Selves.' *Philosophy* 68.

Foot, Philippa. 1978. *Virtues and Vices*. Oxford: Blackwell.

Frank, Robert H. 1985. *Choosing the Right Pond: Human Behavior and the Quest for Status*. Oxford: Oxford University Press.

Frankfurt, Harry Gordon. [1971] 1982. 'Freedom of the Will and the Concept of a Person.' In Watson 1982.

Frey, R. G., ed. 1985. *Utility and Rights*. Oxford: Basil Blackwell.

—— 1985a. 'Introduction: Utilitarianism and Persons.' In Frey 1985.

—— 1985b. 'Act-Utilitarianism, Consequentialism, and Moral Rights.' In Frey 1985.

Fried, Charles. 1985. 'Rights and Common Law.' In Frey 1985.

Friedman, David D. [1973] 1989. *The Machinery of Freedom: Guide to Radical Capitalism.* 2nd ed. La Salle, Ill.: Open Court.

—— 1994 'Law as a Private Good: A Response to Tyler Cowen on the Economics of Anarchy.' *Economics and Philosophy* 10, no. 2:319–327.

—— 1996. 'Anarchy and Efficient Law.' In Narveson and Sanders 1996.

Friedman, Jeffrey M. 1990. 'The New Consensus: II. The Democratic Welfare State.' *Critical Review* 4, no. 4.

—— 1991a. 'Postmodernism vs. Postlibertarianism.' *Critical Review* 5, no. 2.

—— 1991b. 'Accounting for Political Preferences: Cultural Theory vs. Cultural History.' *Critical Review* 5, no. 3.

—— 1992a. 'After Libertarianism: Rejoinder to Narveson, McCloskey, Flew, and Machan.' *Critical Review* 6, no. 1.

—— 1992b. 'Politics or Scholarship?' *Critical Review* 6, nos. 2–3.

—— 1997. 'What's Wrong with Libertarianism' *Critical Review* 11, no. 3.

Friedman, Milton. 1953. *Essays in Positive Economics.* Chicago: University of Chicago Press.

Fuller, Lon L. [1964] 1969. *The Morality of Law.* New Haven: Yale University Press.

Gallie, W. B. 1956. 'Essentially Contested Concepts.' *Proceedings of the Aristotelian Society* 56:167–198.

Gauthier, David P. 1986. *Morals by Agreement.* New York: Oxford University Press.

Gewirth, Alan. 1984. 'A Reply to Danto.' In Paul and Miller 1984.

—— 1984. 'The Epistemology of Human Rights.' In Paul and Miller 1984.

Gibbard, Alan. 1984. 'Utilitarianism and Human Rights.' In Paul and Miller 1984.

Gibbs, Benjamin. 1983. 'Taking Liberties with Freedom: a Reply to Professor Flew.' In Griffiths 1983.

Glover, Jonathan. 1977. *Causing Death and Saving Lives.* Harmondsworth, Middx.: Penguin.

Goldin, Kenneth Darwin. 1977. 'Equal Access vs. Selective Access: A Critique of Public Goods Theory.' *Public Choice* 29.

Golding, Martin P. 1984. 'The Primacy of Welfare Rights.' In Paul and Miller 1984.

Gray, John. 1983. *Mill On Liberty: A Defence.* London: Routledge.

—— 1984. *Hayek on Liberty.* Oxford: Basil Blackwell.

—— 1984. 'Indirect Utility and Fundamental Rights.' In Paul and Miller 1984.

—— 1986. *Liberalism.* Milton Keynes: Open University Press.

—— 1989. *Liberalisms: Essays in Political Theory.* London: Routledge.

—— 1992. *The Moral Foundations of Market Institutions.* London: IEA Health and Welfare Unit.

Gray, Tim. 1991. *Freedom.* London: Macmillan.

—— 1993. 'Spencer, Steiner and Hart on the Equal Liberty Principle.' *Journal of Applied Philosophy* 10, no. 1:91–104.

Green, David G. 1993. *Reinventing Civil Society: The Rediscovery of Welfare Without Politics.* London: IEA Health and Welfare Unit.

—— 1996. *Community Without Politics*. London: IEA Health and Welfare Unit.

Griffen, James. 1985. 'Towards a Substantive Theory of Rights.' In Frey 1985.

Griffiths, A. Phillips, ed. 1983. *Of Liberty*. Cambridge: Cambridge University Press.

Hahn, Frank, and Martin Hollis., eds. 1979. *Philosophy and Economic Theory*. Oxford: Oxford University Press.

Hajdin, Mane. 1987. 'Criminals as Gamblers: A Modified Theory of Pure Restitution.' *Dialogue* 26:77–86.

Hammond, Peter J. 1982. 'Utilitarianism, Uncertainty and Information.' In Sen and Williams 1982.

Hardin, Garret. 1968. 'The Tragedy of the Commons.' *Science* 162.

Hare, Richard Mervyn. [1963] 1972. *Freedom and Reason*. Oxford: Oxford University Press.

—— 1982. 'Ethical Theory and Utilitarianism.' In Sen and Williams 1982.

—— 1985. 'Rights, Utility, and Universalization: Reply to J. L. Mackie.' In Frey 1985.

—— [1952] 1986. *The Language of Morals*. Oxford: Oxford University Press.

Harsanyi, John C. 1982. 'Morality and the Theory of Rational Behaviour.' In Sen and Williams 1982.

Hart, H. L. A. 1979. 'Between Utility and Rights.' In Ryan 1979.

Haworth, Alan. 1994. *Anti-Libertarianism: Markets, Philosophy and Myth*. London: Routledge.

Hayek, Friedrich August von. [1944] 1976. *The Road to Serfdom*. London: Routledge & Kegan Paul.

—— 1949. *Individualism and Economic Order*. London: Routledge & Kagan Paul.

—— [1952] 1979. *The Counter-Revolution of Science*. 2nd ed. Indianapolis: Liberty Press.

—— 1960. *The Constitution of Liberty*. London: Routledge & Kegan Paul.

—— 1978. *New Studies in Philosophy, Politics, Economics and the History of Ideas*. Chicago: University of Chicago Press.

—— [1973-1979] 1982. *Law, Legislation and Liberty*. London: Routledge & Kegan Paul.

—— ed. 1954. *Capitalism and the Historians*. Chicago: University of Chicago Press.

Hazlitt, Henry. [1946] 1979. *Economics in One Lesson*. 2nd ed. New Rochelle, N.Y.: Arlington House.

Heap, Shaun Hargreaves. 1989. *Rationality in Economics*. Oxford: Basil Blackwell.

Himmelfarb, Gertrude. 1995. *The De-moralization of Society: From Victorian Virtues to Modern Values*. London: IEA Health and Welfare Unit.

Hirshleifer, Jack. 1984. *Price Theory and Applications*. 3rd ed. London: Prentice-Hall.

Hobbes, Thomas. [1651] 1943. *Leviathan*. London: Dent.

Hobhouse, L. T. 1964. *Liberalism*. Oxford: Oxford University Press.

Hollis, Martin. 1983. 'The Social Liberty Game.' In Griffiths 1983.

Hoppe, Hans-Hermann. 1989. 'Fallacies of the Public Goods Theory and the Production of Security.' *Journal of Libertarian Studies* 9, no. 1.

Hospers, John. 1977. 'Retribution: The Ethics of Punishment.' In Barnett and Hagel 1977.

—— 1971. *Libertarianism*. Los Angeles: Nash.

Hume, David. [1741–42] 1987. 'Of the First Principles of Government.' In *Essays: Moral, Political, and Literary*. Indianapolis. Rev. ed. Indianapolis: Liberty Classics.

—— [1739–40] 1968. *A Treatise of Human Nature* Ed. L. A. Selby-Bigge. Oxford: Oxford University Press.

—— [1748] 1972. *An Enquiry Concerning Human Understanding*. Ed. L. A. Selby-Bigge. Oxford: Oxford University Press.

—— [1751] 1972. *An Enquiry Concerning the Principles of Morals*. Ed. L. A. Selby-Bigge. Oxford: Oxford University Press.

Hummel, Jeffrey Rogers. 1990. 'National Goods versus Public Goods: Defense, Disarmament, and Free Riders.' *Review of Austrian Economics* 4.Jacobs, E., and R. Worcester. 1990. *We British: Britain under the MORIscope*. London: Weidenfeld and Nicolson.

Jasay, Anthony de. 1985. *The State*. Oxford: Basil Blackwell.

—— 1991. *Choice, Contract, Consent: A Restatement of Liberalism*. London: Institute of Economic Affairs.

Kant, Immanuel. [1785] 1948. *Groundwork to the Metaphysic of Morals*. In H. J. Paton.

Kedourie, Elie. 1960. *Nationalism*. London: Hutchinson.

—— 1985. *The Crossman Confessions and Other Essays in Politics, History and Religion*. London: Mansell Publishing.

Kelley, David. 1984. 'Life, Liberty, and Property.' In Paul and Miller.

Kirzner, Israel Mayer. [1960] 1976.*The Economic Point of View*. Kansas City Mo.: Sheed and Ward.

—— 1989. *Discovery, Capitalism, and Distributive Justice*. Oxford: Basil Blackwell.

—— 1990. 'Self-Interest and the New Bashing of Economics: A Fresh Opportunity in the Perennial Debate?' *Critical Review* 4, nos. 1–2.

—— 1997. *How Markets Work: Disequilibrium, Entrepreneurship and Discovery*. London: Institute of Economic Affairs.

Kleinberg, Stanley S. 1980. 'Criminal Justice and Private Enterprise.' *Ethics* 90:270–282.

Kukathas, Chandran. 1992. 'Freedom versus Autonomy.' In Gray 1992.

Kymlicka, Will. 1990. *Contemporary Political Philosophy: An Introduction*. Oxford: Oxford University Press.

La Boétie, Etienne de. [1577] 1975.*The Politics of Obedience: Discourse on Voluntary Servitude*. New York: Free Life Editions.

Lagueux, Maurice. 1991. 'Kirzner vs. Becker: Rationality and Mechanisms in Economics.' In vol. 9 of *Perspectives on the History of Economic Thought*, ed. R. F. Hébert. Aldershot, Hampshire: Edward Elgar.

Lakatos, Imré. 1976. *Proofs and Refutations: The Logic Of Mathematical Discovery*. Cambrige: Cambridge University Press.

Lal, Deepak. 1995. *The Minimum Wage: No Way to Help the Poor*. London: Institute of Economic Affairs.

Larmore, Charles. 1987. *Patterns of Moral Complexity*. Cambridge: Cambridge University Press.

LeGrand, Julian. 1982. *Strategy of Equality*. London: Allen and Unwin.

Leoni, Bruno. [1961] 1991. *Freedom and the Law*. Exp. 3rd ed. Indianapolis: Liberty Press.

Lepage, Henri. 1982. *Tomorrow, Capitalism: The Economics of Economic Freedom*. La Salle, Ill.: Open Court.

Lester, J. C. 1995. 'Popper's Epistemology versus Popper's Politics.' *Journal of Social and Evolutionary Systems* 18, no. 1:87–93.

—— 1996a. 'Market-Anarchy, Liberty, and Pluralism.' In *For and Against the State: New Philosophical Readings*, ed. Jan Narveson and Jack Sanders. Lanham, Md.: Rowman & Littlefield, 1996.

—— 1996b. 'The Political Compass (and Why Libertarianism Is Not Right-Wing).' *Journal of Social Philosophy* 27, no. 2:176–186.

—— 1997a. 'Liberty as the Absence of Imposed Cost: The Libertarian Conception of Interpersonal Liberty.' *Journal Of Applied Philosophy* 14:3:277–288.

—— 1997b. 'Apriorist Self-Interest: How It Embraces Altruism and Is Not Vacuous.' *Journal of Social and Evolutionary Systems* 20, no. 3:221–232.

—— 1999a. 'Libertarian Rectification: Restitution, Retribution, and the Risk-Multiplier.' *Journal of Value Inquiry* 32, no. 1.

—— 1999b. 'Weakness of Will or Rational Meta-Desire?' *Aristoi* 1:1

—— 1999c. 'Rational Moral Sentiments' *Aristoi* 1:1.

Liggio, Leonard P. 1994. 'Law and Legislation in Hayek's Legal Philosophy.' *Southwestern University Law Review* 23, no. 3:507–530.

Lindley, Richard. 1986. *Autonomy*. London: Macmillan.

Locke, John. [1690] 1966. *Two Treatises of Civil Government*. London: Dent.

Lomasky, Loren E. 1987. *Persons, Rights, and the Moral Community*. Oxford: Oxford University Press.

Luper, Steven. 1996. *Invulnerability: On Securing Happiness*. La Salle, Ill.: Open Court.

Macfarlane, A. 1978. *The Origins of English Individualism*. Oxford: Basil Blackwell.

Machan, Tibor R. 1989. *Individuals and Their Rights*. La Salle, Ill.: Open Court.

—— 1990. *Capitalism and Individualism*. New York: St. Martin's Press.

MacIntyre, Alasdair. 1967. 'Egoism and Altruism.' In *The Encyclopedia of Philosophy*, ed. P. Edwards. London: Macmillan, 1967.

Mack, Eric. 1978. 'Nozick's Anarchism.' In Pennock and Chapman 1978.

Mackie, John Leslie. [1977] 1979. *Ethics: Inventing Right and Wrong*. Harmondsworth, Middx.: Penguin.

—— 1985. 'Rights, Utility, and Universalization.' In Frey 1985.

Maddox, William S., and Stuart A. Lilie. 1984. *Beyond Liberal and Conservative: Reassessing the Political Spectrum*. Washington D.C.: Cato Institute.

Manning, D. J. 1976. *Liberalism*. London: Dent.

McCloskey, H. J. 1985. 'Respect for Human Moral Rights versus Maximising Good.' In Frey 1985.

McElroy, Wendy. 1985. 'Contra Copyright' *The Voluntaryist* (June).

—— 1995. 'Liberty on Copyright and Patents' Unpublished version. (Received 1998 but undated; a version of this paper was published in *The Agorist Quarterly* 1, no. 1:46–55.)

McKenzie, Richard B., and Gordon Tullock. 1978. *Modern Political Economy: An Introduction to Economics*. New York: McGraw-Hill.

McKenzie, Richard B., and Gordon Tullock. 1981. *The New World of Economics:*

Bibliography 235

Explorations into the Human Experience. Homewood, Ill.: Irwin.

Mill, John Stuart. [1859] 1978. *On Liberty*. Indianapolis: Hackett.

Miller, David Leslie. 1984. *Anarchism*. London: Dent.

—— ed. 1987. *The Blackwell Encyclopedia of Political Thought*. Oxford: Basil Blackwell.

Miller, David W. 1994. *Critical Rationalism: A Restatement and Defence*. Chicago and La Salle, Ill.: Open Court.

Miller, Franklin G. 1978. 'Restitution and Punishment: A Reply to Barnett.' *Ethics* 88:358–360.

Minford, Patrick. 1992. 'Gray on the Market.' In Gray 1992.

Minogue, K. R. 1983. 'Freedom as a Skill.' In Griffiths 1983.

—— 1985. *Alien Powers*. New York: St. Martin's Press.

Mises, Ludwig Edler von. [1949.] 1966. *Human Action: A Treatise on Economics*. 3rd rev. ed. Chicago: Henry Regnery Co.

—— [1936] 1981. *Socialism: An Economic and Sociological Analysis*. Translation of the 2nd German ed. of 1932. Indianapolis: Liberty Classics.

Molinari, Gustave de, [1849] 1977. *The Production of Security*. New York: Centre for Libertarian Studies.

Morgan, Patricia. 1995. *Farewell to the Family? Public Policy and Family Breakdown in Britain and the USA*. London: IEA Health and Welfare Unit.

Mount, Ferdinand. 1982. *The Subversive Family*. London: Allen & Unwin.

Mulhull, Stephen, and Adam Swift. 1992. *Liberals and Communitarians*. Oxford: Blackwell.

Murray, Charles. 1984. *Losing Ground: American Social Policy*. New York: Basic Books.

—— 1984. *Underclass: The Crisis Deepens*. London: IEA Health and Welfare Unit.

—— 1997. *What it Means to be a Libertarian*. New York: Broadway Books.

Narveson, Jan. 1995. 'Contractarian Rights.' In Frey 1985.

—— 1988. *The Libertarian Idea*. Philadelphia: Temple University Press.

Narveson, Jan and Jack Sanders, eds. 1996. *For and Against the State: New Philosophical Readings*. Lanham, Md.: Rowman & Littlefield.

Nesbitt, Winston. 1995. 'Is Killing No Worse than Letting Die?' *Journal of Applied Philosophy* 12, no. 1:101–105.

Newman, Stephen L. 1984. *Liberalism at Wit's End*. Ithaca: Cornell University Press.

Nozick, Robert. 1969. 'Coercion.' In *Philosophy, Science and Method*, S. Morgenbesser et al. New York: St. Martin's Press.

—— 1974. *Anarchy, State, and Utopia*. Oxford: Basil Blackwell.

—— 1977. 'On Austrian Methodology.' *Synthese* 36:353–92.

Okun, Arthur M. 1975. *Equality and Efficiency: The Big Trade-Off*. Washington, D.C.: Brookings Institution.

Oppenheimer, Franz. [1914] 1926. *The State: Its History and Development Viewed Sociologically*. Trans. John M. Gitterman. New York: Vanguard Press.

Palmer, Tom G. 1989. 'Intellectual Property: A Non-Posnerian Law and Economics Approach.' *Hamline Law Review* 12:261–304.

—— 1990. 'Are Patents and Copyrights Morally Justified: The Philosophy of Property Rights and Ideal Objects.' *Harvard Journal of Law and Public*

Policy 13:817-865.

Parfit, Derek. 1984. *Reasons and Persons*. Oxford: Clarendon Press.

Paton H. J., ed. 1948. *The Moral Law*. London: Hutchinson.

Pattanaik, Prasanta Kumar. 1988. 'On the Consistency of Libertarian Values.' *Economica* 55, no. 220:517–524.

Paul, Ellen Frankel, and Fred D. Miller, Jr., eds. 1984. *Human Rights*. Oxford: Basil Blackwell.

Paul, Jeffrey. 1977. 'Nozick, Anarchism, and Procedural Rights.' *Journal of Libertarian Studies* 1, no. 4.

Pennock J. R., and J. W. Chapman., eds. 1978. *Anarchism*. Nomos XIX. New York: New York University Press.

Pilon, Roger. 1978. 'Criminal Remedies: Restitution, Punishment, or Both?' *Ethics* 88:348–357.

Plant, Raymond. 1992. 'Autonomy, Social Rights and Distributive Justice.' In Gray 1992.

Polanyi, Michael. 1951. *The Logic of Liberty: Reflections and Rejoinders*. London: Routledge & Kagan Paul.

Popper, Karl Raimund. [1957] 1969.*The Poverty of Historicism*. London: Routledge & Kegan Paul.

—— [1974] 1976.*Unended Quest: An Intellectual Autobiography*. London: Fontana.

—— [1945] 1977. *The Open Society and Its Enemies*. 2 vols. 5th ed. London: Routledge & Kegan Paul.

—— [1963] 1978. *Conjectures and Refutations*. 4th ed. rev. London: Routledge & Kegan Paul.

—— [1972.] 1979. *Objective Knowledge*. Rev. ed. Oxford: Oxford University Press.

—— 1992. *In Search of a Better World*. London: Routledge.

Pressler, Jonathan. 1987. 'Rights and Social Choice: Is There a Paretian Libertarian Paradox?' *Economics and Philosophy* 3:1–22.

—— 1988. 'How to Avoid the Paretian-Libertarian Paradox: A Reply to Kelly.' *Economics and Philosophy* 4:326–332.

Quine, W. V. 1980. *From a Logical Point of View*. Cambridge, Mass.: Harvard University Press.

Raphael, D. D. 1983. 'Liberty and Authority.' In Griffiths 1983.

Rawls, John. [1972] 1983. *A Theory of Justice*. Oxford: Oxford University Press.

—— 1985. 'Justice as Fairness: Political Not Metaphysical.' *Philosophy and Public Affairs* 14, no. 3:223–251.

—— 1987. 'The Idea of an Overlapping Consensus.' *Oxford Journal of Legal Studies* 7, no. 1:1–25.

Raz, Joseph. 1985. 'Right-Based Moralities.' In Frey 1985.

Reeve, Andrew. 1986. *Property*. London: Macmillan.

Ridley, Matt. 1993. *The Red Queen: Sex and the Evolution of Human Nature*. Harmondsworth, Middx: Viking.

Robinson, Colin. 1993. *Energy Policy: Errors , Illusions and Market Realities*. London: Institute of Economic Affairs.

Rothbard, Murray N. 1977. 'Punishment and Proportionality.' In Barnett and Hagel 1977.

—— 1956. 'Toward a Reconstruction of Utility and Welfare Economics.' In *On Freedom and Free Enterprise*, ed. Mary Sennholz. Princeton, N. J.: D. Van

Nostrand, 1956.
—— [1962] 1970. *Man, Economy, and State: A Treatise on Economic Principles*. 2 vols. Los Angeles: Nash.
—— 1977a. 'Robert Nozick and the Immaculate Conception of the State.' *Journal of Libertarian Studies* 1, no. 1.
—— [1970] 1977b. *Power and Market*. 2nd ed. Kansas City, Mo.: Sheed Andrews & McMeel.
—— [1973] 1978. *For a New Liberty: The Libertarian Manifesto*. Rev. ed. New York: Macmillan Co.
—— 1979. *Left and Right: The Prospects for Liberty*. San Francisco: Cato Institute.
—— 1982. *The Ethics of Liberty*. Atlantic Highlands, N.J.: Humanities Press.
—— 1990. 'Concepts of the Role of Intellectuals in Social Change Toward Laissez Faire.' *Journal of Libertarian Studies* 9, no. 2.
Rowley, C. K., and A. T. Peacock. 1975. *Welfare Economics: A Liberal Restatement*. London: Martin Robertson.
Ryan, Alan., ed. 1979. *The Idea of Freedom*. Oxford: Oxford University Press.
—— 1985. 'Utility and Ownership.' In Frey 1985.
Sabine, G. H. [1973] 1981. *A History of Political Theory*. 4th rev. ed. by T. L. Thorson. Tokyo: Dryden Press.
Sanders, John T. 1977. 'The Free Market Model Versus Government: A Reply to Nozick.' *Journal of Libertarian Studies* 1, no. 1.
—— 1987. 'Justice and the Initial Acquisition of Property.' *Harvard Journal of Law and Public Policy* 10, no. 2:367–399.
Sartorius, Rolf. 1985. 'Persons and Property.' In Frey 1985.
Scanlon T. M. 1975. 'Preference and Urgency.' *Journal of Philosophy* 72.
—— 1982. 'Contractualism and Utilitarianism.' In Sen and Williams 1982.
Scheffler, Samuel. 1982. *The Rejection of Consequentialism: A Philosophical Investigation of the Considerations Underlying Rival Moral Conceptions*. Oxford: Clarendon Press.
Schoeck, Helmut. [1966] 1987. *Envy: A Theory of Social Behaviour*. Indianapolis: Liberty Press.
Scruton, Roger. 1982. *A Dictionary of Political Thought*. London: Pan Books.
Seldon, Arthur, ed. 1996. *Re-Privatising Welfare: Welfare After the Lost Century*. London: Institute of Economic Affairs.
Selgin, George A. 1990. *Praxeology and Understanding: An Analysis of the Controversy in Austrian Economics*. Auburn, Al.: Ludwig von Mises Institute.
Sen, Amartya Kumar. [1970] 1979a. 'The Impossibility of a Paretian Liberal.' In Hahn and Hollis 1979.
—— [1976] 1979b. 'Rational Fools.' In Hahn and Hollis 1979.
—— 1987. *On Ethics and Economics*. Oxford: Basil Blackwell.
Sen, Amartya K., and Bernard A. O. Williams., eds. 1982. *Utilitarianism and Beyond*. Cambridge: Cambridge University Press.
Sheaffer, Robert. 1988. *Resentment Against Achievement*. Buffalo, N.Y.: Prometheus.
Siedentop, Larry. 1979. 'Two Liberal Traditions.' In Ryan 1979.
Simon, H. 1955. 'A Behavioral Model of Rational Choice.' *Quarterly Journal of Economics* 69:99–118.
Simon, Julian L. 1981. *The Ultimate Resource*. Oxford: Martin Robertson.

Simon, Julian Lincoln, and H. Kahn, eds. 1984. *The Resourceful Earth*. Oxford: Basil Blackwell.

Simpson, David. 1994. *The End of Macro-economics?* London: Institute of Economic Affairs.

Singer, Peter. [1981] 1983. *The Expanding Circle: Ethics and Sociobiology*. Oxford: Oxford University Press.

—— 1993. *Practical Ethics*. Cambridge: Cambridge University Press.

Skinner, B. 1972. *Beyond Freedom and Dignity*. London: Cape.

Smart, J. J. C. 1973. 'An Outline of a System of Utilitarian Ethics.' In Smart and Williams 1973.

Smart, J. J. C., and Bernard A. O. Williams. 1973. *Utilitarianism: For and Against*. Cambridge: Cambridge University Press.

Smart, R. N. 1958. 'Negative Utilitarianism.' *Mind* 67:542–543.

Smith, Barry. 1986. 'Austrian Economics and Austrian Philosophy.' In *Austrian Economics: Historical and Philosophical Background*, ed. Wolfgang Grassl and Barry Smith. London and Sydney: Croom Helm.

—— 1990. 'Aristotle, Menger, Mises: An Essay in the Metaphysics of Economics.' In *Carl Menger and His Legacy in Economics.*, ed. Bruce J. Caldwell. Durham: Duke University Press.

Sowell, Thomas. 1981. *Markets and Minorities*. New York: Basic Books.

—— 1983. *The Economics and Politics of Race: An International Perspective*. New York: William Morrow.

Spector, Horacio. 1992. *Autonomy and Rights: The Moral Foundations of Liberalism*. Oxford: Clarendon Press.

Steele, David Ramsay. 1992. *From Marx to Mises: Post-Capitalist Society and the Challenge of Economic Calculation*. La Salle, Ill.: Open Court.

Steiner, Hillel. 1983. 'How Free: Computing Personal Liberty.' In Griffiths 1983.

Stroup, R. L., and J. A. Baden. 1983. *Natural Resources*. Cambridge, Mass.: Ballinger.

Sumner. L. W. 1985. 'Rights Denaturalised.' In Frey 1985.

Szasz, Thomas Stephen. [1961] 1972.*The Myth of Mental Illness*. New and abbrev. ed. London: Paladin.

—— 1975. *Ceremonial Chemistry: The Ritual Persecution of Drugs, Addicts, and Pushers*. London: Routledge & Kegan Paul.

Tannehill, Morris, and Linda Tannehill. [1970] 1984. *The Market for Liberty*. New York: Laissez Faire Books.

Taylor, Charles. 1979. 'What's Wrong with Negative Liberty?' In Ryan 1979.

—— [1976] 1982. 'Responsibility for Self.' In Watson 1982.

Taylor, Michael. 1982. *Community, Anarchy and Liberty*. Cambridge: Cambridge University Press.

—— 1987. *The Possibility of Co-operation*. Cambridge: Cambridge University Press.

Tocqueville, Alexis de. [1968] 1997. *Memoir on Pauperism*. Translation of the French original of 1835. London: IEA Health and Welfare Unit.

Trivers, Robert. 1981. 'Sociobiology and Politics.' In *Sociobiology and Human Politics*, ed. Elliott White. Lexington, Mass.: Lexington Books, 1981.

Tucille, Jerome. 1970. *Radical Libertarianism*. Indianapolis: Bobbs-Merrill.

Waldron, Jeremy. 1992. 'Superseding Historic Injustice.' *Ethics* 103, no. 1:4–28.

Watson, Gary., ed. 1982. *Free Will*. Oxford: Oxford University Press.

—— [1975] 1982. 'Free Agency.' In Watson 1982.

West, Edwin G. 1975. *Education and the Industrial Revolution*. London: Batsford.

—— 1994. *Education and the State: A Study in Political Economy*. 3rd. rev. and exp. ed. Indianapolis: Institute of Economic Affairs.

Whelan, Robert. 1996. *The Corrosion of Charity*. London: IEA Health and Welfare Unit.

Wicksteed, Philip Henry. [1910] 1933. *The Common Sense of Political Economy*. 2 vols. London: Routledge.

Williams, Bernard Arthur Owen. 1973. 'A Critique of Utilitarianism.' In Smart and Williams 1973.

—— 1973. 'Conflicts of Values.' In Ryan 1979.

Zandi, David E. Van. 1993. 'The Lessons of the Lighthouse: "Government" or "Private" Provision of Goods.' *Journal of Legal Studies*. Vol. 22.

Index